THE DIVINE NATURE OF BASKETBALL

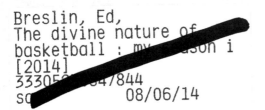
THE DIVINE NATURE OF
BASKETBALL

My Season Inside the Ivy League

by

Ed Breslin

SPORTS
PUBLISHING

Sports Publishing books may be purchased in bulk at special discounts for sales promotion, corporate gifts, fund-raising, or educational purposes. Special editions can also be created to specifications. For details, contact the Special Sales Department, Sports Publishing, 307 West 36th Street, 11th Floor, New York, NY 10018 or sportspubbooks@skyhorsepublishing.com.

Sports Publishing® is a registered trademark of Skyhorse Publishing, Inc.®, a Delaware corporation.

Visit our website at www.sportspubbooks.com.

10 9 8 7 6 5 4 3 2 1

Library of Congress Cataloging-in-Publication Data is available on file

ISBN: 978-1-61321-636-1

Printed in the United States of America

The following page is considered an extension of the copyright page.

This book is for:

Tommy Leonard and Jerry Bernhardt
friends extraordinaire and endless sources of encouragement

and for:

Jimmy Drum and the late Nicky Lapetina
backcourt buddies and running mates beyond compare

and in memory of:

Eddie Leonard
a man ever ready with a hearty handshake
a winning smile
a quick laugh
a kind word
and a helping hand

TABLE OF CONTENTS

"I was the most dedicated basketball player. I don't say the best. In my mind I was terrifically good. In fact I was simply the most dedicated basketball player in the world. I say this because I played continuously, from the time I discovered the meaning of the game until my mid-twenties. I played outdoors on cement, indoors on wood. I played in heat, wind, and rain. I played in chilly gymnasiums. Walking home I played some more. I played during dinner, in my sleep, in movies, in automobiles and buses, and at stool. I played for over a decade...."

Leonard Michaels
"Basketball Player"

"The pleasure of sport was so often the chance to indulge the cessation of time itself—the pitcher dawdling on the mound, the skier paused at the top of a mountain trail, the basketball player with the rough skin of the ball against his palm preparing for a foul shot, the tennis player at set point over his opponent—all of them savoring a moment before committing themselves to action."

George Plimpton
Paper Lion

Foreword

by Rick Telander

FIRST OFF, LET it be known that there are people who like basketball, people who love basketball, and then there is Ed Breslin. The way a dandelion worships the sun, a hammer cherishes the nail, a cue ball loves the cue, that's Ed Breslin and hoops. Maybe it was his Catholic upbringing in basketball-rich Philadelphia, or being one of twelve kids (a tad too short to be more than a school yard player himself), combined with his passion for writing and editing and knowing great literature that gave the now 64-year old Breslin the depth of joy that he gleans from the poetry of Dr. Naismith's game.

Because here's the thing, that near-breathless joy over a simple game that has been described as round-ball-flat-floor can't be faked. You may start off with Breslin on his harebrained quest to be a very unofficial "assistant coach" with the 2011–12 Yale men's basketball team for a season and worry that this is just one of those tag-a-long events we get in the world of sports, a by-the-numbers look at a game without much spirit or drive. But quickly it hits you: this guy *cares*. Breslin drives through the night roads of New England, from one Yale game to the next, taking trains from here to there, sometimes buses, hanging in the gyms and press conferences and coffee shops at the elbows of college hoops fanatics and coaches, in an ever-growing fever of yearning and hopefulness. What does he hope for? Yale wins. What else? For good fortune to befall its likable head coach, James Jones, and the unique players Breslin slowly begins to know and understand.

Ostensibly, Breslin is on a mission to find out what it's like to coach at the D-1 level, but really he's on a mission to have fun and find himself, as refracted through the multiple panes of Ivy League values, sportsmanship, competition and the ecstasy of winning and, yes, the heartbreak of inevitable loss. He describes the ebb and flow of each game as if watching the monitor on a beloved patient in the cardiac unit of a hospital. As we learn the names and habits of the players, and their successes and failures come out, we start to care more and more. We find ourselves getting sucked in by Breslin's passionate observations until the question arises delicately, wistfully in our minds: *What is there in my life that* I *care this much about?*

Schooled on the old-style values from his favorite young adult series— the good old Chip Hilton books by coach and Naismith Basketball Hall of Famer, Clair Bee—Breslin is thrilled to find again, for real, many of the virtues and commitments espoused by fictional coach Henry "The Rock" Rockwell for life success so many years ago right here in these real young men on the Yale team. The Bulldogs are, after all, concerned, intelligent collegians who actually have to study, pass tests and ponder future life outside the fantasy of the NBA. And their mentor, Coach James, himself the brother of an Ivy League coach, is a man Breslin finds to be fair, team-oriented, and full of an enviable "clap-it-up" approach to life.

You will finish this book with a smile on your face, pleased to have spent time with a writer who unapologetically and without the trendiness of irony or the falseness of sentiment has led you on a journey that, unequivocally, was the greatest of his life. And because that journey revolves around the game of basketball, it revolves around the world, as well. And because Ed Breslin loves it, you can't help loving it too.

Prologue: "Don't Step on the Y"

THE POWER OF basketball to make me happy leads me to suspect that its underlying nature is at least somewhat divine. That is why I didn't question the reason I was shuttling back and forth to New Haven on the Metro North commuter train three straight days starting on Friday, October 14, 2011. In a span of sixty hours that extended weekend I spent thirty-four of them either commuting to and from Yale, or having lunch on campus with Coach James Jones, or in the gym watching him conduct the initial practices for the men's basketball team. It was as exhilarating an experience as I'd had since being a starter on the St. Francis Xavier grade school CYO basketball team in the spring of 1961. We won the championship of the inaugural Roman Catholic High School Tournament that year. That tiny and dusty old bandbox gym on the third floor overlooking Philadelphia's Broad Street is still a part of me.

At Yale that super weekend I was delighted to rediscover that basketball could transform my mood and elevate my spirits even in a practice session without a formal scrimmage. It was enough to sit in the shadowy gym with the stands all to myself and listen to the snick and screech of seventeen pairs of sneakers on the polished hardwood. The symphony the sneakers created reminded me of listening drowsily to predawn birdsong on a summer morning in the country. Only now the percussive thuds of basketballs bouncing off the oak floor or smacking off the glass backboards stirred me fully awake and fully alive, loving every minute of the old sights, sounds, and smells of being a gym rat.

Before that first afternoon of practice Coach Jones and I ate lunch at Box 63, a restaurant in an old Victorian firehouse, two blocks from his office. After the lunch, and before practice began, he dispatched Assistant Coach Jamie Snyder-Fair to give me a tour of the facilities. In the home team's locker room there was a dark blue rug with a big white Y in its center. Coach Snyder-Fair, leaning all his weight into the statement and towering over me at six feet nine inches tall, said: "Whatever else you do in here, don't step on the Y."

That old high-school gym at Roman, like the gym at Yale, had large lancet windows in the Neogothic style. In the backstory of how I came to be writing this book, the gym at Yale plays a starring role. The first time I was there I was riveted to the spot, just inside the main doors on the balcony overlooking the court. I was trying to take it all in and didn't even walk over to the railing and get a better eyeful. For what must have been a full fifteen or twenty seconds it seemed a piece of paradise had fallen to earth and landed on the Yale campus. The John J. Lee Amphitheater, or JLA as it is called, struck me as the most beautiful venue for basketball, even though I loved Penn's Palestra and was practically a fixture there while growing up. And I had been in Cameron Indoor Stadium at Duke and in the hallowed old Rose Hill gym up at Fordham in the Bronx. They all pale in comparison to JLA.

My first glimpse of JLA came at the end of the 2009–2010 season. I went up to Yale to satisfy my curiosity about its gym and to watch Coach Joe Jones's Columbia team play his older brother James's Yale team. At the time I had written to Joe to ask if I could take him to lunch to discuss the possibility of bird-dogging him and his Columbia team for a season as a kind of auxiliary coach. I wanted to be an unofficial assistant coach assessing close-up the job of what it is like to be a head coach of basketball in the highly underrated Ivy League.

My writer friend Bruce Feuer had tipped me about the attractiveness of Yale's gym. Like me, he followed the Ivy League basketball season by strolling up Broadway from his Upper West Side apartment and taking in the Friday and Saturday night games at Columbia's Levien Gym. Bruce and I used to work out in the same Crunch gym on Eighty-third Street. Whenever we bumped into each other, we would compare notes on writing and on book publishing and, during the season, on Ivy League basketball. I told Bruce once that I rated the Palestra the greatest venue for basketball and that I liked to take in at least one game a year there, combining it with a weekend trip down to Philly to see my mother. He told me I should take a trip up to Yale and see their gym before I made such a broad statement. He found aspects of what he called "Yale's gym," not using its official name, to be cathedral-like. He loved the way its churchy windows looked against the night sky.

Columbia's Levien Gym is the right size and scale for maximum appreciation of college basketball. Like JLA, Levien is intimate and has great sight lines. Also like JLA, it accommodates only a little over two and a half thousand spectators, so there isn't a bad seat in the house. Yet, because Levien is relatively new, and because it has mainly bench seating made of molded plastic, it is uncomfortable when crowded, lacking JLA's old-fashioned, pre-war, and roomy theatre seats. They're wonderful, though their wooden rigidity can get to your keister in overtime or while watching four straight hours of practice. Levien's newness also lacks the patina JLA wears with such effortless aplomb.

The night I first saw JLA, I also met Coaches James Jones and Joe Jones for the first time. I had entered the Payne Whitney gym and been directed to the ticket office on the opposite side of the lobby from the basketball arena. In walking back across the lobby I spotted a tall man coming toward me in a blue warm-up suit with white stripes running down the sleeves and the pant legs. I had watched Coach Joe Jones of Columbia many times from the higher stands at Levien and, in the shadowy light of the stone lobby, I thought the man approaching me was Joe, who, from our recent correspondence, knew I was coming up to the game in New Haven. By that time Joe and I had discussed via letter and phone the possibility of the book I wanted to do, and we had arranged to meet in person that night. As the man in the blue warm-up suit and I drew abreast of each other, I said, "Excuse me, you're Coach Jones, aren't you?"

"Yes I am," the man replied. I stuck out my hand and told him I was the guy who had written to him.

"I'm James Jones, the coach of Yale. You want my brother Joe. I think you'll find him downstairs in the visitors' locker room."

Embarrassed, I thanked him, remembered to wish him luck in the game, though then still rooting for Columbia, and moved on. Yale won the game, 65-48. I didn't want to disturb Joe before the game, so I hadn't gone downstairs to introduce myself. After the game I found the visitors' locker room and asked a student manager to tell Joe I was outside. This was after I'd waited for silence on the other side of the door. I knew enough not to interrupt a losing team's post mortem.

A few minutes later Joe came out and we introduced ourselves and arranged for me to call him after the NCAA Tournament ended in three weeks. We intended to set up a lunch date to discuss my book idea. I walked out of the building back through the vaulting stone lobby feeling as though I could have windmilled or three-sixtied a dunk in JLA. I'm five seven, having lost half an inch to age, and could only, the best day I ever lived back in my youth, put my fingers in the twine above the lower mess where the tongs lead up another eight inches to hook on the rim of the basket. Now fifty pounds heavier than my playing weight, I might not have been able to touch the net at all. Yet I offer this as evidence of that divine power I mentioned that basketball has when it comes to making me happy.

On the train ride back home that night I was flying and in my exhilaration I couldn't concentrate to read and instead plotted the book. It would be a challenge to get it right. My own athletic résumé wouldn't be much help. In high school I made the junior varsity basketball team as a sophomore guard. The previous year as a freshman I was a pine-riding halfback on the freshman football team, all five feet one inch and eighty-eight pounds of me. Coach Joe Herkness hung a nickname on me, "the mighty midget." By sophomore year I had added only one inch and four pounds. And no speed. Also, right in the middle of that year I found out I needed glasses. I was near-sighted. Since I was a good outside shooter (provided I could get my shot off without having it blocked), this development was more bad news. The point is: I was a bench warmer who mostly took in the games while sedentary, all suited up and nowhere to go. And the next year was worse. I tried out for basketball and didn't make the cut for the varsity.

No matter: I loved trying out for the teams. I loved the participation. I especially loved basketball.

When the NCAA Tournament ended that spring of 2010 I duly called Columbia and asked for Coach Joe Jones, only to be told that he had resigned to take a coaching job at Boston College. That put an end to my plans to write that book. Deflated, I had to abandon the idea or try to rebuild it with another coach, maybe with the new Columbia coach. But my obligations on another book intervened and I had to place the basketball book, as I called it, on the back burner. I got embroiled in finishing a book I was helping to write on American railroad stations and their outstanding architecture.

This challenge was so engaging that I didn't get to see as many college basketball games as usual the following year, the 2010–2011 season, though I had a strong hunch about the Harvard-Yale game in late February and hopped the train to New Haven. I also wanted to be in JLA again. My hunch proved right and Yale upended a really good Harvard team, one I'd seen earlier that winter in Jadwin where Princeton nipped them in a thriller. Yale's upset of Harvard that night was also a thriller, Yale a single point better.

So excited was I on the train back to the city that I emailed Yale Coach James Jones my congratulations. He responded. Next thing I knew we were discussing my aborted book scheme involving his brother Joe. I asked would he be interested in considering my idea to write a book on Ivy League basketball with my Walter Mitty stint as a shadow coach, an unofficial assistant coach; in other words, the kind of thing that George Plimpton perfected: participatory journalism featuring an eyewitness account of sports by an amateur fully engaged with an actual team. He said we'd talk after the season.

I sent him copies of books I'd written. Then I got busy promoting one of those books. Meanwhile he took his Yale team on a tour of China, where they played several amateur and one professional team. Two months had passed by now since the end of the 2010–2011 season. Then I called and arranged to have lunch in early June. I met him at his office and we walked down New Haven's Broadway and ducked into a place called the Educated Burgher, very casual, collegiate, and sports-minded. Jones fans staffed the place and he returned their enthusiastic greetings.

Our meeting that day was brief and to the point. I gave him my thumbnail bio and explained what I hoped to do with this book. He asked sharp questions. I gave my best answers. I told him I had followed Ivy League basketball since the early sixties, when I was a Big Brothers' ball boy at the Palestra and immersed myself every winter, like half of Philly, in the battle for the Big Five championship. To this he responded, "I like basketball but I'm not a fanatic."

"Neither am I," I said truthfully, "but I love the game, and as a boy it helped me learn a lot of life lessons. It's also given me hours of joy since then, watching it played, especially when played well. It still lifts my mood whenever I stroll up Broadway to Levien and watch a good game."

This was also true, and painful in one respect: his brother Joe had raised the level of Columbia basketball to the point where games were selling out. More than once in the 2009-2010 season I trudged through the slush and snow and stood shivering outside the Dodge Athletic Center only to be told: sold out. But I was persistent that year with Cornell's Sweet Sixteen team and got into the arena in time to see the tail end of the first half and all of the second half, even if I did so on my dogs in standing room only. That Cornell team featured lightning ball movement, deadeye outside shooting, and a clawing defense, and when they did go into the NCAA Tournament as

Ivy champions they progressed to the round of sixteen, knocking off mighty Big Ten powerhouse Wisconsin along the way. They made me look like a prophet to all the people I had told to look out for them, that they were dangerously good.

My predictions about that Cornell team drew the usual skeptical looks accorded Ivy League basketball teams by the uninformed ESPN "Top Ten Highlights" crowd. Coaches knew better. I was to learn this fact firsthand, and soon, because Coach Jones, at the end of our lunch, agreed that I could write my book, provided Yale approved and that he introduced me to the team gradually and at his pace. Later that fall as the season started, I followed Yale in the early weeks during its nonconference schedule, and opposing coaches would wax eloquent in their postgame interviews about the quality of Ivy League teams.

That sunburst lunch with Coach Jones lasted only forty-five minutes but we covered a lot of territory. I told him about my modest achievements as an athlete and he seemed to enjoy the jokes at my own expense. He sensed, I believe, that I had been permanently uplifted by even this limited athletic career, and that I loved basketball and had benefited from the exposure to my coaches. I left the restaurant with my determination to write this book surging, my hopes soaring that the authorities at Yale would give James, as he insisted I call him, the green light for us to go ahead and try it. I felt confident that I knew enough about basketball and enough about writing to pull it off. I rode the train back to the city that beautiful early summer day determined to get James a letter I'd promised him explaining my intentions.

As it turned out I had the usual interruptions and delays and didn't get the letter out for eight weeks. In truth I had trouble with the letter. My projected book was difficult to plan and even more difficult to explain. Exploratory and experiential books are hard to describe in advance. I felt inadequate about this until George Plimpton posthumously saved me. I ordered an old copy of *Paper Lion* and discovered in rereading it that Plimpton had gone through the same experience. He had difficulty in pitching his book to publishers and, as a consequence, met with an enthusiastic lack of interest. Finally *Sports Illustrated* and Harper & Row took a flyer on *Paper Lion* and the book became an instant classic.

I doubted I'd be that talented or that lucky. But I had a feeling these days that everything in life happened for a reason, as my intelligent and very religious maternal grandmother, Julia Drakeley Kelly, used to tell me all the time when I was a boy. And it did seem fortuitous that I had ended up soliciting the help of Coach Jones once his younger brother Joe had moved on from Columbia to coach at Boston College, and once I'd glimpsed JLA. On top of that good fortune, Yale was picked to contest Harvard for the Ivy League championship in 2011–2012: Harvard the favorite, Yale the runner-up.

A flood of boyhood associations hit me when I considered that the planned book might now revolve around Yale, with its rich tradition in athletics, its top-tier academics, and its colonial beginnings. I remembered reading some young adult novels for boys called, I believe, the "Wynn Wingate of Yale" series. Wynn was a lot like his more celebrated fictional predecessor at Yale, Frank Merriwell, the hero of the "Frank Merriwell at Yale" comic strip that also turned into a series of young adult novels. Like Frank Merriwell, Wynn Wingate was an all-around all-star athlete back in the days when the Big Four—Harvard, Yale, Princeton, and Penn—set a hot pace in intercollegiate sports. Few people realize that the genesis of big-time collegiate sports lies in the Ivy League, even back before the league was formalized in 1954. Big-time college frenzy in sports, especially in football, had its origins among the famous old-line eastern schools where the distinguishing ivy clings to the walls. Frank Merriwell and Wynn Wingate inspired young boys to emulate their dedication to scholastic and athletic excellence, a sound mind in a sound body.

The Wingate books were given to me by Bill "Rip" Collins, the coach of CYO football and basketball at St. Francis Xavier grammar school on the Parkway in Philly opposite the art museum. Rip, besides being the president of Germantown Savings Bank, was a gifted coach and a great mentor. He also gave me stacks of Chip Hilton books, written by legendary LIU basketball coach Clair Bee, who'd won national titles with his Blackbirds back in the 1930s when LIU, CCNY, and NYU dominated college basketball, including the NIT, then its crown jewel at season's end before the NCAA Tournament eclipsed it.

The Chip Hilton books, also gifts from Rip Collins, were written along the same lines as the Frank Merriwell and the Wynn Wingate books, exhortations to young boys to clean living, athletic effort, and scholastic diligence. I loved them. No matter how predictable, these books always held my interest until Chip had struck out the last batter, with the bases full in the bottom of the ninth, and a slim one-run lead to protect, to win the state baseball championship; or until Chip fired a touchdown pass with no time left on the clock to break a deadlocked game and secure the state football championship; or, finally, until Chip hit a buzzer-beater from the top of the key with the final horn sounding to, you guessed it, clinch the state basketball title.

Would that I had kept those values. Had I stuck to them I might have got to play a little intercollegiate basketball at Drexel University as a third-string guard, and I might well have ended up as a college basketball coach, the alternate reality, the persistent fantasy, that this book is designed to gratify and exorcise. Another great mentor of mine, my uncle Tom Leonard, said to me in the summer of 1965, before I entered Drexel, "Ed, you should be able to play some basketball there." Those words have haunted me for forty-seven years and counting, because I didn't go out for the team and have regretted it ever since. Uncle Tom had been a cheerleader for Roman Catholic High back when my father was a starting guard there in the 1937-1938 season, their senior year. Uncle Tom knew the value of participation in life, of lending support, and of rendering service. But back then I didn't know the value of such things.

Don't misunderstand me. I've led a lucky and delightful life, full of many blessings. This book, far from being a sustained lament or a tortured dirge about opportunities lost, will be a celebration of basketball, of participation in life, of gifted mentors and coaches, and of the proper approach to collegiate athletics exemplified by Yale and its seven confreres in the Ivy League. My late buddy Al Strausman, a successful sculptor, professor of art at the Fashion Institute of Technology, and demonically possessed fan of the New York football Giants, once said to me, "Always remember what they say about sports, Ed. You have to be smart enough to understand them and intelligent enough to realize that they don't matter."

Yes and no, Al. As laboratories for preparing you for life's disappointments and triumphs, as challenges that present you with the task of mastering a formidable skill set, and especially as activities that expose you to coaches capable of mentoring and instilling lasting values in you, sports are very important and they matter a great deal. I offer proof of this in a remark made at lunch in that same Box 63 restaurant in New Haven on December 15, 2011 by Assistant Coach of Yale basketball Justin Scott. While seated with Coach Jones and Assistant Coach Jamie Snyder-Fair and me, Justin said: "Aside from my father, Coach Jones has had the greatest influence on my life."

Justin as a sophomore was a member of Coach Jones's 2002 Yale team, the Ivy League basketball co-champions, the first of what I hope will be many such championship teams for him.

At any rate, I was launched and eager to turn my body clock back half a century and once again participate with a team, anticipating each game, living day to day or even hour to hour during the buildup to the next game, checking averages, keeping stats, discussing strategies, suffering heartache with each loss and thrilling to ecstasy with each victory, dropping an encouraging word to a player now and again, maybe even a tiny word of technical advice, on shooting or rebounding or defending, or even putting in my two cents with Coach Jones or his assistants as long as it wasn't invasive or annoying. I wanted to experience again the power and influence, the energy and life-altering investiture of values you get from placing yourself under the aegis of a great coach, and I even wanted, by fantastical proxy extended to me by Coach Jones, to feel a little, even at a large remove, what it was like to be that kind of coach, mentor, and influence on the lives of young people. I was definitely pumped, even if the price turned out to be making a fool of myself.

And, by the way, if you ever visit the Yale locker room, remember: "Don't step on the Y."

"What attracted me was the sound of the swish, the sound of the dribble, the feel of going up in the air. You don't need eight others, like in baseball. You don't need any brothers or sisters. Just you. I wonder what the guys are doing back home. I'd like to be there, but it's as much fun here, because I'm playing. It's getting dark. I have to go back for dinner. I'll shoot a couple more. Feels good. A couple more."

Bill Bradley
As quoted in John McPhee's
A Sense of Where You Are

PART ONE:

THE PRESEASON

CHAPTER ONE

North of Grand Central

THE PATTERN WAS set that very first Friday. I would hustle to Grand Central Terminal, rush across the Grand Concourse to the platform out back and catch the New Haven express train. The two-hour train ride became an integral part of the whole experience of participating once again in the fate of a basketball team from the inside, as a member, not from the outside, as a spectator. As soon as we emerged from the underground tunnel at Ninety-sixth and Park Avenue it was all basketball. First would come the crowded courts between the tall buildings of the Harlem projects. Then the single backboards and nets hung above the garage doors of the near suburbs. Then, finally, we would hit the huge recreation center at Bridgeport with its multiple basketball courts hedged in by baseball diamonds and soccer grids.

As much as I loved to see baseball diamonds, especially from the air when flying, I loved to see the geometry of a basketball court from the slightly raised roadbed of a passing train. There would be the rectangle divided down the center into two equal squares. There would be the six circles: two at the foul lines, two at center court—the smaller within the larger—and two formed by the hanging baskets. Behind the baskets hung the two opposed squares of the backboards. In turn the two foul circles formed the tops of two keyholes. Under the baskets the two ellipses of the restricted areas faced off at either end of the court like two reversed and opposed parentheses. At either end of the court the giant parabolas defined the arcs beyond which three-point shots must be taken. No one had made better use of geometry since Euclid invented it than had Dr. James Naismith when he invented basketball in December 1891 in Springfield, Massachusetts. He had simply hung two peach baskets to balcony railings at either end of a YMCA gymnasium and the deed was done, the miracle completed.

On the train trips to New Haven, when passing the geometric scheme that constituted a basketball court, I was always reflective. For young players, this oh-so-familiar geometric scheme was, depending upon their geographic, economic, and demographic situation, either a blueprint for escape, a passport to an education, the diagram of a challenge, an outlet for obsession, or an invitation—often their first—to strive for proficiency, sometimes even for perfection, in one of the earliest undertakings in their lives. Often it was all of these in various combinations and permutations.

For me as a boy it had been all of them. Along with learning to balance and control one's body well enough to ride a bicycle, it had presented the first serious challenge to teach me the importance of practice when striving to master difficult tasks. It was a simple template inviting complex mastery.

When I told my father that I found it difficult to learn the art of dribbling, he exhorted me not to expect perfection "right off the bat," but instead to practice until I was "blue in the face" at any challenge that was proving difficult. He had finished our row house cellar in North Philadelphia to make it a proper basement, with whitewashed walls and a smooth tile floor, and he banished me to its thirty-five feet of uninterrupted length to practice dribbling obsessively around chairs he arranged as stand-ins for defenders. I had to dribble rapidly through them, weaving and never looking down. He forbade me to look down at the ball as I dribbled, assuring me that my hands would learn to sense and control the ball without any visual contact.

At first, failing constantly, losing control of the ball incessantly, I doubted him; but little by little, the result of endless hours spent in the basement, what he told me started to come true. Eventually I didn't need to look down at all. I could control the ball instinctively; it became as natural to me as breathing, a function of my dribbling hand as easy to control as my opposed thumb. Sooner rather than later, mastery of dribbling, mastery of shooting, mastery of body control when leaping to tap in deliberately missed shots became a narcotic: hours of practice sweetened the challenge and vanquished both boredom and teenaged angst. Later in life, when I sought to meet the challenge of my lifelong ambition to write, this lesson in dribbling would reappear to save me.

* * * * *

When Naismith blew the whistle and conducted the first basketball game ever played, the ball he used was a soccer ball. There were also nine players on each side, instead of five. His boss had given him fourteen days to come up with an indoor game capable of being played in a small space, at minimum expense, with no violence and scant chance of injury. The game was to involve no excessive contact.

As a boy in Canada, Naismith had played a medieval children's game called "Duck on a Rock." The object of the game was to lob, not throw, a smaller stone and knock a larger stone, the duck, off its platform on a very large rock or on a tree stump. In his new invention of basketball the object of the game was to lob, not throw, a round ball into an elevated peach basket. Today we call lobbing shooting, and the basket is open-ended, not enclosed.

Naismith scribbled thirteen original rules for the new game on a scrap of paper. That scrap of paper sold at auction a few years ago for two million dollars. The original rules disallowed players running with the ball. They could only transfer it to one another by handing it off or by throwing it. Throwing is called passing today. Because the original ball used was a soccer ball, dribbling was out of the question, not yet even thought of. The patent on what we call today a basketball took thirty-eight more years before its issuance in 1929. By that time the game was played in a big steel cage that, though rectangular and larger, somewhat resembled in construction the wire mesh batting cages used today on baseball diamonds in recreation centers. Naismith's original rules specified penalties for fouling. Running with the ball was the usual early culprit when it came to committing a foul, but tackling, though expressly forbidden, was in the game's earliest days also hard to eliminate, so rambunctious were Naismith's early male charges, hemmed in with cabin fever in the severe New England winter and beset with an excess of teenaged testosterone.

When you think about it, what Naismith basically did was to shorten the pitch for soccer, move it indoors, and elevate the goals ten feet in height, the approximate height of the original peach baskets hung from the balcony railings. He also reduced the elevated goals to small round baskets instead of, as is the case with soccer, large boxes anchored in the ground and festooned on three sides with netting. Yet netting too would appear in basketball in 1903, when the iron rims of the goals that replaced the original peach baskets were draped with open-ended netting. This improvement speeded up the game enormously. The ball returned to the floor immediately instead of having to be fetched after each goal from the bottom of the peach basket.

By 1930 YMCAs worldwide had spread the new game internationally, and Naismith lived long enough to see basketball contested as an official sport at the 1936 Berlin Olympics. Today three hundred million people play basketball, its global popularity topped only by soccer. Though invented by a Canadian, basketball is the quintessentially American game. Baseball was first played in England; in fact, a game called baseball is played in summer twilight in Jane Austen's novel *Northanger Abbey*, published in 1817. English cricket is also clearly the prototype for American baseball. Equally, American football evolved from another English forerunner, rugby. In contrast basketball had no precedent until played in America.

* * * * *

Anxious not to be late, I got to JLA for that first practice on October 14 more than half an hour early and took up a seat on the south side, in the permanent seats in the balcony, content to sit and study that nonpareil gymnasium, its proportions perfect, its design inspired, its aura sacred, especially in the muted half-light on an autumn afternoon. There was a festive air to the place that I sensed but couldn't document until suddenly the full lights flashed on and a man carting a lot of photographer's equipment trundled through the swinging floor-level doors below me and walked to center court along the near sideline. There he proceeded to set up twin light stands and a camera tripod. Soon another man in shirtsleeves and slacks joined him, and then the gym started to fill up with players dressed in dazzling new uniforms, snowy white with dark blue lettering on the chest spelling out "Yale" above the player's number. Shortly thereafter the assistant coaches wandered in, dressed in business suits: and then Coach Jones came in, his impeccably tailored suit draped on his carefully maintained physique as smartly as it would have been on a professional model or on a tailor's mannequin. As I would later learn, when I asked him about it, Coach Jones "worked out every single day."

While I watched, the players were photographed first individually and then in groups of various sizes with Coach Jones beaming a smile in the very center of each group. This happened four times and, no detective, I didn't glom to the groups being arranged by class year until the man in shirt sleeves and slacks who had chatted with the photographer came through the upstairs balcony doors and walked over and introduced himself. He was Tim Bennett, the Yale sports information director for men's basketball, or SID. He explained to me that the groups were freshmen, sophomores, juniors, and seniors. As we sat chatting the finale below took place as all seventeen players flanked Coach Jones in the center, with the assistants ranged on the wings, for the official team photo. I didn't know at the time that I would recollect this moment five months later and be grateful that my fantastical adventure had begun with such a magical moment. When the team shot was over, like everyone at Yale, Tim told me to let him know if I needed anything, then we shook hands again and he left as the players and coaches scattered below me and the photographer started to break down his equipment and pack up.

Once again I was alone in the gym, now brightly lit. But my solitude this time was short-lived. As I watched, the players—dressed now in drab practice uniforms—drifted back into the gym and started to shoot individually at the four baskets, two temporary practice baskets having been set up on the sidelines opposite center court. In minutes the assistant coaches wandered in, dressed in big baggy shorts and T-shirt, Coach Jamie Snyder-Fair looming large at six feet nine inches tall. I knew from asking him on our earlier tour of the facilities that Jamie had played center at Colby College in Maine during his undergraduate years. I also knew from tracking the Yale basketball website over the summer that Justin Simon had been hired as the third assistant coach. Having played center for Yale, Justin was ridiculously easy to recognize at another towering six feet nine inches tall.

The third assistant coach was a short guy I knew from reading the website: Matt Kingsley. An eyelash under six feet, Matt started to circulate and shoot in a desultory way, mixing advice to the players with an odd shot of his own. Fluid and graceful, he was deadly accurate. As a result of my narrow escape from dwarfdom, I always and instantly identify with short basketball players. Never having passed a word with Matt, I liked him on sight for the endless obsessive hours he had invested to achieve the eye-hand coordination and muscle memory behind that kind of shooting accuracy.

No sooner had I made a mental note to ask Coach Jones about Matt than in Jones walked in his blue shorts and gray T-shirt and strode right over in my direction. Why, I couldn't imagine. He handed up two sheets of paper and I stretched down over the balcony railing and took them. They were ordinary letter-size sheets of white bond. On them the agenda for practice was itemized. A glance provided the first hint I had that I was in over my head. The entire practice to come was rigorously organized and laid out on the two sheets of paper with a timeline running down the left margin. Each exercise and activity had an allotted segment of time to be conducted, some segments as short as four or five minutes, others as long as fourteen or fifteen minutes. Every detail was spelled out, including the opening half hour for photos and the twenty-minute interval for changing uniforms in the locker room followed by a team meeting. Even the time allotted for the players to shoot baskets individually right then was specified, the third item on the agenda: ten minutes. Not having said a word to me after handing up the practice agenda, Jones turned and strode to center court, where the three assistants joined him. For only a few minutes they watched and chatted before Jones blew his whistle and, on cue, the players all joined him and his assistants in a cluster at midcourt.

From my theater seat I could hear the murmur as Jones addressed the players, but I could not distinguish the words. Right here I want to make it clear I am not an investigative reporter. Gossip or "dirt" or "dish" on people bores me rigid. I wasn't trying to get any on James Jones or his staff or his players. I wasn't trying for an "insider's expose." I've no interest in the foibles and failures of human nature, except where politics and evil are concerned. There I think investigative reporters are the greatest.

I had entreated Coach Jones to let me shadow him and bird-dog his team for a full season for one reason: I wanted to appease the nagging suspicion I have that I would have enjoyed my life more and invested it with more meaning had I been a college basketball coach, influencing young people's lives, rather than having spent my life as an editor and publisher improving and then publishing authors' books, but having had no formative or lasting influence on the already formed lives and values of the authors. I feared that I had misspent my life in a selfish and futile, and arguably an elitist, manner. I believed that Coach Jones, in contrast, hadn't.

His natural and understandable reluctance to grant my wish to become a fourth, if faux, assistant coach was firmly grounded in his seriousness about his mission. His professionalism, as I would find out, always came first. Moreover, as I would learn, he had a beautiful family to support in a job involving considerable pressure. The Ivy League is guided by gentlemanly sportsmen and scholars, but feckless, wanton, and constant losing is most assuredly not an option. Accommodating and coping with failure is admirable but settling for it beforehand is not.

Because of the serious considerations Jones had to weigh into his decision about my request, and in light of the appropriate reservations he had about my whole scheme, I had vowed to myself and assured him verbally that I would not impede him or his real assistant coaches in any way, or in any way interfere with the tutoring of the players. I would get as close to the coaches and players as I could while respecting the team's privacy. Jones had told me we had to integrate me carefully and at his pace so we wouldn't disrupt the players or distract them in any way. Team chemistry came first, my fantasy job second. What's more, this suited me because I didn't want the players aware of me right away and I didn't ever want them to "play" to me because they were aware of what I was up to with the planned book.

This is a memoir, not a report. Keep in mind I was on a leaning curve, not an investigative quest. I trusted the gradual approach to integrating me that Coach Jones wanted to take. I also thought I would learn enough inside stuff eventually about what it was like to be a Division I college basketball coach. That, after all, was my goal. As it turned out, I did. And it was the right stuff to learn. More important, it turned out to be the right stuff to pass along.

* * * * *

As soon as the players broke the midcourt huddle they retreated to either end of the court, having split into two groups that would become so familiar to me. The taller post players filed to the eastern end of the court under the direction of coaches Snyder-Fair and Simon. The shorter perimeter players stayed at the west end under the supervision of Coach Kingsley, with frequent assists from Coach Jones, who hovered near center court but roamed into either half-court whenever he wanted to make a point with any of his players or coaches. Having played on the perimeter as an undergraduate at the University of Albany, Jones tended to work more with Coach Kingsley and his perimeter guys and leave the post men to his two towering assistants who had played center, the ultimate post position, as undergraduates. In certain of the drills for the perimeter players the team's student manager helped Coach Kingsley. As I would come to learn, the team manager was a terrific kid named Will Manville, a freshman whose work was intense, essential, and extensive. Will was a better than fair basketball player and could have played at the Division II level. On the court with the team he blended in perfectly. I hoped and prayed all season long that one day he would be a walk-on for Yale, whether it took one more or three more years.

The two groups then practiced their designated "Post-Perimeter Shooting," as the exercise was called. The smaller perimeter guys practiced long shots, the taller post guys short shots. Post players consist of the fours and fives as they're numerically designated: meaning centers, the fives, and power forwards, the fours, collectively also called the "Bigs." They play under the basket or to the sides of it along what is called the front line. I was fascinated to watch the post guys shoot in close, nearly beneath the basket or slightly to either side of it. The two small and narrow areas either side of the basket in close are called the low posts, left or right; or, collectively, the blocks. The areas straight up from the blocks toward the ends of the foul line are called the high posts, left or right; or, collectively, the elbows.

Either Coach Snyder-Fair or Coach Simon would grab a dark blue foam rubber pad the size of a baseball umpire's chest protector. After slipping their forearm into a sling at the back of the pad, they would hold it out before them like a medieval warrior with his battle shield. Whenever a post player attempted to get off a shot on the blocks they would ram the pad into him as he went up in the air, simulating the rough and tumble melees under the backboards that post players encounter in actual games. The object was to accustom the post player to control and balance his shot even as his body went one way and his arms and hands the other.

Just as post guys play near the basket on the "inside," perimeter guys play far away from the basket on the "outside." They operate in the backcourt, or, put more concretely, along the curve of the three-point shooting arc, or even beyond it. Guards and small forwards make up the perimeter players: numerically, point guards are ones, shooting guards twos, and small forwards threes. Swing guys can play shooting guard, the two position, or small forward, the three position. Tall and athletic enough to play small forward, they usually have better than average leaping ability, enabling them to snatch rebounds and score on put-backs of missed shots by their teammates. Equally, they are shifty, quick, and adept enough at handling the ball and driving to the basket to play the shooting guard position.

Additionally, a good swing guy can step in as a third guard in a three-guard offense, which utilizes a second shooting guard, and only a single forward—the power forward—to complement the traditional center, point guard, and shooting guard arrangement. A three-guard offense has no small forward and instead uses three players on the perimeter, and only two on the front line, as opposed to the traditional two perimeter players and three front line players. That is, in the three-guard offense the small forward retreats from the front line and plays in the backcourt, out on the perimeter. If the player retreating from the front line and instead playing on the perimeter is the same player, and not a substitute, he is a swingman.

After precisely ten minutes the post-perimeter shooting drill ended on a command from Coach Jones, and the players all hustled to the baseline under the western basket, where the perimeter guys had been shooting. On another signal from Jones they all started to "walk" to midcourt loosening up along the way and back. "Walk" is in quotes because I came to refer privately to this exercise as "The Ministry of Silly Walks," in honor of John Cleese's immortally funny sketch on *Monty Python's Flying Circus*. The players would raise one leg at a time exaggeratedly high, wiggle it slightly while balancing on the grounded foot, and then plant the wiggled leg back on the floor and repeat the process with the opposite leg. Often along the way they would alternate this stretching exercise with an aerial knee bend, bringing up one leg at a time, then cupping the raised and bent knee at its apex with their clasped hands before pulling it toward their torso. After holding this position for a moment, they would release their hands and let the stretched leg return to the floor in order to bring the other leg up and repeat the process. Watching seventeen young men perform this exercise, some of them seemingly as tall as giraffes, has its humorous aspects; but, intent on observation, I skipped the laughs.

On a signal from Jones the players next streaked at full speed around the outside of the court several laps before they fanned out along the baseline and slightly up the two sidelines, hit the floor, and did push-ups, counting them off to themselves softly, creating a nice murmur. After only a few brief minutes of this, Jones clapped loudly and ordered them to dribble-run around the perimeter of the court, bouncing the ball in front of them while moving at top speed. For a watcher in the stands this exercise had a stereopticon effect as pleasing as watching a photo sequence unfurl rapidly, looping and repeating itself at dazzling speed, like those primitive strips of early movie film.

Next, Jones issued a command in his alto voice directing the guys to form two lines near either sideline and cut toward the basket, alternating with the guys cutting from the other line. As they cut they were fed a pass to "finish" by making a good shot, either laying the ball in off the backboard or dunking it. The exuberant ones went for the dunk and this led to much banter and jibing among the players. Their enthusiasm was marvelous and I attributed it directly to Jones. All season this insight sustained itself: Jones could motivate.

After exactly ten minutes elapsed, Jones redirected the players to perform a six-minute drill called "Chase the Ball." It was designed to improve rebounding skills by simulating a scrum beneath the backboard for a loose ball, in this instance a deliberately missed shot that three players would scramble to secure.

Another rebounding drill, "Blockout and Chase," immediately followed and lasted ten minutes. Two players positioned under the basket contented for the deliberately missed shot. While doing this they practiced blocking each other out to gain inside positioning and an edge in snaring the ball midair as it caromed off the backboard; or, failing that, they jockeyed to gain an advantageous position to chase down the loose ball quicker than their opponent if it managed to reach the floor in a freefall. Blocking out is massively important. It means positioning oneself nearer the basket and simultaneously forcing an opponent farther out from the basket to gain a serious advantage in grabbing rebounds. The team that gets the most rebounds in a game increases its chances of winning, provided the opposing team is not shooting so accurately that the majority of its shots are going in and thereby not generating many rebounds.

* * * * *

For the next two and a half hours I sat fascinated and watched as Jones drilled his team. They practiced all the basic skills, offensive and defensive, they would need in the coming season, sometimes individually but often in small groups, simulating front line situations for the post players and backcourt situations for the perimeter guys. The defensive drills especially interested me, and I liked that Jones kept urging his guys to "communicate" on defense. "Talk it up, boys, talk it up," he would holler while standing a few steps behind the apex of the three-point arc, about five paces back from the top of the key. The top of the key is the area at the top of the circle above the lane. The lane, often painted in, hence the expression "in the paint," is the area that extends up from the baseline on either side of the basket in two straight lines to the opposite ends of the foul line. The foul line is the horizontal diameter midway up and straight across the circle that forms the top of the key. The foul line, also called the free-throw line, is exactly fifteen feet out from the front rim of the basket.

Jones would stand beyond the top of the key and especially exhort the players to "talk to each other" during a drill called "5 on 5 Shell," which is what it says: five players on defense forming an impenetrable shell in front of and around the basket. After forming the shell the defenders try to force "stops" on the five players on offense. The best stops are stolen dribbles or intercepted passes or blocked shots or deflected shots forced wildly off course. Such stops result only from playing avid, chest-to-chest, in-your-face defense, especially on the shooter.

There were also defensive drills to develop individual skills in closing out shots on the wings, or in the lanes, or along the baseline, or down on the blocks in the low post, or even in the corners. The corners are obvious. The wings are the areas on either side of the half-court between the top of the key and the corners. The wings have "seams" that are ideal for offensive players to drive through toward the basket when making what is known as "dribble penetration." Dribble penetration uncontested often ends up in a score, either by lay-up, dunk, floater, or teardrop, all variations of close-in shots fairly easy to make off a dribble penetration drive by an offensive player. During a game the seams shift, opening and closing, depending upon the positioning of the defensive players and their movements to counter openings the offensive players are trying to create, either by rapid passing or rapid dribbling.

The object of any offensive strategy is to create "openings" to get off "uncontested" shots. Defensive players need to shout out to each other to "deny" or to "seal" the seams by coordinating their movements. Jones, correctly, was emphatic that denying and sealing seams can only be accomplished with constant chatter among the defenders, alerting one another to what they are doing so the alerted players will know how best to position themselves to aid and fortify the defensive position taken and shouted out by the communicating defender, who is often the man guarding the offensive player with the ball.

Like all good coaches, Jones knew that defense wins championships, so he concentrated early practices more on defensive skills and philosophy than on offensive skills and philosophy. Naturally, players would prefer it the other way around because to most kids it's more exciting to score than to stop a score. Kids who feel otherwise are often the most valuable players on the floor, shutting down skilled scorers and winning games and championships for their side. Because I've watched basketball devotedly for over half a century, I know that well played defense is the most exciting aspect the game can present. In the way, baseball aficionados thrill to a pitcher's duel.

That's why I loved watching Jones teach his players to "get low" in a full crouch while guarding their man. I loved to watch him, when he got the players low enough in their crouches, make them practice shuffling their feet by taking short choppy steps as they backed up rapidly to prevent the attacking player on offense from getting around them, especially if he had the ball. Arms also had to be fully extended and hands held high, to impede the opponent's vision and, if he attempted a shot, to thwart it, deflect it, or block it. Never shy and always assertive, a driven teacher, Jones would halt action repeatedly and instruct his players, often by self-demonstration, in the defensive techniques he wanted employed. If their defensive crouch was too high, or their feet positioned wrong, or their hands held too low, he would stop action, step in, and demonstrate the exact approach to defense he wanted taken. Lesson finished, he would scan all the players besides the specific one under instruction to ensure that they had all understood the point he was making.

Sitting in the balcony I couldn't get enough of this. I watched as Jones put his team through a variety of other drills, some emphasizing offense, but most emphasizing defense. Over the course of the season these exercises would become familiar to me, though some of them would be de-emphasized or even phased out as practices concentrated on more advanced techniques and on the insertion of offensive and defensive ploys and stratagems to counter those of opposing teams. When I talked to Richard "Doc" Sauers, who had coached Jones in his undergraduate days at the State University at Albany, it came as no surprise that Jones had been a defensive standout, a specialist often inserted late in the game to shut down the opponent's hottest scorer. Demonstrating defense, even at age forty-seven, Jones was fast, driven, and maniacal.

* * * * *

Psychologically keen as well, Jones, after nearly three hours of strenuous practice, rewarded the guys with an eighteen-minute "controlled" scrimmage. "Controlled" means that the action can be stopped at any point for the coach to deliver instruction, which typically involved showing the offending player or players how to correct their mistakes by employing the proper techniques. First, Jones divided the squad into two teams: one wearing white, the other blue. The reversible jerseys worn for practice were perfect for this, white on one side, blue on the other. In fact, for any intra-squad drills pitting offense against defense, whether half-or full-court, Jones would divide the players into a White team and a Blue team. Same with full-court "controlled" intra-squad scrimmages.

The kids cut loose during this first practice-ending scrimmage, officiated by the assistant coaches. Every player attempted to strut his stuff. This for me was a joy to watch. Not so for Jones. He kept stopping the action to correct this or that mistake, teaching passionately, blowing his whistle and screeching in his alto voice to underscore a point of instruction. Sometimes these exchanges had comical aspects, but, again, I always stifled the laugh for fear it would be misinterpreted and hurt some kid's feelings. During this first controlled scrimmage Jones underscored "motion starters," meaning techniques to start the offensive assault on the basket, usually by means of what is called an "entry" pass from the perimeter to the post, or by means of dribble penetration. Such motion starters are the job of the offense to perfect and the job of the defense to impede or stop.

When the controlled scrimmage ended, Jones rewarded the players a second time with six minutes to practice "Bulldog shooting, " another sweetener based on honing offensive skills. Then he cracked the whip again with the "35 Second Drill," during which the players had to sprint cross-court from one sideline to the other as many times as they could within the allotted thirty-five seconds. This exercise would acquire punitive—and comical—aspects throughout the season as it was used to punish the players for lax performance or shoddy techniques or bad attitude. Jones would set a goal for everyone to attain within the thirty-five second span. If even one player failed to fulfill the goal, the entire squad had to repeat the drill until the requirement was met. This exercise increased the team's overall fitness and built up their wind, strength, and stamina, just as punitive push-ups would also do all season long. This system of imposing discipline I loved, believing as I do that a team can't be too fit. Like defense, fitness and stamina win championships.

The last time-segment on the practice agenda, spanning fifteen minutes from 7:45 to 8:00, read simply "Extra Credit." The description stated: "Individual Work with Coaches." I liked the serious academic tone of that, like the name of a course in a syllabus followed by the course description. It was so Ivy League and so right, so in balance: sports and mind.

In that vein I had giggled earlier in the day when, waiting for practice to begin, I noticed a piece of lined notepaper on the floor beside my seat. I picked it up and grinned as I scanned it. On it were handwritten notes and crude little pie charts and bar graphs on economics, comparing and contrasting macroeconomics and microeconomics. Discovering such an academic scrap in a college gym fortified my admiration for the seriousness of the Ivy League. The Ivy League is a throwback to another era, when amateur athletes who were serious students played true college basketball while pursuing an education over the course of four years. In an era when true college basketball is vitiated by big programs recruiting classes of high-school all-stars in a group, with promises that the group recruited to the one college can snare the NCAA championship the following year and thereby ensure each group member a high NBA draft position two months later, the college game has been debased to a semiprofessional recruitment lottery, dull, exploitative, and cynical, with the recruited players departing the school after a nine-month tour of duty. This travesty is a source of pain for all true fans of college basketball.

* * * * *

As a handful of players practiced their shots and moves with the coaches at the four baskets below, I packed up my briefcase and put my sweater and sports coat back on, preparing to leave but reluctant to do so, having had so much fun. When I stood up Jones saw me and smiled and nodded in my direction. I gave him a thumbs-up and mouthed in broad pantomime the words "See you tomorrow."

I sauntered out through the stone lobby with the wonderful ribbed arches and walked across campus and across the town green and through downtown until I reached the railroad station. It was comforting to me that I left one great railroad station in New York and traveled to another in New Haven each day, only to reverse the process each night. That very month the book I had worked on—on America's great railroad stations and their remarkable architecture—had been published, and in the book pride of place had been accorded both stations.

On the train I was still high from watching the practice. At the top of the agenda Coach Jones had highlighted in bold type, under the rubric "Word of the Day," the word "**Goal**: Something that someone wants to achieve." This practice of inserting and defining an inspirational word would continue all year, with each new agenda festooned with a meaningful word Jones intended his players to embrace and personify. At the bottom of the agenda in large bold type he had written: "**CENTRAL CONNECTICUT #1.**"

The Blue Devils of Central Connecticut were our first regular season opponents. The "#1" targeted them as our first victory. We had only four short weeks to prepare.

CHAPTER TWO

Laying the Groundwork

OVER THE COURSE of the next two weeks I attended nearly every practice, totally absorbed and delighted to be there. That very first intense weekend had set the tone. Because the women's basketball team also needed to practice in JLA periodically, the men's basketball team sometimes practiced in the new wing built behind Payne Whitney and called Lanman Recreation Center. This new annex was so spacious it held four full-length basketball courts laid out parallel to one another on its ground floor. Coach Jones would have a large blue curtain extended across the side of the second nearest court to the entrance and so sequester the two far courts exclusively for the use of his team. Once as I watched, a handful of young invaders violated this reserved space and Jones vanquished them with dispatch.

At first it was uncomfortable to watch in Lanman. Leaning against a wall it was hard to scribble my notes. If I squatted down and used my knee as a small writing tablet I risked toppling sideways when I attempted to rise, such was the state of my knees from an old football injury and from the relentless pounding of my years of compulsive jogging and marathon running. Though some of my athletic activity was as many as four decades in the rearview mirror, I still paid for it every time I tried to emulate a limber young athlete. Watching the players, I would often envy their agility and youth, the way you do when you're starting to circle the drain: when you start to get into movie theaters and onto public transportation for reduced rates. This intermediate state precedes the one where you're fully enfeebled. It's a sort of last hurrah for your vanished athleticism if, like me, you are afflicted with galloping arthritis and a waistline fighting to expand. Three years earlier this physical decline had been dramatically impressed on me. While on vacation with my wife at the Arizona Biltmore, one of my favorite places to relax, I put on my high-tops and strolled across the tennis courts until I reached the outdoor basketball court on the far side. There, with the first dribble, I instantly felt the old thrill, the magnificent rush, the unmatchable charge I always got on a basketball court.

Naturally, having by then suffered two frozen shoulders and acute bursitis in both, my shot was not what it had been. I had to adjust the arc upward to compensate for my lack of proper follow-through and elevation. My accuracy was nothing like it had been. Even when I practiced foul shots I hit only an appalling 50 percent, a huge drop-off from my youthful and routine mid-eighty-plus average. I used to be able to win quarters at games of PIG, HORSE, and best-out-of-ten foul shots. That proficiency was gone. What was worse was this: When I whipped the ball up on the side of the backboard for a deliberate miss so I could tap in a put-back, I got no lift on my leap and had to compensate with an extra upward push on the ball to get it high enough to drop into the basket after it caromed off the backboard.

My vertical leap had been pretty good once. Now it was a bunny hop. Instead of surging with exhilaration on going into the air, I returned to terra firma so quickly I felt like a toddler trying to alert a parent through over-articulated body language that I needed to go potty. My leap now was hardly more than toe walking. I had been a hundred and thirty pounds back when I could really get up; these days I was fifty pounds north of that, saddled with a slow metabolism, and restricted, in my ability to exercise, solely to walking. Yet walking still left me with a cherished gift, and lots of gratitude for it, since it is one of the great activities in a New Yorker's life, and one of my favorite things to do, achy knees and falling arches notwithstanding.

* * * * *

Overnight I had demonstrated the presence of mind, before reporting to the second practice in Lanman early Saturday morning, to print out from the website the roster of players, listing their position played, class year, height, weight, hometown, and high school. The previous afternoon at practice I had recognized only a few players from last year's team: the star center, Greg Mangano, predicted to be the Ivy League Player of the Year in the upcoming season; Reggie Willhite, like Mangano a senior and a starter the previous year; and two undergraduates, a small outside sharpshooter named Austin Morgan, a junior, and a sophomore power forward named Jeremiah Kreisberg. All four had played sizable roles in the upset of Harvard back at the tail end of last season. During the entire Saturday practice, and for several to come, I would drill myself in player recognition. At first I simply matched the players to their uniform numbers. Then, gradually, I studied each player's face, physique, posture and carriage, and his proclivities on the court, so I could identify all of them, before too long, at a glance, in uniform or out. I also committed to memory their hometowns and high schools.

The practices grew more complex as Jones hastened to instill his defensive philosophy and then his offensive strategy. Since defense wins or loses more games than offense, Jones concentrated on defense. Hour after hour of practice was dedicated to perfecting an aggressive man-to-man defense, my favorite form of defense, the classic form, the form that shuts down more offenses than a zone does. The man-to-man is what it says: each defender guards a specific man on offense. In a zone each defender is assigned instead a specific area of responsibility, and the man he guards depends on the offensive player or players that enter his designated area of responsibility within the overall zone configuration.

Zones come in many configurations: a three-two, a two-three, a one-two-two, a two-two-one, and other slight variations on these basic formations. There are also zones in which one defender is assigned a man to guard at all times, usually the highest scorer on the offense. In this instance one defender plays a man-to-man while his four teammates play a zone, each defending a specific area. The two most famous such combinations of man-to-man and zone are known as a box-and-one or a diamond-and-one. The fifth defender, sometimes called the roamer or chaser, pursues the man he is defending one-on-one wherever he goes.

Jones spent the majority of the time trying to perfect the aggressive man-to-man. He roared at his players to stay low, to extend their arms and hands, and to shuffle backward as fast as possible using short choppy steps to stay between their man and the basket. To watch remarkable defenders do this is exhilarating. Reggie Willhite and Austin Morgan were super quick, resembling dancers on steroids doing a backward jitterbug. Opposing players could not get around them. The metric for the effectiveness of any man-to-man is the synchronicity it achieves. All five defenders have to move in concert like the gears meshing in a Swiss watch.

Offensive players counter the aggressive closeness of a man-to-man defense with their own synchronicity by setting picks and screens on unwary defenders. In setting a pick, another player on offense comes up quickly behind the defender guarding the man with the ball and plants himself, standing dead still. The man with the ball then cuts toward the basket, simultaneously running his backpedaling defender into the man setting the pick. In setting a screen the offensive teammate without the ball comes up quickly to the side of the man with the ball. The man with the ball then cuts laterally toward the man setting the screen, simultaneously running his sidestepping defender into that screening teammate.

For a man-to-man defense to prove effective it must counter picks and screens with rapid "switching." Each of the two defenders, the one guarding the man with the ball and the one guarding the man who has just set the pick or screen, must instantly exchange men to defend, each now guarding the other's original man. Think of basketball as a game of chess between the opposing coaches, with each having only five players, instead of sixteen pieces. The five players on each side must perfect an amoeba-like movement in response to whatever the opposing five are doing to outmaneuver them. The ever shifting offense is attempting to capitalize on openings in the defense's ever shifting movement in response; the defense's reactive movement is designed to close any openings nearly instantaneously, before the offense can capitalize and score. The object of the offense is to move with total synchronicity at warp speed that the defense cannot match.

On defense Jones varies his preferred man-to-man with two classic zones: the two-three and the three-two. Although a team must have a preferred defensive system, either man-to-man or zone, all good teams can shift adequately from one to the other when necessary. To simplify, a zone is often necessary when the offensive team is composed of good post players and perimeter players good at dribble penetration and scoring off drives, but poor at perimeter shooting. In that instance the zone is designed to shut down the inside game and force the opposing offense to beat you with outside shooting, often referred to as "beating you over the top." The inside game is always composed of good post scoring and good scoring off dribble penetration and drives. To clarify, dribble penetration is classed separately from drives because all drives derive from dribble penetration but dribble penetration also leads to scoring when the penetrator feeds an open player in the low post or an open man on the perimeter.

The open man, either in the post or on the perimeter, results from the penetrator drawing defenders other than the man guarding him toward him to thwart his effort to score himself off his drive. When the penetrator passes the ball back outside to the open man on the perimeter, or when the post player receiving the initial pass from the penetrator whips it out to the open man on the perimeter, that is known as an "inside-out" game.

Although a man-to-man is usually more effective than a zone, a zone must be in a team's repertoire to sometimes break an opponent's offensive rhythm. This is true especially when the offensive team is scoring at will with its inside game, but it also holds true when the defenders are clearly at a sharp disadvantage in athleticism compared to the attacking offensive players. A coach will also shift into a zone, often temporarily, when forced to use a substitute who is a lesser athlete than the man being replaced; in that instance, the zone can mask a weak link in the chain of defense. A zone can compensate for lesser athleticism in one, or several, or all of the defenders.

Jones knew that a good team needed both forms of basic defense. Yet he also knew that a great man-to-man defense was superior to a zone when well synchronized and energetically played. When that happened the man-to-man was hard to penetrate and beat. Throughout the season Jones worked his players in the demanding "5 on 5 Shell" exercise, honing and polishing their man-to-man skills, never failing to exhort them to "talk" to one another to enhance coordination and increase synchronicity, all in the cause of attaining the "shell" for which the exercise was named. This shell was to be impenetrable, with its every amoeba-like, shape-changing move designed to stymie any offensive move so that the shell remained unbreachable. When the shell was totally sealed the only option left to the offense was to shoot low-percentage shots from far out. A well played man-to-man achieves the same goal as a tight zone in forcing the offense to "beat you over the top."

But a great man-to-man has another advantage. If you have the athletes to pull it off, it can be quick and agile enough to extend outward to harass the perimeter shooters and sometimes even deflect or block their long distance shots. When such proficiency is achieved in the classic man-to-man, the opponent's offense is shut down. The shell's tightness and instant expandability suffocate the opposing offense, in the post and on the perimeter, choking off any chance of penetration and eliminating the possibility of long shots taken in the clear. A perfect man-to-man shell spells curtains for any offense, no matter how good, talented, or coordinated.

* * * * *

The offense Jones installed was founded on what is called the "Flex," with variations and wrinkles blended in. These were random borrowings, mostly from the Triangle offense, the Motion offense, and the UCLA offense. The strength of the Flex is that it is basic, adaptable, and fairly easy to teach and learn. Its weakness is that it is predictable and easy to defend provided the opponent knows it well and has the talent to "match up" well with the offensive players executing it. Bear in mind that any variety of offense deployed in basketball is designed to lead to a score on every possession, just as in football every offensive play on the drawing board, executed to perfection, is designed to result in a touchdown. Of course in the heat and chaos of game action these designs only rarely work out to perfection.

On offense the goal of any system is to draw five defenders to four offensive players, leaving the fifth offensive player open to score. On offense the ballhandler has three basic options: pass, dribble, or shoot. All offensive systems are designed to max out on these three options, aided by the movements and actions of the four offensive players moving without the ball, so that one player winds up open for a scoring shot. In the Flex, two players—the point guard and the shooting guard—are stationed out front on either side of the top of the key. The small forward is down in the corner. On the same side of the court the center is on the near block parallel to the basket but just outside the lane. The power forward is on the opposite side of the court on the far block parallel to the basket but just outside the lane. No offensive player is allowed to stay in the lane for three consecutive seconds, so players on the low posts have to stay just outside the lane until they cross it rapidly or move into it rapidly to shoot. Offensive players can stay in the lane if the ball has been shot, once or repeatedly, and, if the shot or shots miss, they can stay in the lane to position themselves to contend for the rebound or for the put-back shot.

In the Flex, the point guard will initiate the offense to either side of the court. The side chosen, where the ball is in play, is called the strong side.

The side without the ball is called the weak side. The Flex is designed to run through options quickly and result in low post scores off screens and picks, or in open shots on the perimeter when the low post is defended. When the low post is defended the ball is quickly passed back out to an open player on the perimeter. He will shoot or pass the ball back to the man open in the near corner or to the player open on the perimeter on the opposite side of the court.

When the ball is passed rapidly to the player open on the opposite side of the court it's called "reversing the ball." This is crucial. Rapid ball movement is the most important element of effective scoring. A thrown ball is faster than any defender. A pass thrown back to the weak side must be countered by a defender rushing to the weak side and thwarting the open offensive player set to take the shot. The weak side on offense is the help side on defense. Like fluid in a hydraulic system, the defenders tend to cluster on the strong side, where the ball is and the pressure needs to be applied, and in doing so they slack off the weak side. With a rapid ball movement reverse the ball ends up on the weak side faster than the defenders can get back to that weak side, a.k.a. the "help side" for them. Recall: drawing five defenders onto four offensive players is the object of ball movement, the key to scoring with the "open man" on offense.

That simple principle is the cornerstone of offensive basketball. Rapid passing combined with syncopated movement by all five offensive players is the key. The four offensive players moving without the ball must set screens and picks before the defenders can switch men to defend and thereby "help out." The slight time lag before the defenders can rearrange themselves results in an open man and a good scoring opportunity.

The Flex offense has nice advantages to exploit if there are tall and talented post players on the team executing it. The reasons for this are two. First, the options designed to feed the post are plentiful and easy to learn; and, second, these low-post scoring options depend on screens that often result in a taller post player being guarded, after the defensive switch, by a shorter defender. The taller post player can then usually score fairly easily. On Yale, Greg Mangano and Jeremiah Kreisberg were tall and talented post players.

Another advantage of the Flex is that it endlessly renews itself when executed properly. Its options are designed to end with the five offensive players positioned on the court so that, should the original set of options be exhausted without a score, to reset the offense quickly involves only minimal player reshuffling. After a simple rotation and a ball reversal, the five offensive players restore the original two-out, three-in formation on the opposite side of the floor.

Because syncopation and speed are so important to the proper execution of any offensive system, Jones drilled his players endlessly. He needed to inculcate in them a feel for one another's movements on the court in any and all situations. This mutual awareness, this "feel" for one another's movements, has to become second nature. Great players sense one another's presence and movements as surely as the blind do. Only then can they facilitate rapid ball movement and the speed of execution that lead to the five-on-four defensive overload that results in the open man. As Jones drilled the players, he rotated them in different combinations so they acquired this feel for the movements of all their teammates. Each combination would explore all the different ways to initiate the Flex and exploit all its options.

Jones drilled mainly the five-man combinations he thought would play together most frequently, especially the starting five. That's why he would begin with the starting five and then substitute players in the most likely order they would be inserted into a game. Learning how to deploy your players for maximum effectiveness depending on who else is on the floor at any given time, and what strengths and weaknesses the opponent possesses, is a skill every good coach must have. Jones had it: he knew how to choose the best overall set for his team, and he knew how to mix and match this set in light of the opponent's strengths and weaknesses. Timing is incredibly important here. A good coach must have an innate and unerring sense of when to substitute.

Jones would rely on the Flex as his team's basic offense. But he added to it—gradually, as the players became more proficient at executing it. He first installed elements of the Motion offense. Similar to the Flex, the Motion allows the players more freedom to improvise using a larger and more varied set of options. While the Flex is a continuous offense, the Motion is an interpretive offense. Along with being less predictable, the Motion can be executed at a faster tempo. In short, it is more sophisticated, and requires the players to take more initiative. The Motion is more fluid and improvisational than the more strictly choreographed Flex. Harder to defend, the Motion is harder to master. And because the Motion depends on players being highly familiar with one another's moves and preferences, it usually only works well for teams that have been together for long periods of time.

Jones also incorporated the sideline triangle from the Triangle offense, where a post player comes up to the elbow while another player, either a guard or forward, retreats to the near, or "short," corner, and the guard at the near wing initiates the offense with an entry pass to either of these two players "overloading" that side of the court. When this three-man sideline triangle is in place, the remaining two teammates set up on the opposite or "weak" side of the court and position themselves one out, one in, with the perimeter player out on the far wing and the post player in on the low block or the elbow. These two players on the weak side are ready, when the triangle side is defended, for the ball to be reversed to them for open shots, the defenders having clustered on the overloaded strong side.

To add yet a third wrinkle, Jones later grafted the high post alignment from the UCLA offense into his team's repertoire. In this alignment, a post player with good passing, shooting, and dribbling skills comes out "high," meaning far from the basket, and forms the fulcrum of the offensive maneuvering and flow. Usually this offense works best with a tall center coming out to either elbow or to the center point on the foul line, thus "high" as opposed to down low on the blocks. The other four players then align themselves along the perimeter. This offensive configuration is the same as the triangle but with the fulcrum of the offense rotated ninety degrees from the low blocks on one side, so that the point of the "triangle" is centered on the post player in the middle of the foul line or on either elbow. Also more complicated than the Flex, this beautifully balanced offense is harder to defend, especially if all five players executing it have outstanding passing, shooting, and dribble penetration skills.

* * * * *

After two weeks of intense practice, Jones had the fundamental offensive and defensive strategies in place. He had also spent hours practicing the fast break. By splitting the team, Jones could practice offense and defense on the fast break at the same time, constantly switching the players back and forth. The fast break occurs when the team on defense steals, intercepts, or rebounds the ball and hastily "breaks" down court—running and dribbling at maximum speed or passing rapidly forward—before the team that had been on offense can recover and run down court in time to set up its defense. Following Jones's agendas, the three-on-none fast break had been practiced for hours, as had the four-on-three. The three-on-none is obvious.

The four-on-three occurs when the team that had been on offense recovers enough to have three of its players scramble back on defense, usually in disarray, where they will be outnumbered by the four formerly defensive players now sprinting down court to execute the offensive fast break.

It was now time to take the team on the first of two shakedown cruises before the start of the regular season. These took the form of scrimmages against outside competition. The first occurred on October 29 against the New Jersey Institute of Technology in Newark, and the second a week later, November 5, back at JLA against the State University of New York at Stony Brook.

CHAPTER THREE

"It'll Happen Fast"

ON OCTOBER 29 a freak snowstorm hit the Northeast. In New Jersey it was not too bad but Connecticut was hit hard. The storm started early that Saturday and did not prevent the Yale team bus from arriving at the New Jersey Institute of Technology gym in Newark for the scheduled morning scrimmage against the Highlanders. The scrimmage itself was a bit chaotic at times, despite the presence of three pinstriped referees, all professionals. This was to be expected with both teams trying out their offenses and defenses for the first time against outside competition.

NJIT was essentially overmatched. The school plays in a minor Division I conference, the Great West Conference. What a school based in New Jersey is doing in a conference called the Great West with teams from near or beyond the Continental Divide says volumes about what is wrong with college athletics today, but that's the way it is. The NJIT team was somewhat undersized though it had a handful of able outside shooters and a few guards who could penetrate well off the dribble. The opposing coaches had agreed to play two twenty-minute periods, or the length of a regulation game, with an additional "overtime" period spanning ten minutes. This extended playing time allowed each coach to rotate his players and try them in different combinations.

In the first period Jones played Yale's starters and the "first guys off the bench." They acquitted themselves well enough to "win" that period 49-41, though the score was not as pertinent as in a real game. In the second period Jones went with his second team and his "down the bench guys," players who rarely get into a game. NJIT "won" that period 46-42, mostly by keeping a handful of their starters on the floor. For the overtime period Jones gave his starters more work and the tally ended 20-12 in Yale's favor.

All the while the scrimmaging continued in the Fleischer Athletic Center, the size of a high-school gym, the snow whirled against the glass doors in the foyer, propelled by gusts of wind. Slush accumulated outside on the sidewalks and in the parking lots. The hallmark of this scrimmage was the lack of cohesion from both teams, and Yale's highly accurate outside shooting. Yale's star center, Greg Mangano, scored twenty-three points, as did lightning quick shooting guard Austin Morgan. Point guard Michael Grace chipped in twelve points and reserve guard Sam Martin scored thirteen, going a perfect four-for-four beyond the three-point arc and adding a foul shot for good measure, prompting me to nickname him "Sharpshooter Sam."

Neither team's defense was impressive. Yale allowed four NJIT starters to combine for 71 points, eighteen from Isaiah Wilkerson, who would go on to win the Player of the Year award in the Great West Conference and wind up as the only player on any of New Jersey's eight Division I teams to win Honorable Mention on the Associated Press All-America team. What's more, NJIT would go on to have a good season, losing the conference tournament championship game to North Dakota in their final game. No doubt the Highlanders were much better later in the season than they were that snowy day.

My reward for trekking out to Newark in this filthy weather arrived suddenly and unexpectedly when Jones walked across the court and said, "Come into the locker room, Ed." I was the only spectator in the stands save one other man, a very tall one. Half an hour later, talking to this man on the inanely run Newark subway system, I learned that he was a Yalie and the father of the tallest player on the team, seven-foot freshman center Will Childs-Klein. I told him that when his son put twenty to twenty-five pounds on his torso and ten to fifteen on this thighs and buttocks he would not be knocked off the low blocks so easily and would be too quick for Ivy League centers. Over the next couple of years I hope to track that prediction, on which his dad and I heartily agreed.

When I got to the locker room I stood in the back, behind all the players, while Jones addressed them for about ten minutes. Letting them know he was extremely disappointed in their play, he told them, barring improvement, they would win few games against the stiff competition they would soon face in their non-conference schedule, let alone against their over-determined, hyper-competitive, rivalry-ridden Ivy League foes. It was an effective speech and I noted that Greg Mangano, seated directly in front of me, shook his foot, in either anger or frustration, from first word to last. During the scrimmage he had seemed at different times agitated and discomfited, most likely from the rough handling he got without fouls being called on the NJIT players and from his teammates' lack of entry passes to him in the low post. The Yale perimeter guys had declined to work the offense and instead hoisted up too many hasty long-range, low-percentage shots, though this day they made a lot of them. Such selfishness is to be expected when every player is trying to make his mark and impress Jones to use him more, or even to promote him to the starting lineup. The game was not a pretty sight, and Yale should have played better.

Jones concluded his speech by saying that it was "the twenty-one of us against them," alluding to his seventeen players, three assistants, and himself. Under my breath I added, "twenty-two."

* * * * *

The following week in practice Jones was animated and firm, pushing his team very hard; yet, admirably, he never became a martinet about it. Certainly I never saw him be abusive. That doesn't mean he wasn't dissatisfied, and very vocal about it. The more I thought back on the haphazard quality of play at NJIT, the more I disliked it and apparently for Jones it was even more vexing to think back on it. We had only a week to get ready for Stony Brook and the days were flying by, and along with them the number of practices left to get the team up to speed and in sync.

The snowstorm had crippled central Connecticut, dropping a weird twenty October inches that paralyzed homes and communities. Roads were blocked and power lines downed by fallen trees. The result was havoc. The Monday following the NJIT scrimmage, the 31st of October—Halloween in fact, now that I reflect on Mother Nature's mischief—Jones notified me that the Connecticut Six Press Conference scheduled in Hartford for the next day, Tuesday, November 1, had been postponed because of the statewide emergency the governor had declared. The conference would convene instead in Hartford the following week, on Tuesday the 8th.

Because of the emergency I didn't get to really talk to Jones until Friday of that week, when I met him for lunch at his office. We went to the Educated Burgher again and sat in a back booth and reviewed everything so far, including his animated take on what he wanted to happen the following day against Stony Brook and what he saw against NJIT and never wanted to see again all season. He knew and enumerated the team's problems in detail and discussed how he planned to correct or eliminate them. I listened intently and then gave him my take on all the players so far, especially the freshmen, who referred to themselves, half mockingly, half seriously, as the Fab Five.

I told him I saw a great deal of potential in a rugged freshman named Brandon Sherrod, a muscular post player to reckon with in years to come if his footwork improved and his offensive repertoire expanded. I also told him my evaluation of Will Childs-Klein that had so pleased Will's dad in the Newark subway system. He smiled but acknowledged that Will was not yet ready to play much. A tall, unselfish point guard named Javier Duren had extraordinary dribbling and passing skills and "saw the floor" at six-feet-four-inches better than any other guard we had. He was quick, he could drive well, and he sensed, as well as saw, the movement around him. "Seeing the floor" meant he had good peripheral vision, very important in a point guard. In short, he had a high basketball IQ. Armani Cotton at six-seven would evolve into a swingman with exceptional quickness and grace for his size; his wingspan led me to nickname him the "Baby Raptor." When he defended, he crouched very low, moved backward and laterally at amazing speed, and enveloped the man he was guarding. He brought these same athletic gifts to his offensive game, to which he added good passing skills and a good shooting touch.

When the lunch ended, I realized as soon as we parted that I never mentioned the fifth freshman, Matt Townsend, a polite and well-bred kid whose game I admired for its polish. Like Brandon, Matt, six-feet-seven-inches tall, was a well-built post player. He had exceptional footwork for his age and experience, and a butterfly touch on his finishing shots in the low post. He had an especially deft jump hook on which he scored most of the time when he relaxed infinitesimally before he shot it. Freshman excitability from lack of game experience at the Division I level could impair Matt's effectiveness, but that was true for most freshmen, and true for the four other members of Yale's Fab Five. With playing time they would all outgrow it.

During that lunch I remember asking Jones if he planned to run a lot, using lots of substitution because the freshmen added such athletic ability and speed. Cagey yet open, Jones did not commit. With a wait-and-see grin he kept his own counsel. To my question whether he had decided on a starting unit he essentially said that he had. I told him that his sophomore guard Isaiah Salafia was an immensely impressive young athlete. I estimated his vertical leap in the thirty-six-inch range. I had tracked him carefully in practice and he was the fastest kid on the team, faster even than Reggie Willhite, the senior captain with outstanding agility, speed, and leaping ability. Jones agreed with me.

At our initial lunch back in June I recapped how two books had formed my basketball philosophy, Branch McCracken's *Indiana Basketball*, given to me over half a century earlier by Rip Collins, my CYO football and basketball coach, and by Jack Ramsay's *Pressure Defense*, which I had bought and read when it came out in the early sixties. Both books were classics on how to win basketball games and championships via pressurized man-to-man defense. The seventeen rules of fundamental defensive techniques enumerated nearly six decades ago by McCracken are all dead-on applicable today, and thanks to a wonderful man named Tony Alfonso you can pluck them off the Internet, as I did to refresh my memory, having foolishly lost both books over the years.

Ramsay's book was a gem on how to practice, apply, and master the trapping man-to-man and its application in the half-court and in the full-court press. As a ball boy in the Palestra I had seen Ramsay's St. Joe's teams topple team after team with superior talent simply by applying relentless pressure in trapping man-to-man defenses. For such pressure defense to be devastating to the opposition it must be practiced ceaselessly by the team applying it; that team must also be superbly conditioned and blessed with able substitutes who can give the exhausted starters a blow on the bench when winded and their legs weary from applying frenzied energy full bore. As a player who had played both point and shooting guard I knew firsthand the havoc a pressing, trapping man-to-man defense could inflict on an offense that had not drilled against it incessantly in its own practices. Then again, even when a team had done this, an athletic, gifted, and prepared offense could still falter and turn the ball over repeatedly against a masterfully applied trapping and scrambling press.

I told Jones such pressurized defense was a great equalizer but he countered—as many knowledgeable basketball people do—that it was too often a sign of weakness and an admission that the opposing team had superior athletes. If the press backfired, games could get out of hand against you, he maintained. I acknowledged his point but silently demurred. I believe a team can't be too good at applying the press or at coping with it, whether half-or full-court.

We closed that lunch with Jones agreeing that his team had good senior leadership, not just with the two stars, Greg Mangano and Reggie Willhite, but with the two senior reserves, power forward Rhett Anderson and shooting guard Brian Katz. Jones smiled his patented smile and said we'd find out more about this team tomorrow morning when we scrimmaged Stony Brook.

* * * * *

When I got to JLA early the next morning autumn sunlight streamed through the windows and added highlights to the already shiny and floodlit hardwood. Players from both teams were out on the floor warming up and taking shots, Stony Brook in scarlet and Yale in white. Scheduled for ten o'clock, the scrimmage started right on time. It was immediately obvious that Stony Brook was a cut above NJIT. Bigger and stronger, Stony Brook had a much better front line and a much better post presence. They also played in a better conference, the America East Conference.

Jones used his starters again but substituted freely, as did Stony Brook's head coach. The teams played three intense periods of twenty minutes each, all contested fiercely and all finishing with the score nearly even. Yale took the first period and Stony Brook the last two, with the third period contested principally by substitutes for both teams, most of them third-string freshmen and sophomores. Stony Brook ran a smoother and more disciplined offense than NJIT, but Yale played infinitely better defense than it had the previous Saturday in Newark. Yale looked like a different team on defense and it was clear Jones had drilled his players fiercely all week long. On the other side of the ball Yale was equally improved, with the offense not so haphazard and helter-skelter but more controlled and rhythmic. More patient, the guys worked the ball not only into the post better but moved without the ball better and got into position for uncontested shots not only on the perimeter but midrange, at ten to fifteen feet from the basket.

Greg Mangano led all Yale scorers with twenty points and played tight defense on the Seawolves' post players, blocking several shots, a tactic he was extremely adept at. The rest of the Yale scoring was spread evenly, with five other guys in double figures, led by Greg Kelley's fourteen points. Greg was a slender but agile six-foot-eight sophomore with quick and effective post moves and a fluid and accurate midrange and perimeter shot. He needed to fill out a little more but even if he didn't, he was an effective scorer if not burly enough to be a rugged post rebounder or defender. Yet his quickness sometimes compensated for his lack of bulk even under the boards and he managed to pick off the odd rebound. Of the players who would become

Yale starters for most of the year, deadeye shooting guard Austin Morgan had nine points, swingman and captain Reggie Willhite had ten, point guard Mike Grace scored thirteen, and power forward Jeremiah Kreisberg chipped in with four. Jerry also snared six rebounds, only one fewer than Greg Mangano, who, as with blocking shots, was skilled and adept at rebounding. Each six-feet-ten-inches tall, Greg and Jerry formed a pair of twin towers in the post. One of the other players in double figures was senior shooting guard Brian Katz, with thirteen points.

All things considered, Yale had looked like a different, more polished team. The players had apparently listened. It was obvious that Jones had "coached them up" with a vengeance. His stern diatribe a week ago, informing them that they would have their heads handed to them by the upcoming competition if they didn't come together as a team, had hit home, both on offense and defense. Stony Brook would go on to have the best season in school history, finishing with a 22-10 record and a two-point loss in a first-round game at Seton Hall in the postseason National Invitation Tournament. But for a loss to Vermont in the America East Conference tournament championship game, Stony Brook would have snared a trip to the NCAA Tournament. All of this couldn't be known right then leaving JLA that sunny autumn Saturday but clearly, only one week later, Yale had played far closer to its potential against a much better team than NJIT.

One incident in the scrimmage had upset me a great deal, and I wasn't ready for it. Near the end of the last period Matt Townsend had driven hard for the basket and crashed into an oncoming defender. Down Matt went, screaming in pain. Sprawled on the floor beneath the basket, he clutched his knee, writhing and yelping as he rolled back and forth. In my balcony seat I feared that he'd torn his meniscus or his anterior cruciate ligament. I feared his freshman season was over before it had begun. I was crushed for him. All the rest of that Saturday I worried and all of Sunday. Then I emailed Jones and he told me Matt had a severe sprain and that he was "a tough kid" who would be back on form in a few weeks. It surprised me how quickly I had become so concerned for these kids, so fond of them, but I had. Here was yet another thing coaches, like doctors, had to inure themselves against: the prospect of heartbreaking injury.

In six days Yale would play its first regular season game at the Connecticut Six Classic. Walking to lunch with Jones the day before I had remarked that bird-dogging the team had made time fly. He looked at me and said, "Winter is short when you're this involved with basketball, Ed. It'll happen fast."

"In America today, coaches are judged by whether they win or lose and not by how well they teach. So winning is what you worry about most—winning and all the factors that affect the chances of winning: the character of the players, recruiting, admissions, financial aid, academic pressures, luck. I define success as having a chance to win every game."

Pete Carril
The Smart Take From the Strong

PART TWO:

THE NONCONFERENCE
SEASON

CHAPTER FOUR

Wheel of Fortune

NOVEMBER 11, 2011, Veterans Day, was one of the greatest days I've ever lived. At the Mohegan Sun Casino in eastern Connecticut, the Connecticut Six Classic commenced, three games right in a row, starting at three in the afternoon and going straight on into the evening. Hartford played Sacred Heart in the opening game, followed by Quinnipiac against Fairfield, then Yale wrapped up the festivities at eight against Central Connecticut.

A jumble of nerves and anticipation, I drove over to the casino from my house in the Hudson River Valley, not knowing what to expect but more excited than I'd been since I'd started my first CYO basketball game in the fall of 1960. The casino complex was so vast it took me nearly forty-five minutes to find the basketball arena. It was quite beautiful and large, the home of the Mohegan Sun women's professional team in the WNBA and the venue for many successful rock concerts and other entertainment events. I found the press window, picked up my credentials, and wound my way to press row, my heart pumping hard enough to clear out all my arterial plaque.

I was in Walter Mitty heaven, and had to remind myself I wasn't yet fledged to rub shoulders with the ghosts of Red Smith, Shirley Povich, Sandy Grady, Jim Murray, Dan Jenkins, Jimmy Cannon, A. J. Liebling, and Grantland Rice. You see, when I wasn't woolgathering that I should have been a college basketball coach, I fantasized that I should have been a sportswriter. Ingrid Bergman remarked once that the secret to a happy life was good health and a bad memory, but I think another ingredient is a must: an active fantasy life. Sitting along press row with a lanyard around my neck and a laminated card flapping against my chest declaring me a writer was heady stuff.

I was thrilled to be learning a lot. My rush was so strong I felt like a bulimic at a Roman banquet. But the old feelings of being a fraud and an impostor were surging as well. Every time I walked along press row to the media room in the bowels of the arena beneath the stands I thought the security guards were going to stop, frisk, and escort me out. Of course this never happened. I went to and fro between the halves and between the games and gorged on pizza, pasta, and oatmeal cookies. Had I pinched myself a thousand times I still couldn't have believed what Coach Jones, SID Tim Bennett, and the Yale community had done for me.

Three days earlier I had attended the postponed press conference in Hartford where I'd heard all six coaches interviewed. When Jones initially invited me to attend I had no idea why. I soon found out and was most grateful for his foresight. As each coach took to the podium I got a whole new perspective on the skills required to be a head coach of men's basketball in Division I. Every coach impressed me with his analytical and verbal skills, and Dave Bike, the longstanding coach of Sacred Heart, hit the wittiest zinger when asked what had changed in college basketball over his thirty-four-year coaching career: "The pants are longer."

Each coach in turn had expressed his hopes for the season, and each was as zesty and enthusiastic as a big league manager in the spring training sunshine of Florida or Arizona. Dreams abounded. I remembered driving back from Hartford after the press conference immersed in a kind of passionate curiosity about the future. I knew the folly of wishing your life away like that but I wondered where everyone's season would be four months hence—how it would end: in triumph or in tears, or maybe in just plain old mediocrity.

What I knew for certain was this: everyone—players, coaches, trainers, student managers, statisticians and band members—all of them by spring would have enhanced their lives through sheer participation, win, lose, or draw. And in the process they would have banished the winter blues, which was part of the original plan when the YMCA boss told James Naismith to invent an indoor game back in 1891.

* * * * *

When the first game started, there I was on press row excited and beaming and clueless. I knew enough to have a notebook in front of me but I wasn't sure what to write in it. Did I just put down impressions, or did I score the game as I used to score baseball games in old Connie Mack Stadium in Philly when I was ten? Back then I was so well versed in the art of scoring baseball that the game could be reconstructed from my scorecard. I wasn't sure if I needed to be that elaborate scoring a basketball game. I only knew I was overmatched if I had to remember all the stats and facts the coaches and announcers and color men could cite in games I watched on television.

Not sure what to do, I sat and wrote a few impressions of the Sacred Heart and Hartford players. Both teams were on our schedule for November games, so I could scout them now and get a foretaste of what we'd be up against shortly. Then young women, student volunteers, came along press row distributing running stat sheets on the game. The sheets had all the dope on them the coaches and announcers and color men cited during the televised games. What a great boon this was, I thought, and semi-relaxed as I studied the sheets, updated every few minutes. All the stats you needed to analyze the game were on the sheets, categorized and clearly laid out. I watched all the professional sportswriters seated along press row study the sheets and tap their laptop keyboards. Same with the radio and TV guys. Obviously I had a lot to learn about covering sports but I knew the human element was more important than flat numbers, and that was what I was really after, the human drama. This realization was a great consolation for what I realized were my reportorial inadequacies.

The first half between Hartford and Sacred Heart was the worst half of basketball I watched all season. It ended with the score Sacred Heart 26, Hartford 15. Ineptness was steep on both sides but Hartford pushed it to its limit. A single player can frequently score fifteen points in a half, let alone a whole team having only fifteen points for an entire 20-minute half. Even ascribing much of this ineptness to nerves in the season's opener, Hartford was stinking up the arena, and Sacred Heart was adding to the overall odor. At the intermission I counted the house as I walked to the media room and estimated the crowd at 350 people. It was an afternoon game on a holiday but still the competing schools were fairly short drives away and I thought there'd be more students. In the media room my spirits spiked when I overheard two student reporters enthusiastically discussing the upcoming season and noting that Drexel was picked preseason to win the Colonial Athletic

Association title. I hadn't known that but I hoped it would come true for my much-loved alma mater.

When I got back to my seat for the second half I scanned the arena and thought it was the perfect size and configuration for good viewing. It held 10,000 and was laid out in the familiar modern two-tiered oval, yet it was intimate, not airplane-hangar cold the way so many modern arenas are. Thankfully the game picked up. Settled down, no doubt by helpful words from their coaches, both teams played much better, though Hartford lost the second half as well, 44 to 35. That meant Sacred Heart walked away with a convincing 20-point win, the final score being 70 to 50.

My overriding impression was that Yale could beat both these teams. I expected, naturally, that Sacred Heart would be the more difficult of the two. They had more and better athletes, and very good guard play. I had especially been impressed by Shane Gibson, a six-two guard who could score in bunches, and they had a six-nine center named Justin Swidowski who, agile and quick, had managed to top all scorers with eighteen points. He was a transfer from Philadelphia University, what used to be called Philadelphia College of Textiles and Science, and I had great memories of the early sixties when Herb Magee had set NCAA Division II scoring records at Textile that lasted for decades.

Hartford had played too poorly to make much of an impression. I knew only that senior point guard Andres Torres was expected to lead the team but he had played so erratically that he was ineffective. On offense his passing was often wild and on defense his impulse to lunge for steals too often failed, leaving a five-on-four situation for his teammates to contend with on a break while he tried to scurry back down court to help defend. It did register on me that Hartford was a very young team and had played a number of freshmen for considerable stretches of the game. Obviously the Hawks were in a rebuilding year.

Between games I spotted Coach Jones sitting on the opposite end of press row chatting with a friend. He caught my eye as I passed on the way to the media room and we greeted each other. I leaned down and whispered to him that the first half of the game just completed had been a sloppy mess, and he agreed with me, adding that this sometimes happened in the first game of the season. I hoped it wouldn't happen to Yale and wondered if the same fear had occurred to him.

* * * * *

The second game had rough spots but was much better played and more closely contested, though it seemed clear early on that Fairfield had the better squad, deeper and more experienced on the front line. Fairfield had a new head coach, Sydney Johnson. The year before, his former team, the Ivy League co-champion Princeton Tigers, had won the winner-take-all single playoff game against Harvard to earn the Ivy's automatic NCAA tournament bid. Then they nearly upset eventual tournament runner-up Kentucky in the first round but fell two points short. During the offseason Johnson had been lured to Fairfield. Because his recruiting season had been foreshortened by the change in jobs, Johnson's Fairfield team consisted mainly of inherited players. His upperclassmen were seasoned, and a seven-foot senior center anchored the front line and commanded the post, aided by two able small forwards, Rakim Sanders, a senior star with outstanding scoring and rebounding skills, and Maurice Barrow, a gifted athlete who could also rebound and score with consistency.

Quinnipiac was no slouch either. The school was coming off its second straight 20-win season and, though there were eight new players on the roster, a handful of talented upperclassmen returned, including high-scoring senior point guard James Johnson and rugged sophomore forward Ike Azotam. Unfortunately, Johnson had been suspended one game by head coach Tom Moore for disciplinary reasons. This mishap did cost them any chance they had to win the game, though Fairfield would likely have prevailed anyway had Johnson been on the court. As it was, Quinnipiac had to start freshman guard Zaid Hearst, talented but untested.

Fairfield took quick control of the game, led at halftime 38-29, and, when Quinnipiac made a late run in the second half to narrow the lead to two points, pulled away with an 11-0 run over the last three minutes-plus, to win by a final score of 72-60. My one thought was that we could beat Quinnipiac the following Tuesday. I was also grateful Fairfield wasn't on the schedule.

* * * * *

When Yale ran out of the tunnel and paired off in two lines for pregame warm-ups I hadn't been this excited about basketball since my Uncle Tom decided to cut down an unused utility pole in the early sixties and plant it in the center of what was called "the back lot." The back lot was actually a trapezoidal-shaped plot of land behind a block of two-story row houses lining the south side of Brown Street between Pennock and Twenty-eighth streets. This block of houses sat directly opposite the house I grew up in in Fairmount, as our neighborhood in North Philly was called after the park it fronted, the largest urban park in the world.

The back lot stood where the foundries and workshops of the Baldwin Locomotive Works had been, before the company decamped to Chester, thirty miles south of Philadelphia on the old Wilmington Pike, a.k.a. Route One. In spots on the back lot remnants of the old stone foundations of the Baldwin buildings loomed above the cinder surface like outsize stepping-stones in a gray and dirty brook. This didn't deter guys from playing baseball there, or from sliding into a base and skinning their entire upper thigh and worse.

Uncle Tom was bighearted and brilliant. His plan had been to plant the utility pole in the middle of the back lot after adding a plywood backboard and a metal basket with a chainlink net. Brilliant but naïve when it came to things mechanical, Uncle Tom strolled down Brown Street and into our kitchen to check his plan with my father. One man was to cut the pole and the other to catch it. Uncle Tom planned to do the catching. The minute my dad heard this scheme he roared with laughter. When he managed to stop, he said, "Hell, Tom, it'll kill you. You gotta rig it with guy wires and lower it slowly and carefully to the ground."

I heard this exchange because I was standing in the kitchen at the time. So was my Uncle Bill, my mother's younger brother who lived with us. Uncle Bill had laughed hard too. I'd just listened, not knowing enough one way or the other and not wanting to laugh at Uncle Tom, about whom I was crazy. My dad and Uncle Bill loved Tom, too. He was married to my mother's and Uncle Bill's older sister Mary, the gentlest and most loving person imaginable. But my dad and Uncle Bill, both mechanically gifted, found brainy Tom endlessly amusing. My dad was a first-class machinist and Uncle Bill a spectacular auto mechanic who'd been a crackerjack Seabee in the war. Between them they could build or fix practically anything.

In contrast Uncle Tom was pure gray matter, a great administrator and analyst and solver of problems. Years later he went on to head the City of Philadelphia Department of Procurement for nearly two decades. He was also a master psychologist and could read people instantly. Above all, he understood boys as well as any American, possibly excepting Mark Twain and Father Flanagan. I put that qualifier in to moderate any tendency on my part to hyperbole, but in a showdown with those two my money would have been on Uncle Tom. In four decades living in New York City I've audited hundreds of claims asserting that this fellow or that woman was smarter than anyone else ever, but not in New York, Los Angeles, or London was I ever in a room with someone I thought was smarter than my uncle Tom.

The following Saturday the pole came down, my father calling the shots. He worked with riggers at his job, and had strung ropes and wires to the pole and stationed men from the neighborhood strategically around it with the ends of the ropes and wires secured in their hands. Once the pole was cut near its base these men gradually and gently lowered it to the ground, completely under control the whole time. Then they picked it up waist high and marched it half a block into the back lot, far enough into the middle and far enough back from the row houses not to impede Uncle Tom's outdoor amphitheater for movies.

Every summer Uncle Tom showed outdoor movies on the back lot on a large portable screen using a thirty-two millimeter Bell & Howell projector he had acquired after it fell off the back of a truck, as the folk saying goes. A hat would be passed to cover the film rental fee. Everyone would then settle in to watch classics like *Kill the Umpire, Mighty Joe Young, The Babe Ruth Story, Thirty Seconds Over Tokyo, Gungha Din, King Kong, Pride of the Yankees, The Sands of Iwo Jima* and any number of John Ford westerns starring John Wayne. Duke was a big hero in Fairmount in the late fifties and early sixties. At the time, Uncle Tom still worked for the Budd Corporation up on Hunting Park Avenue and would sometimes borrow an industrial film Budd had made to promote its rail cars and show that for free. The film was called *The Silver Streak* and starred a fast prototype train making a timed run against horrendous odds to beat a terrible deadline and secure a production contract. The bullet train beat the deadline by a whisker every single showing but the Fairmount crowd still cheered it on every time with a thunderous roar.

Starting an hour and more before nightfall, people would stream to the back lot from every nook and cranny of our neighborhood. They would parade down Brown and Pennock streets carrying beach and kitchen chairs under their arms. Some from nearby houses hauled out armchairs, love seats, and sofas. Others carted backseats from cars, usually flivvers or junkers of one sort or another.

The Italian man selling snow cones docked his cart curbside with a big slab of ice on it. He shaved balls of ice from the slab to put in pointed paper cones dowsed with the customer's favorite fruit-flavored juice: orange, lemon, cherry, raspberry, or lime. The Good Humor truck would also pull up alongside the back lot, as would the Mr. Softee frozen custard truck. They would do a landslide business serving customers from their trucks. My cousin Jimmy, nicknamed Jungle Jim, Uncle Tom's second oldest son, would always set up a card table off to one side and cover it with a white cloth. He'd pile it high with big vintage Philly soft pretzels and sell them slathered with French's mustard applied with a wooden dipstick the size of a hatchet handle.

The erection of the basketball court that fateful Saturday was every bit as exciting as cheering on the Silver Streak. Watching the pole and backboard go up was as stirring in its urban way as the barn raising sequence in screen-writer Walt Kelley's masterful film *Witness*. With the men all pulling the guy wires and ropes in timed sequences directed by my dad, the pole was righted and plumbed, then sunk into the cinders, Uncle Tom having grasped it like a drunken dancing partner on wobbly legs and wrested it into the pre-dug hole.

Within the hour Uncle Tom had a team of guys raking away madly and smoothing cinders in a "half-court" square in front of the iconic pole with the big square backboard supporting the orange metal basket and its meshed chain netting. Every few inches the rakers had to stoop and extirpate clumps of random but hardy crab grass and dandelion that sprouted against all odds in that hostile cinder-encrusted excuse for topsoil. Pretty soon a half-court five-on-five game was in progress and not one player minded the patina of cinder dust adhering to his legs from the knees down and coating his white Keds dark gray.

The basketball court lasted for several weeks before the Philadelphia Electric Company got huffy about the miscarriage of justice accorded its hijacked, yet formally abandoned, utility pole. A huge truck and workmen showed up and in minutes deconstructed the basketball court so lovingly imagined and erected with Uncle Tom as the conceptual artist and prime mover. The irony was that my dad, the chief engineer on the project, worked for the Philadelphia Electric Company and would for nearly four decades. Still, it was their pole and that was that. They confiscated the bright orange rim and chain-mesh net too, driving off in their huge truck with the whole works, including our shattered dream of having our own private court among the crowded, scarce, and contentious playgrounds of North Philly.

Seeing Yale hit the floor in their snowy white home uniforms had trig-gered this memory and galvanized my already surging enthusiasm and my throbbing sense of anticipation. The nonconference season was on. The quest to ready ourselves and hone our skills and teamwork for the challenge of finishing on top in the daunting and exhausting Ivy League round-robin tournament was about to commence. I could scarcely wait for the ball to go up for the center jump to open the game.

* * * * *

In a flash we were down 9-2. Central Connecticut came out fast and hot, hitting their early shots; we came out sluggish, tentative, jittery and cold, missing our early shots. Somehow I felt no concern. I knew this was simply opening game nerves. I had watched these Yale players in practice for countless hours over the course of a solid month and I knew they were much better than they showed early on. Coach Jones knew too, and stayed calm.

Our only score had come on a cutting lay-up in the low post by Jeremiah Kreisberg. Then the senior stars, Mangano and Willhite, went to work. Reggie stole the ball and scored on a driving lay-up. Greg tipped in a put-back. After a media time-out Greg stole the ball and whipped an outlet pass to Mike Grace. Mike fed a streaking Willhite for an easy fast-break dunk. Off the bench Sam Martin hit a three. Greg made a lay-up. We were all even, 13-13.

But Central Connecticut struck back. They kept hitting their shots, led by Kenny Horton, their star senior forward who had won Player of the Year honors the previous season in the Northeast Conference. They also had another thousand-point scorer in senior guard Robby Ptacek. He added seven points to Horton's dozen and at halftime we trailed by four, 34-30.

Still, we were in good shape and I was bullish, feeling that the game was ours for the taking. Jones had started Isaiah Salafia, the sophomore point guard whose outstanding athletic skills I so admired, but Isaiah had accumulated two quick personal fouls and played with too much recklessness and not enough control. Junior Michael Grace had replaced him at point guard and sparked the team with six quick points by hitting two three-pointers to go along with two good assists. Shooting guard Sam Martin had also come off the bench and nailed a three on the only shot he attempted.

All things considered, despite shooting for only 38.7 percent, we were in good shape. We had not played anywhere near our potential, yet were down only four points. Coach Jones had also used eleven players, so no one was exhausted; even better, no one had more than two fouls. What's more, starting shooting guard Austin Morgan had been held scoreless, a development unlikely to be sustained for the rest of the game.

* * * * *

Yale came out for the second half and took control, reeling off a 16-1 run. At the 11:47 mark we were up 53-39 after Austin Morgan sank a three-pointer. Our defense was outstanding. In the first six minutes of the second half Central Connecticut managed to score but a single point; in the next two minutes, they managed only four more. In effect Yale had shut their offense down.

Yet the Blue Devils were not done. Horton would score nine more points in the half and their freshman guard, Kyle Vinales, would pour in sixteen more points before the game ended, many of them scored down the stretch. Vinales was so good that by season's end he would make the All-NEC first team with Horton and win the conference's Rookie of the Year award. Against Yale he was so good that he nearly pulled the game out singlehanded. In the closing minutes he hacked away at our lead by hitting shot after shot. When he canned two foul shots to narrow our lead to six points with 4:05 to go, I was agitated and scared that the game would slip away from us. A media time-out occurred seconds later. Out of the time-out Mike Grace got open in the right corner in front of my seat and I jumped up and shouted, "Take it, Mike." He did and made it, restoring our lead to nine points. As soon as I clapped, the reporter seated next to me snapped, "You can't do that here. That's not allowed. As a member of the media you have to remain impartial."

"Why? The last thing I am is impartial."

"It's against the rules. You might get away with it here, but you won't later in lots of other places." I ignored this, turned back to the game, and resumed rooting, but only silently, wondering if this reporter had a point. When I learned after the game that I was in the wrong I feared I could have embarrassed Coach Jones and Yale. I would have to quit it. But I did want Yale to win.

And by playing smart in the closing minutes Yale did win. After the lead dwindled to a single point, Willhite, Mangano, and Morgan hit six foul shots in the last minute and ten seconds, preserving the lead at three. Greg Mangano then missed two free throws with thirteen seconds left that gave Central Connecticut a chance to tie the game by hitting a three. When they missed the three-point shot, and fouled Greg again, he added drama by clanking the first of his two shots before extinguishing all hope for the Blue Devils by hitting the second, extending the Yale lead to four points and making it a two-possession game with 5.09 seconds left.

Now came the first installment of what I would come to call "Reggie to the Rescue," a scenario that would recur with regularity. This first time it occurred right in front of me. Reggie intercepted a Central Connecticut pass but threw the ball out of bounds attempting a pass up-court to a teammate who could have dribbled out the clock. No matter. With 2.5 seconds left Reggie intercepted the ball again, then crouched and cradled it till the buzzer sounded.

Ecstatic, I saw from the final stat sheet that we had shot 53.6 percent in the second half, making fifteen of twenty-eight shots. I hadn't felt this good about a sporting victory since Tug McGraw pitched the Phillies to the World Championship in 1980. Across the court I saw Reggie Willhite and Greg Mangano brace the announcer from CPTV for their postgame interview. To me it was a magical moment. I went beneath the stands and stood outside the Yale locker room.

Soon Coach Jones emerged trailed by Greg and Reggie. Jones stopped and introduced me to his wife and his two children, then told me to come to the media room. As I trailed behind Greg and Reggie I mentioned how great the senior leadership was on their team, asking them to convey that message to fellow seniors Rhett Anderson and Brian Katz. I had studied Rhett and Brian closely in practice and noted the example they set for the younger players. In the interview room I listened as Jones explained how, after the slow start, his team settled in, handled the pressure Central Connecticut applied, and, in the second half, stopped firing up hasty three-point shots and instead worked the ball for a high-percentage shot by an open man, often in the low post. He praised Greg for hitting the crucial foul shot that extended our lead to four with only five seconds to play. He also lauded Greg for his solid minutes played, his twenty-three points, his thirteen rebounds, and his two blocked shots. Mentioning Greg's two blocked shots, Jones added that Reggie was still annoyed with him for designating Greg the team's outstanding defensive player the year before. Then he praised Reggie for the defensive job he had done on senior guard Robbie Ptacek, who had not scored one point for Central Connecticut in the second half once Reggie clamped down on him.

In closing, Jones reemphasized how pleased he was that his team had handled Central Connecticut's pressure defense. He cited the difference a year can make. The previous year, he said, when Yale scrimmaged Central Connecticut, the Blue Devils had "manhandled" them. This was in keeping with their coach Howie Dickenman's approach to defense. For years he had coached the post players for Jim Calhoun at UConn, after having been a formidable post player for Central Connecticut, and he really knew how to

intimidate an opponent, control post play, dominate the boards, and suffocate an offense with relentless pressure. On this night Yale had coped with
all of it.

As I walked out of the arena I knew I had experienced again the supremacy
of amateur athletics over industrialized sport. The NBA could never match
the excitement of college basketball. All spectacle and sensation, nothing
but entertainment—gaudy, overstated, and boring—the NBA left me flat.
In contrast, college ball was a genuine contest, all effort, drama, tension and
suspense, authentic, understated, and glorious. Despite the four-hour night
drive ahead I felt nothing but exhilaration. Next up was Quinnipiac in four
days. It couldn't come fast enough.

CHAPTER FIVE

"How Do You Coach That?"

QUINNIPIAC WAS A revelation. After battling gridlocked traffic for most of an hour, I finally found the TD Bank Sports Center, a modern gem that held a 3,254-seat basketball arena recessed into the earth next to a matching ice hockey arena, also recessed. Above them the two arenas shared a common glass-enclosed, ground-level lobby with a food court and restrooms. As far as modern midsized college basketball arenas went, Quinnipiac had the best I'd seen except for Bucknell's masterpiece in Lewisburg, Pennsylvania, which is also recessed and built along the same lines, but about twice the size.

As soon as I walked into the arena I had a funny feeling Yale was up against it. There were already a few scattered groups of Quinnipiac students and fans in the stands, though it was an hour before game time. Decked out in Quinnipiac gear it was clear they intended to loudly support the Bobcats' effort to upset near neighbor Yale. About fifteen minutes later when I chatted with Yale SID Tim Bennett I mentioned my suspicions to him. He immediately shot back, "It's always tough to win on the road in Division I."

This only made my sense of foreboding worse. In the back of my mind I remembered that at the Mohegan Sun Arena a press release had circulated before Quinnipiac's game against Fairfield stating that head coach Tom Moore had suspended star guard James Johnson for one game. That suspension was now over and Yale would face the Bobcats at full strength. In looking over the press kit for the game I was not encouraged to see that Yale was winless in three previous attempts to beat Quinnipiac. My assumption last Friday at the casino that we could beat this team seemed dicey, or maybe it was just my saturnine nature casting its usual dark scenarios. My gloom unchecked could escalate to the point where I regretted the future.

I watched as the three assistant coaches took Yale through the pregame warm-ups. The players did the "Ministry of Silly Walks" exercise and it lightened my mood. So too did meeting a young man who came in and sat down beside me. His name was Charles Condro and he was a reporter with *The Yale Daily News*, "the oldest college daily, founded in 1878." I knew this tagline distinction from reading the paper on campus at lunch while waiting for practice to begin. Charles was a delight and I quizzed him and learned that he was merely a freshman. He had grown up in Richmond, Virginia and had been a reporter, covering many sporting events, on his high-school newspaper. His knowledge of basketball and how to report it was impressive, and far exceeded mine, as I intuited that first night and had confirmed many times during the season. Sharing comments and insights with him increased my pleasure that night and many others.

When the game started the speed at which it is now played impressed me again. This was especially noticeable sitting courtside. At Mohegan Sun Arena I had marveled at it. My memory of my own playing days recalled a more deliberate and slower pace. At the Connecticut Six Classic press conference in Hartford coach Dave Bike of Sacred Heart had remarked that the men's game had become more unstructured, like the women's game. As I watched this game I thought what Coach Bike meant was that the game was now more spontaneous and used far fewer set plays. Much less time was spent setting up the offense and the more rapidly executed offense ignited a more rapidly responsive defense. The overall effect was an accelerated game. Speed was at a premium.

But this night that wasn't such a good thing. The game was "ugly." Both teams played sloppily. Yale had seventeen turnovers, Quinnipiac only two fewer. Thirty-two turnovers is not good. Nor is a combined fifty-seven personal fouls, Quinnipiac with thirty and Yale with three fewer. The time for the game was two and a half hours, much too long for a crisply played and smartly executed contest. The two teams banged and flailed away at each other way too much. In fact, Quinnipiac played a very rough brand of basketball and should have been called for more personal fouls, especially in defending Greg Mangano in the low post, where he was manhandled and hammered far too much.

Yet the game was exciting. Yale jumped out to a solid lead at 16-8 after seven minutes. Reggie Willhite had gone on a 7-2 run at the very start, after Jeremiah Kreisberg again scored Yale's first basket, this time off a jump shot. But Quinnipiac quickly answered now, scoring seven points in a row and making it a one-point game, 16-15. The rest of the first half was tight, with numerous ties and multiple lead changes. Ominously, Reggie Willhite picked up two personal fouls by halftime, but he was doing an outstanding defensive job on star senior point guard James Johnson, containing him well and limiting him to nine points. The half ended with Yale trailing by a single point, 32-31.

Yale seemed able to handle this team and cope with the partisan crowd. As expected, the crowd was loud and out in force, the arena nearly 90 percent full. The game was also being telecast on SNY, the New York City-based sports network serving the tri-state area. That Yale trailed by a single point yet Greg Mangano had scored only two points seemed encouraging; it was unlikely Greg would score so scantily in the second half. Yale's chances of winning appeared good and stayed that way until the 13:20 point of the second half with the score tied at 43.

Coach Jones had to pull Willhite because he had picked up too many quick fouls. When Reggie went out James Johnson went off. Threading through Yale's full-court pressure he went on a scoring binge. With three minutes to go Yale trailed by a dozen points. Yet Yale narrowed the gap to 64-59 with 1:18 left. That's when James Johnson drove the left side and banked in a twelve-foot jumper. It was the deathblow. Down seven points, Yale called time-out with under a minute left.

When play resumed, Austin Morgan missed a three-point attempt. Ike Azotam grabbed the rebound and Greg Mangano fouled him. Azotam made both shots. Yale brought the ball up-court and Greg Mangano attempted a three that Azotam blocked. Isaiah Salafia snared the rebound and fed the ball to Jeremiah Kreisberg, who missed a lay-up. Willhite grabbed the rebound and passed the ball out to Morgan, who hit a three-pointer with sixteen seconds left. Quinnipiac reserve guard Evan Conti then missed a pair of foul shots. Morgan grabbed the rebound but Ike Azotam, a thorn in Yale's side all night, stole the ball and cradled it as the horn sounded.

In the postgame wrap-up an obviously pleased Tom Moore, the Quinnipiac coach, extolled his two stars, James Johnson and Ike Azotam.

They had accounted for forty-two points between them, and Azotam had pulled down eighteen rebounds to go with his seventeen points, two blocks, and three steals. He had also manhandled Greg Mangano and should have been called for more personal fouls. A muscular six-foot-six kid from Boston, Azotam had used a lot of playground tactics to maul Greg. Yet, humble and polite, Azotam was charming in his postgame interview. Not so teammate James Johnson. In responding to a reporter's query whether having Willhite on the bench in foul trouble had freed him up to score sixteen of his game-high twenty-five points at crunch time, Johnson dissembled and said he wasn't aware all game who was guarding him. Taking back the microphone, Moore emphasized the great advantage in rebounding his team had enjoyed as the key to winning the game.

There was a long interval between the time Moore and his two stars left the media room and Coach Jones showed up. Those of us waiting were told he was "on the way." The media room was only a short distance down the corridor from Yale's locker room. I knew he was furious and likely letting his players have it with both barrels. Still, when he appeared he was dignified, if obviously still furious, and he rightly pointed out that Yale was impatient on offense and did not work hard enough with ball movement to facilitate the entry pass into the low post to Greg Mangano. Jones said as a result Mangano didn't have a good, clear shot all night. He also criticized Willhite for getting into foul trouble "because he was trying to do some things he shouldn't have been trying." He said Quinnipiac "put a lot of shots back. We didn't." That was the crux of the matter: Quinnipiac had fifty-four rebounds to Yale's forty-one. In the second half alone Quinnipiac scored twelve points "in the paint," meaning in the lane. Many of these points came on offensive rebounds put back up for scores in the low post. Twelve points scored this way was exactly double Yale's total scored on put-backs.

After James left the media room I drifted in the corridor, a little stunned by the loss. I was also eager to comfort him. Yet when he came down the corridor one glance at his face told me to keep it short. I said, "The guys just had a bad night, Coach. There won't be another game like this."

"There better not be."

He went straight past me and out to the bus.

* * * * *

Two nights later Yale routed an outgunned Lyndon State team in our home opener in JLA. Lyndon State I'd never heard of. At least with Quinnipiac I knew the school beforehand from its political polling prowess, always cited in the media. With Lyndon State I had to resort to the Net to learn it was a former "normal" school in Vermont originally dedicated, as were all "normal" schools, to the education and training of teachers. When I learned that the school played in Division III my foreboding increased. Watching the kids from Lyndon warm up added to my discomfort. The tallest player was only six-five. Most were only about six feet tall or an inch or two more. As soon as the game started I knew it was over. Division I Yale went off like a cannon. At halftime the score was 56-13. The final was 101-37.

Yale did as Yale wished. The two things I remember about the game are Will Childs-Klein dunking to put us over the century mark, a kind of totem, and my writing an email to Jones afterward telling him the guys should not have shucked and grimaced at calls against them in the second half when their lead ballooned to half a hundred points and more. Viewed from the stands this behavior made a negative impression. The referees at that point were legislating more than officiating the game to keep it within bounds, fearing the kids from Lyndon State might return home and, lemming-like, commit mass suicide by throwing themselves off a cliff above Lake Champlain and perishing in a mass drowning. The game was not just a case of men against boys, it was Yale men against boys and the Yalies didn't act right.

Jones wrote back and said it was doubly bad because he was his players' advocate with the officials, and the players had no right verbally protesting or acting-out with contemptuous body language or verbal guff in the first place. Scheduling a creampuff game like this is always debatable. On the one hand, for a coach your team can gain confidence against a hapless opponent while acquiring a feel for proficiency and a taste of victory. On the other hand, your team isn't tested, can freelance wildly, and can fall into a pattern of selfish and bad choices. Since Lyndon State wasn't a fraction as talented as any team Yale played all year, I left the arena consoling myself with the thought that the Lyndon kids could tell their grandchildren they had played Yale in their incomparable gym. I was sure James would not have scheduled this squad had he known how outclassed they were. In the lobby I overheard disapproving murmurs to this effect.

Yet that night on ESPN the streamer reported a rout nearly as bad by the semi-pros from eventual national champion Kentucky under their recruiting renegade, Coach John Calipari. He had left both Division I schools he'd previously coached, UMass and Memphis, on probation. I consoled myself with the thought that I'd rather watch hapless Lyndon State than a big-time bandit program staffed with bartered athletes. In the Age of Spectacle and Sensation such contrarianism put me in a minuscule minority, I knew. Still, the coach in me had wanted to leave press row and slide onto the Lyndon State bench and help them do better.

* * * * *

Our next opponent was storied Seton Hall from the mighty Big East Conference. We played them five days later, two nights before Thanksgiving, in the biggest venue we visited all year, the Prudential Center in Newark. I had to slog through an autumn deluge to get there, and I arrived semi-soaked from the lashing monsoon-like downpour, the wind whipping the rain sideways and the gutters overflowing the curbs and flooding four feet out. Yet it was worth any amount of inconvenience once the game started. Yale got going quickly, and within seven minutes took a 15-7 lead. Reggie hit a baseline jumper, Greg dropped a jumper just shy of the three-point arc, Austin hit a three from the right perimeter, Jeremiah finessed a hook in the left lane, Reggie arced a three from the right perimeter, Brandon Sherrod made one of two foul shots, and then Greg feathered a short jumper in the lane. The guys were cooking, cooperating, weaving and moving the ball, feeding one another and hitting the open man. My spirits spiked, and I recalled James telling me that the Lyndon State game might have put his team in a "buoyant mood." So far he looked to be right.

Then Seton Hall got into high gear when their star power forward, Herb Pope, slammed in two alley-oops off gorgeous feeds from point guard Jordan Theodore. Yale flagged as the Hall forged ahead. With 3:24 left in the half it was a tie-game at 28 apiece after Pope dropped a plus-one foul following a lay-up off a perfect backdoor feed. By the time Greg hit a three-pointer with twenty-eight seconds left Yale trailed 36-31. Seton Hall's talented sophomore forward Fuquan Edwin hit a foul shot with ten seconds left to make the halftime score 37-31. During a 12-0 Seton Hall run Yale had seen its lead evaporate, going from six points up to six points down, and it looked like the Pirates of Seton Hall were about to hijack the game.

Amid the rousing atmosphere, I hoped this wouldn't prove true. Seton Hall had a great mascot in full buccaneer garb gallivanting all over the court along with comely dancers and cheerleaders working frantic routines during time-outs. There were also ball boys who had retrieved the stray shots during the team warm-ups, just as I used to do in the Palestra half a century earlier. The cheerleaders had shot bazookas into the stands with rolled-up T-shirts for ammo, and there was a carnival atmosphere to the whole affair that reminded me of the raucous days in the Palestra during Big Five games in the sixties. That Big Five atmosphere had been so rollicking that *Sports Illustrated* did a memorable feature on it, emphasizing in the lead paragraph the sports-crazed nature of Philadelphia in general, and mentioning that the Eagles were pronounced "iggles" in the Quaker City. Back then in the Palestra the long and insulting "streamers" unrolled by fans on opposing sides of the court were legendary for their wit and venom. The school bands blasting fight songs were especially loud in the Palestra, with its barrel-vaulted ceiling imparting a repercussive and amplifying effect. Seton Hall home games had some of that pizzazz.

Yale came out for the second half on fire. Austin scored an old-fashioned three on a driving lay-up and a foul shot. Greg tallied a soft jump hook over Pope in the low post, added a fade-away jumper from the left lane, and capped matters off with a soft lay-up off a feed from Jeremiah. Then Jerry added a lay-up off an entry pass from Austin to make it a two-point game, 44-42, favor of the Pirates. Yale had come nearly all the way back. After a tip-in by Pope made it 46-42, Jeremiah hit both foul shots of a one-and-one to pull us back within two points with just under eight minutes gone in the half.

That's when an elephant fell on Yale. Seton Hall reeled off a 15-0 run and looked to put the game away. Yale rallied again but could only reduce the lead to seven when Austin hit a three with 1:48 to go. Moments later Austin again whittled the lead to seven by hitting a lay-up after Jordan Theodore made two foul shots. That finished the night's scoring except for Theodore banging home four free throws following deliberate fouls as Yale pressed full-court in desperation. Senior Theodore was too good a ball-handling point guard for Yale to turn him over and steal the ball cleanly. While Seton Hall poured in fifteen points in a span of seven minutes Yale scored zilch. Such lapses of concentration on Yale's part I called "dead zones." There had been one in the first half and another in the second. Combined, they killed any chance of victory. Yale might have survived one but never both.

In the postgame press conference Seton Hall coach Kevin Willard, a good point guard for Pitt twenty-five years earlier, praised Yale for being well coached and for having the pluck to come back twice. He rightly praised

Herb Pope and Jordan Theodore, and said he feared his team was tired after playing its fourth game in six days. They had lost the championship game of the Charleston Classic to Northwestern two days earlier. He also singled out Fuquan Edwin for scoring a quiet but decisive twenty points to top all scorers. Adding, "Thanks, and Happy Thanksgiving," he exited the media room.

Seconds later James came in, not visibly as angry as he had been following the Quinnipiac meltdown but not happy. He noted the devastating effect when Seton Hall went to a zone and "shut down Reggie." Until then Willhite had dribble-penetrated the seams and the baselines. He added that Reggie had played thirty-eight minutes, "too much," causing him to have lapses. The 12-0 Seton Hall run at the end of the first half had crippled Yale. There was much work to do against the zone. About his team's looseness with the ball, Jones noted that the Pirates had scored twenty-five points off twenty-two Yale turnovers. He "had to make guys understand what we're trying to do." After acknowledging his team's great defensive job in the half-court, he said, "There's no defense, though, on lay-ups in transition off turnovers."

There was no getting around that Yale had gift-wrapped the game through giveaways and mental lapses. In Herb Pope, Yale had faced a future pro, and post players Greg Mangano and Jeremiah Kreisberg had acquitted themselves well, each scoring fourteen points. Jerry had added thirteen rebounds for a double-double before fouling out with seconds left to play.

A week later after practice I remarked to James that we might have won both the Quinnipiac and the Seton Hall games if the team could learn to avoid mental lapses and not fall into "dead zones."

He looked at me incredulous and said, "Yeah, but how do you coach that?"

CHAPTER SIX

At the Point

FEW PLACES THRILL me as does West Point. To see a football game in autumn in Michie Stadium is a great privilege and I have been blessed to do so three times, having seen the Black Knights play Syracuse, Colgate, and Southern Miss. If lucky and you attend a game on a sunny October day with a backdrop of multicolored autumn foliage you have won the best New York lottery going, forget the one offering swag. To join the crowd in singing "Fight On, Bold Army Team" sends chills down the spine.

So when Yale pulled into West Point for the game with Army on Saturday night, November 26, two days after Thanksgiving, I was disappointed that Christl Arena was empty of the cadet corps, almost all of them away on holiday leave. Christl Arena is a good facility but the crowd that night fell far short of the slightly over five thousand capacity.

Arriving over an hour early for the game I had stood in the dark outside Michie Stadium, across a narrow driveway from Christl Arena, and thought again of all the legends, both military and athletic, who had played there. It stung me again that since Division I football had gone semiprofessional, Army, with its high academic standards, had been largely unable to compete for national championships as it had in the forties, winning three, and as late as the late fifties, when it won one with a team featuring Heisman winner

57

Pete Dawkins, the even greater but unheralded halfback Bob Anderson, and the legendary "Lonely End," Bob Carpenter, a Philly guy, I'm proud to add. To watch that masterfully efficient Red Blaik-coached team play had been gratifying. It was a fully coordinated example of team play at its highest.

Before our game started Coach Jones's young son Quincy practiced his shot on a lowered portable basket pushed into one corner of the arena, beneath the stands. A preschooler, "Q," as he was affectionately called, was a sort of mascot and good luck charm for the team. His father's vigilant and affectionate guidance of him never failed over the course of the season. His dad was a man with his values and priorities in proper alignment. As superstitious as only the spiritually awed can be, I dreaded every game we played when Q was not around. It was enormously comforting to watch him heave his shots up at the lowered practice baskets pregame, and it was reassuring to glance into midgame huddles and see him leaning jauntily, like a diminutive Frank Sinatra, one foot crossed over the other, on his crouching father's shoulder as James instructed his players, clipboard and pen in hand.

Offsetting the fun of watching Q fire up shots pregame was my growing concern about the absence of three players: guards Mike Grace, Javier Duren and Brian Katz were nowhere in sight. I kept glancing toward the corridor under the stands that led to the visitors' locker room. Mike, Javier and Brian never showed. It turned out that Mike had to fly to North Carolina for his grandmother's funeral. Though saddened for his family loss, I was relieved that he hadn't been injured. Javier I had seen take a hard fall, a thumping header, in practice a few days earlier, but I hadn't realized the resulting concussion knocked him out of this game and, worse, would linger all season long. Brian's news broke my heart. A senior, he had to take permanent medical leave of the team for dual operations, one on each eye, having suffered detached retinas in both. His playing career was over. A gifted shooting guard who had been the Catholic League Player of the Year on Long Island as a high-school senior at St. Dominic's, Brian was a committed team player, mature and composed beyond his years; and I rightly feared, as it turned out, his loss of leadership, and his scoring power, for the remainder of the season.

* * * * *

The key to beating Army was shutting down their perimeter shooting. James had instructed the guys to play out "high," to fight through screens and picks, and to get a hand in the face of any three-point shooters. Army did not run a lot of "pick and rolls," where the screener breaks for the basket and is fed a bounce pass for an easy driving lay-up by the would-be three-point shooter. This meant defenders did not have to "hedge" against the screen, holding back in case the screener "rolled" toward the basket for the easy lay-up; instead, the defender could "fight through the screen" by pushing the screener to the side and, hands up, confronting the shooter behind the three-point arc, harassing, deflecting, or blocking his shot.

Army led halfway through the first half, 22-15. They had already hit three quick threes. Then Yale exploded for a 23-8 run highlighted by great outside shooting from Austin Morgan and Greg Mangano. Reggie Willhite added two beautiful low-post feeds, one to Greg Mangano, the other to Greg Kelley, facilitated by one of Reggie's lightning quick steals. Jeremiah Kreisberg then fed Greg Mangano in the low post for a picture-perfect reverse lay-up. Our offense started to click and resulted at halftime in a 44-38 Yale lead.

When Army roared back in the second half to tie the score at 53, Greg Mangano went off and took over the game, pouring in six points, snaring four rebounds, and blocking two shots as Yale tore off a 17-5 run that settled the issue. When the media time-out occurred with under four minutes to go, Yale led by twelve, 70-58. Out of the time-out Julian Simmons of Army hit a three-pointer, reducing the deficit to nine. Jesse Pritchard answered with a three. Jeremiah Kreisberg slammed home a dunk to push the lead out to fourteen, and in the waning minutes Yale scored off a driving Willhite lay-up before Morgan, Mangano, and Willhite combined to drop in seven free throws. The final was Yale 84, Army 75.

Yale had played its best game. As Jones said, "It was a good team win." Our size resulted in a 48-34 advantage in rebounds, a good many of them leading to second-chance baskets. In Army's three-guard offense the two tallest starters had been six-six and six-seven, too short to battle the six-ten Mangano and Kreisberg. Another big plus was Austin Morgan's hot hand from outside; he scored a career-high twenty-seven points, two more than Mangano. Between them they dropped fifty-two points on the cadets. Kreisberg had his second double-double in a row, eleven points and ten rebounds. Willhite scored only six points but had seven assists, seven rebounds, two steals, and a block. Starting point guard Isaiah Salafia had five points and played a solid all-around game, dishing off two assists, handling the ball intelligently, and directing the offense with maturity.

* * * * *

Driving home from the game I eschewed the thruway and stayed on the secondary roads until I reached Poughkeepsie. There I ducked into the Barnes & Noble superstore. I had a discount coupon burning a hole in my pocket and used it to buy a copy of *Hemingway's Boat*. When I got back on the road I quickly found the thruway entrance and drove home to Coxsackie in a pleasant reverie, one triggered by being at West Point. I had asked Army's Associate Athletic Director, Brian Gunning, where the cadets had played basketball back when Bob Knight coached the Black Knights. The games had been played in Gillis Field House. For me Knight is the greatest coach ever, and I thrilled to his 1969 NIT Army team. Though badly undersized because of the limit on maximum cadet height, which I believe in those days was six-five, Knight's Army teams were models of intelligent play, precise execution, and total teamwork in unselfish, unstinting synchronicity. Knight had the knowledge of the game and the commanding presence to implant such peerless virtues in his teams, as his three NCAA championship teams later at Indiana proved. His 1976 champions were the greatest collegiate men's basketball team I ever saw, and they provided me with one of the sweetest memories of my father.

The Final Four that year was held in Philadelphia. I had offered to take my dad to the game. But he, a Depression kid, refused to attend any basketball game where tickets cost fifty dollars. So we watched in our living room, thirty minutes by car from the site of the game, South Philly's Spectrum. To win the championship Indiana topped Big Ten rival Michigan for the third time that year. That alone was a feat. Beating a team three times in a season is extremely difficult, especially a team as outstanding as Coach Johnny Orr's Michigan squad was that year. The Wolverine star was Rickey Green, a magnificent guard who could score from anywhere on the floor. But offense and scoring was not the reason I consider that championship game as great a collegiate contest as any ever played. Defense was.

Michigan had a guy named Wayman Britt at small forward. For me he has no equal as a college defensive forward. Oddly enough I met him in 1990 at the Frankfurt Book Fair. He was attending with his wife, Diana, who, like me, worked at the time for HarperCollins publishers. When Wayman introduced himself I immediately recognized him. I told him how I regarded him and said that Phil Sellers, the Rutgers legend and scoring machine, would leap off his deathbed and flee should anyone hold a picture of Wayman up to him. In the semifinal Britt had shut Sellers down, cutting down the floor on him and chicken-chesting him so tight that Sellers couldn't get a good look or a clean shot all game. Sellers was like a man caged. Defense played that well I could watch around the clock, so beautiful is it, and so difficult to do. A defender as great as Britt is for me always the key man on his team, taking nothing away from Rickey Green.

The irony is that Britt was the second best defender on the floor in that championship game. All four other starters on the opposing Indiana team—Kent Benson, Scott May, Tom Abernethy, and Quinn Buckner—received more press and bigger billing than did Bobby Wilkerson, the top defender I ever saw play college basketball. Humble and generous, Wilkerson would hang back and let his four teammates garner the accolades and pile up the attention-grabbing points until the game was on the line. Then he came to life. The defensive jobs he had done on Green in the two regular season Big Ten games that year had been magnificent. As luck would have it, Wilkerson had to leave the championship game early when he was injured badly. Watching him in those regular season games on Green and watching Britt on Indiana's star forward and top scorer, Scott May, was a memory to cherish forever for anyone lucky enough to appreciate virtuoso defensive basketball played by two masters. Britt and Wilkerson proved the supreme importance of the "key man" in basketball, though neither was the star of his team.

So marvelously coached, so synchronized, precise, and proficient was Indiana's 1976 team that, near the end of the championship game, my dad looked across the living room at me and said, in awe, "I don't know if God himself could outcoach this magnificent Knight." This quote is bowdlerized. My father actually stated—he never implied anything in his life, he simply stated it—that Knight had been born of a female dog. This was no slight to Knight, and certainly not to his mother. It was my father's highest form of praise, his form of eloquent emphasis. Like me, my dad thought Knight was the greatest coach ever, and my father had played and watched basketball since the late 1920s at the Warwick Boys Club in North Philly. At the club he had played in a cage, hence the nickname "cagers" for basketball players. For him there was only one form of defense: an aggressive man-to-man. If a team played a zone defense for more than three minutes, my father would turn the TV off, protesting a "lazy man's excuse for playing defense, just standing around."

My dad had gone on to play guard well enough at Roman Catholic High School to earn a half-scholarship to college in 1938, the year he graduated. But he couldn't afford, because of the Great Depression, to accept it. Instead he took his first full-time job, having worked part-time jobs since the age of nine. That's when the big crash hit in October 1929 and his father, a boil-ermaker, was put out of work. In 1945, when he got back from the Pacific, having earned a Silver Star, a Purple Heart, and a parade, he married my mother and set to work producing my three brothers, my eight sisters, and me. He appreciated life keenly, probably because, before a Navy search team rescued him, his mother had been notified that he was missing in action and presumed dead. When he was shot up in the Marianas after rushing up on a beach under machinegun fire to drag a wounded kid back to my dad's landing craft, the Japanese installed shrapnel in his fingers, legs, and ass. My mom said she never noticed it slowed him down any. Refusing a GI disability pension, he went to work for Westinghouse in West Philly, but found assembly line work boring. So he apprenticed himself to the Philadelphia Electric Company and worked his way quickly up to "first-class"—he always insisted on this designation—machinist until retirement in 1985 at age sixty-five.

Next to God, my mother, and his children, he loved basketball best, and for the moments of unalloyed pleasure watching Bob Knight coach basketball gave him, I will always be grateful to Coach Knight, lament his bad temper though I do, just as his many detractors exaggerate it with too much virulence. Since there has never been an NCAA violation or scandal attached to Knight's name, since he insisted his players graduate, since there is no record of an underprivileged kid of any color, race, creed or religion being exploited by Knight, who would go so far as to storm across campus and drag his oversleeping players out of their dorm beds to attend class, and since Knight proved his humanity in so many ways, especially in the case of Landon Turner, the center paralyzed in an auto accident while playing for Knight and still looked after and cared for today by Knight, it is very hard for me to see him in a pejorative light. Like another great coach with a temper problem, the admirable Al McGuire, Knight did the right thing ethically at all times when it came to guiding young men under his charge, especially underprivileged kids. Regrettable as his loss of self-control could be, he always taught his charges to do the right thing, the responsible thing. One other thing, based on personal experience: kids don't play that hard, that intensely, that passionately, that beautifully for a coach they don't love.

* * * * *

On Yale's basketball team Reggie Willhite was the key man, though Greg Mangano was the star. Three days after we topped Army I drove across the

Mass Pike and down Interstate 91 in pouring rain to Hartford. Along the way I heard Representative Barney Frank, in announcing his retirement from Congress on NPR, cite America's progress in overcoming prejudice as its outstanding achievement in his lifetime. I agree. It thrilled me to see so many coaches and players of color in prominent roles in the Ivy League. Before the season Coach Jones proudly told me that he had seven minority kids on his team. This was a long way from my boyhood when John Edgar Wideman was a rare African American playing in the Ivy League. He played guard for Penn before moving on to Oxford as a Rhodes Scholar. He's the same John Edgar Wideman celebrated today for his novels and memoirs. In his playing days he formed a formidable backcourt with Sid Amira, though they never got around the Bill Bradley-led Princeton Tigers to win the Ivy League championship. Back then, when black players in the Ivy League were rare, the league had no black coaches. Today there are four, or half the coaches in the league.

Even in the rain and the dark it was clear Hartford had a stately campus. The school also had a classy mid-sized gym in Chase Arena. The instant I sat down along press row the welcoming place card caught my eye: It said that, in accordance with NCAA regulations, any cheering from the media was grounds for removal. I thought back to the rebuke from the reporter at Mohegan Sun and determined for the remainder of the season to act right.

The game itself was a revelation. I went into the gym under the impression Yale would run Hartford off the court, judging from Hartford's abysmal performance two and a half weeks earlier against Sacred Heart at Mohegan Sun. Instead, no game all year demonstrated the supreme importance of good coaching as did the seesaw struggle between Yale and Hartford that night. Hartford Coach John Gallagher, in a matter of mere days, had transformed his young team into a force to reckon with, despite starting four freshmen. Instead of being erratic, disorganized, and scattershot, the Hartford Hawks were synchronized and smooth and aggressive, on both offense and defense.

The game was so closely contested it featured ten ties and nine lead changes. The difference came down to one factor: Yale's superior experience prevailed when things got very tight in the last four minutes. Once again the deciding factor was Reggie Willhite. He broke a 65-all tie with a driving lay-up right before the final media time-out at 3:51 to go. Out of the time-out Greg Mangano floated in a jump hook in the left low post. Then Reggie electrified the crowd by stealing the ball at midcourt and driving for a breakaway dunk. That 6-0 run sealed the issue, though Hartford fought back with a three and a foul shot to make the final 74-69. In the last few seconds Austin Morgan dropped in two free throws following an intentional foul. Jesse Pritchard added another free throw after the desperate Hawks fouled him intentionally too. All season, whenever a game got tight, I prayed that Austin would have the ball in his possession when the inevitable intentional fouls came. For the season he would shoot 90 percent from the foul line and finish fifth in the nation in free throw shooting accuracy. This night he also poured in twenty-six points, one shy of matching his career high of three nights ago against Army.

* * * * *

In the postgame interview I waited until the real reporters finished questioning Coach Gallagher, then told him how impressive his job of "coaching up" had been, citing the Sacred Heart debacle. It was a complete turnaround, as good as any instance of coaching excellence I would witness all year. In researching his background I discovered that Gallagher is a Philly guy who started his college coaching career under former La Salle coach Bill "Speedy" Morris. Like me, Morris is "a Roman guy" and is even in the Roman Catholic High School Hall of Fame, where he played and coached before moving up to La Salle. Gallagher had played his college ball at St. Joseph's, whose hyperactive teams under Coach Jack Ramsay had been such a formative influence on me, with their classic pressing defenses, both full- and half-court. Ramsay would sometimes open in a full-court press, a move akin to running across the ring and nailing an opponent with a knockout punch before the opening bell has stopped reverberating.

Playing Philly ball all the way—pressing on defense; moving the ball rapidly on offense—Coach Gallagher's Hawks had nearly upset Yale for their first win of the season. Yet their bad luck would continue through the first thirteen games. Then they would finish with a nine-win, nine-loss run that saw them take eventual America East champion Vermont into double overtime in a tournament semifinal before losing by four points. That's coaching. Look out for Coach Gal and his Hawks in the future, when the freshmen mature, including NBA standout center Jack Sikma's younger son Nate, a smooth and agile small forward with a diamond cutter's touch on his mid- and long-range shots.

CHAPTER SEVEN

Hat Trick

As it happened, Vermont was our next opponent, in JLA that Saturday afternoon. On Friday I took the train to New Haven and had a crisis of nerves along the way. Confidence is not my long suit. The nefarious voice in my head said I was a hopeless idiot with no chance of delivering an interesting book on college basketball as played in the Ivy League. I well know that in a game like writing, where you sit down and face a blank screen, you can't afford to pick up the first doubt. Yet keeping doubt at bay when it comes to writing is a daunting task.

I was early and so ducked into Trinity Church on the corner of the town green. The stained glass windows alone are worth a visit, the deep blue of the one in the apse a breath-robbing masterpiece. I took a seat in a back pew and started to pray, mostly for my two friends battling cancer, Ahouva and Ariella; for my fabulous cousin Eddie, Uncle Tom's son, fighting back gallantly in Fairmount against Lou Gehrig's disease; and for a writer friend of mine blocked on her latest book. I also prayed for a friend immersed in a toxic divorce. Then I prayed for Coach Jones, his family, and all the assistant coaches and their families, then for the guys on the team and their families. I asked God vulgarly to help Yale "whup ass" and realized yet again I need a delay button like they have for radio and TV when I'm praying. I fear this character flaw of mine is the result of North Philly, or of generalized derangement from anger; but, then again, I'm horribly disfigured in this praying business and whenever I do the Christian thing and pray for my enemies, real or imagined, I usually wish them dead within three verses. I realize this must be a great disappointment to God but character is fate, as the Greeks knew. Quickly I picked up *The Book of Common Prayer* and read "A Prayer of Saint Chrysostom," sneaking it in selfishly at the end of my laundry list of things for God to help with. Chrysostom is the patron saint of writers. I always remember the nuns telling me Chrysostom in Greek meant "golden mouth." This helped, as did recognizing that the root of the name spelled SOS.

The day was windy and clear. This had caused my eyes to tear up on the walk from the train station. As a result I wiped them now, kneeling in the pew. Revitalized I went back out into the wind feeling better about being a literary wuss and walked up to Payne Whitney reading myself the riot act about the importance of coming through on this book. I did this in my head only, not aloud—praise the Lord; I'd succumbed to talking aloud in public before, back before the cell phone era, when such behavior marked you for a loon. When I reached Payne Whitney I went straight into the Yale locker room, where James had told me to come early for the pre-practice Vermont "scout."

The "scout" is where the coaches review the game strategy with the players. There is a written report of several pages for the players to read beforehand. Then the points emphasized in the report are demonstrated with video clips on a large-screen TV. Standing quietly in the back I loved every minute of this. On every scout an assistant coach takes the lead and does most of the work. For Vermont, Jamie had done this. For me inclusion on a scout provided a major epiphany. I put such openness and generosity down to James's secure sense of himself. The next day I saw a basketball game as I had never before seen one: I had a fuller understanding because I saw, in a way, the text and the subtext. I saw not only the action but the underlying strategy. It was like looking at a finished building one had observed going up and being able still to visualize the underlying steelwork.

The next day I got to the gym at noon, two hours before game time. This was only Yale's second home game of the season, having played three straight road games and another on the neutral site at Mohegan Arena. The early December day was clear, bright, and beautiful, and from my seat in the second row of the press section I could see shafts of sunlight shooting down from the portals opposite me in the south stands. Behind the portals loomed the lancet doors in the corridor with their handsome wrought iron grillwork.

The architect of Payne Whitney, John Russell Pope, was a disciple of Thomas Jefferson. In fact Pope designed the Jefferson Memorial in D.C., plus the National Archives, and the west building of the National Gallery. He also designed the Broad Street Station in Richmond, Virginia, one of my favorites in the railroad station book I'd worked on. I found few things in life more beautiful than Palladian buildings well executed. When I was a graduate student at the University of Virginia I never tired of studying the Rotunda and the Ranges, and a trip up the mountain to Monticello was always a tonic, banishing my then catastrophic depression at the nadir of the Vietnam tragedy.

* * * * *

The game against Vermont was a kind of Palladian masterpiece of coaching. Yale played in total harmony and balance, with structure and control, serene in its calculated and choreographed proficiency. In all phases of the game, Yale soundly beat a good Vermont team that would make the NCAA tournament three months later. To date it was by far the best game Yale played. At halftime we led, 38-20, having imposed clamped-down defense on the Catamounts. Vermont had beaten Yale the three previous years. In the second half our defense was just as good. Vermont shot a paltry 35 percent for the game, and made only three of thirteen three-point attempts.

Scoring twenty-two points and pulling down fifteen rebounds, Greg Mangano dominated the game while notching his third double-double of the season. Jeremiah Kreisberg threw in fourteen points with his masterful footwork in the low post, and Austin Morgan hit four of five three-pointers and two of two fouls to match Kreisberg's fourteen points. Reggie Willhite and Mike Grace, making his first career start, scored eight points apiece to complete the totally integrated and balanced scoring by the starters. Brandon Sherrod added the only other two points off the bench. Yet as well as the offense played, the defense was the story. Typically, Willhite had three steals, four rebounds, and four assists, while functioning as the team's key defender and its very able point forward.

After the game James, as I'd finally started to call Coach Jones, praised his team, citing the first half as one of the best played in recent years and rightfully singling out the defense as the principal cause of Vermont's distressed and inept performance. Equally as pleased, I couldn't get over how beautifully the game had played out for Yale according to the scout. Jamie had so ably compiled the report and selected the illustrative video. After the game I told him how accurate and intelligent it was. He gave me a look I never figured out. It meant, I believe, that he'd either chuck me under the chin or crush my skull.

Here is what I scribbled in my notebook before heading to the train station, feeling, perhaps risibly, like a real coach: "The Vermont game was where I saw the effects clearly of Jamie's 'scout' analysis the Friday before. The point especially well made was to front Vermont's handful of big guys in the post. This Yale did in the first half to near perfection. Jamie said that only the Vermont freshman Four McGlynn would offer problems on the perimeter and that proved true. McGlynn hit several outside shots and wound up as the leading scorer for Vermont with sixteen points. I saw the game scheme play out and the strategy come alive."

Having done essentially nothing, I nevertheless flattered myself, on the train ride home, that I was rocking this coaching thing pretty good.

* * * * *

The following Monday I drove up early to Sacred Heart University in Fairfield and worked on a project in the library all afternoon while it drizzled outside. A matter of only a few short miles from New Haven, Sacred Heart has a rival's edge for Yale, as have all the Connecticut Six schools. Like Penn's fierce rivalry with the other four schools in Philadelphia's Big Five, Yale's annual contention with the other five schools in the Connecticut Six gave it two separate "conferences" to compete in, one informal, the other official. The Ivy League was the official and more important conference affiliation. But local rivalries in college basketball are always special, mainly because many of the players involved have competed against each other since high school and sometimes even since grade school.

After I drove across campus to the gym in the early evening I had to wait in the lobby for the doors to open. While sitting there I spotted Sacred Heart head coach Dave Bike sitting opposite me on a leather couch, chatting with friends. The previous year I had read an article on him in the *New York Times*. It increased my determination to follow my plan and actualize my faux coaching fantasy. Not sure what I wanted to say to Coach Bike I waited patiently for the admiring friends to leave so I might talk to him. But, as it turned out, he was too popular and I was too shy to butt in.

The game was a barnburner not decided till the final shot. At halftime Yale trailed by nine, 44-35. That was better than after the first seven minutes, when Yale had trailed by thirteen, 20-7. I foolishly remembered not being worried at halftime and expecting Yale to win. My instinct was initially confirmed when Jeremiah Kreisberg threw the ball inbounds to start the second half and Reggie Willhite drove the left baseline for a lay-up. Moments later Reggie drove again and laid the ball in while being fouled. He sank the foul to complete a 5-0 personal run to start the half.

He wasn't finished. After Yale took a time-out, Greg Mangano stole the ball and passed to a breaking Reggie. He again drove in for a lay-up while being fouled. He hit the plus-one foul shot. On Yale's next possession Jeremiah Kreisberg fed Reggie in the low post for another lay-up. Austin Morgan then hit two foul shots and followed with a jumper in the lane. Sacred Heart called a time-out. Out of the time-out, Reggie, returning the favor, fed Jeremiah in the low post for a lay-up. Off a 16-2 run Yale had seized the lead, 51-46.

Sacred Heart rallied but Yale countered with ten answering points, seven of them by Reggie. With roughly ten minutes to go, Greg Mangano sank two free throws and the score stood at 63-58 in Yale's favor. But, ominously, Greg, who had a hot shooting hand, not unusual for him, had also picked up three personal fouls with a full quarter of the game to go. Playing through the fouls, Greg hit a lay-up with four minutes left to put the Bulldogs up, 70-65.

But then Justin Swidowski poured in six consecutive points to give Sacred Heart the lead, 71-70. Mangano hit two answering foul shots to put Yale ahead by a single point. Sacred Heart failed to score on its next two possessions. Then, with 9.2 seconds left, Swidowski fouled Mike Grace. The foul was Swidowski's fifth and put him out of the game. Mike hit the first foul shot but missed the second.

The score stood at 73-71 when Shane Gibson launched an off-balance, desperation three-pointer. Reggie Willhite was all over Gibson impeding his vision and forcing a midair adjustment that threw Gibson's shot off line. Yale prevailed by two points but would have lost had that last shot fallen. Lucky for us the shot clanked off the rim and Mike Grace grabbed the rebound and dribbled out the clock. At last Yale could breathe easy after sweating through a second half with five ties and nine lead changes.

Reggie had topped all scorers with twenty-three points and all rebounders with seven. Since he had added a game-high three steals to complement his five assists, it was another case of "Reggie to the Rescue." Greg Mangano played magnificently as well, scoring twenty-one crucial points. For the second game in a row Yale had balanced scoring from all five starters, with Kriesberg and Grace tallying eight apiece and Morgan adding nine. The starters scored sixty-nine of the team's seventy-three points. The other four points came from Isaiah Salafia's three-pointer and from Sam Martin's single foul shot. Isaiah had also intercepted a critical pass with only minutes left to break Sacred Heart's momentum when they were on a late scoring run.

James was on the money in the postgame interview when he characterized the game as "chippier than normal." There had even been two technical fouls, one on Sacred Heart and one on James for protesting a foul on Matt Townsend that should have been called a charge instead. The important thing was that Yale had broken a three-game losing streak to Sacred Heart and run its own current winning streak to four straight.

* * * * *

In JLA two nights later we were right back at it against Bryant for our third home game of the season and the last before an eleven-day break for final exams. It was also our third game in five days. Trying to experience college coaching in all its aspects I had asked James if there was a walk-through scheduled that morning and he told me there was, at ten. So I hopped an early train and arrived on a dark and drizzly December morning to find JLA as brightly lighted as it would be later that evening for the game. I took my usual balcony seat on the south side and watched as the guys, mostly in sweats, walked through Bryant's sets on offense and their alignments on defense. James and Justin took the lead, Justin having done the scout on Bryant.

Once again I wanted to see the underlying strategy for the upcoming game, not just the surface reality. Even as far back as watching the early practices, I had thought of what James was trying to do as the equivalent of watching a photo come to life in an old pan full of developing solution in the pre-digital era. You could watch his team come into focus. It was like seeing the cartoon—the elaborate outline for a mural—and then coming back months later and seeing the finished painting on the wall. I was especially intrigued to watch Justin instruct the guys on how to counter two favorite moves Bryant had when inbounding the ball.

The walkthrough ended just short of an hour and left me with a day to myself. I walked through the steady rain to the campus post office and mailed out some material. Then I got lunch at Au Bon Pain on the corner of York and Broadway before retreating to the Starbucks café in the campus bookstore on Broadway run by Barnes & Noble. Settling at a seat in a back corner along the bench I worked on a project and then took a power nap. When I woke there was a comely young lady, very tall and dressed in athletic gear, working her laptop at a table in front of me. This reminded me that tonight the Yale women played a game before the men. I wondered if she was on the team but thought better of asking her. As much as I liked talking to the kids on campus I restrained myself because she was absorbed in what I assumed was schoolwork. I had liked it at the walkthrough that morning when James told me sometimes guys couldn't attend morning walkthroughs if they had a scheduling conflict with a class. Class attendance took precedence over athletics, he said, and he would fill them in later.

When I got to JLA that afternoon early enough to see the women play, the comely young woman from Starbucks was indeed on the Yale team. She was a rangy and quick freshman reserve with the lovely name of Hayden Latham. It pleased me when she got in the game. Very graceful and an accurate shooter, she canned eight of nine foul shots and added two field goals to help Yale rally back against Boston University from a twenty-point deficit in the second half only to fall five points shy of victory, 59-54. I love to watch women play basketball for their superior unselfishness and their instinctive predilection for synchronized teamwork over individual stardom.

My original revelation about this had come when watching the Immaculata College women's teams from Philly in the early seventies win national championships with unstinting teamwork. Nicknamed the "Mighty Macs" for the Immaculate Heart of Mary order of sisters who founded and ran Immaculata, those teams I especially loved because the "Macs," as Immaculate Heart of Mary sisters are called, had taught me in grade school. They were great teachers and what they taught me about math, history, geography, art appreciation, and the writing of prose in English I still treasure and rely on daily.

A small northern women's college like Immaculata winning national championships at basketball replicated the history of men's college basketball. In its early years men's basketball also made possible competing on a national level in intercollegiate athletics for small schools. Unlike football, basketball is much cheaper to underwrite and you need only five starters and five backups, ten players in all. Also, as Pete Axthelm, a Yalie, proved in his wonderful book, *The City Game,* basketball is as metropolitan as subways, gridlock, and fire hydrants.

Immaculata's seventies success in women's basketball on the national stage reprised my father's enthusiasm for St. Joe's early success in men's basketball in the thirties. Those "Mighty Mites" teams were led by Philly legend Matt Goukas, Sr., another "Roman guy." My dad had a scrapbook he kept when he was a boy full of Mighty Mites stories of games against the great New York City dominant teams of that era, especially CCNY, LIU, and NYU. I can still remember him showing me that scrapbook. Believe me, if you grow up in Philly, basketball is set deeper in you than your DNA.

Sheryl Swoopes provided my second revelation about women's basketball. Watching her play for Texas Tech in the early nineties proved once and for all that women were every bit as athletic as men. Jaw-droppingly great, she was as gifted and polished in every aspect of the game as possible. Seeing her play prompted me to think of her as the female equivalent of the Big O, Oscar Robertson, my favorite player of all time. In North Philly there was always an Anglo-Saxon adjective between the "Big" and the "O," and he deserved this emphatic encomium. Unlike too many later stars, Robertson was like the proverbial tide that raised all boats. Every teammate he ever played with was markedly better for being on the same floor with him. The only other guy I'd ever say that about is Magic Johnson. And Sheryl Swoopes was just like them, unimaginably elevating to her teammates and to the game of basketball itself.

Thank God for feminism, I say. When I was in high school "girls' basketball" was played in "modest" uniforms like slightly shortened pinafores. The court was sectioned into six areas, there were six players to a side, and not one of the six, or her defender, was allowed to leave their assigned area. Contact was verboten so reproductive organs would not be injured. No kidding. That was the thinking back then.

Significantly, Coach Jones came out to watch the Yale women play too, to lend his support. Q sat beside him, a bit rambunctiously, like any six-year-old. Infinitely patient and unfailingly attentive with his son, James pointed out things in the game for Q to note. It impressed me too that Rhett Anderson sat near them rooting the women on. He is a magnificent young man, a backup forward from California who has done charitable work as a missionary for his faith, the Church of Jesus Christ of Latter-day Saints.

★ ★ ★ ★ ★

After the Yale women lost, the men took the floor. In the early stages of the game both teams were laughably sluggish and ineffective. At the midway point in the half Bryant was up, 13-11. Like fledgling actors from their world famous drama school, the Yale guys were doing an impressive improv of *The Night of the Living Dead.* After the game James correctly attributed this torpor to playing three games in five days.

At the half the score was tied at 27 but I knew we had the game in hand. We had trailed at the half in three of our previous six wins. Instead of fretting during the halftime break I reveled in watching the little guys from the Waterford CYO team play an intrasquad game. I recalled my CYO days wearing the midnight blue and bright gold uniform of the St. Francis Xavier team. We played in the school auditorium that doubled as a gym. The floor was always powdered with super-fine cigarette ash from the weekly bingo games played there. Each week I picked up a few bucks cleaning up after bingo orgies. I emptied the always overflowing and lumpen-shaped metal ashtrays that resembled small World War I helmets turned upside down. I swept the empty coffee cups, dirty hot dog wrappers, and empty soda containers off the floor and into big black plastic bags. When we played basketball there the super-fine cigarette ash made the floor dangerously slippery.

In the second half Yale rallied. Greg Mangano powered the rally, scoring fifteen of his twenty-one points while Austin Morgan chipped in eight of his ten. The bench came through in a big way, accounting for twenty-four points all told. Freshman Brandon Sherrod hit a career high ten points in the first of what will likely be many double-digit scoring nights for him. A 7-0 Yale run in the middle of the second half broke a 52-52 tie. Though Bryant fought back to pare the later double-digit lead down to three, Yale pulled away again and closed the game effectively, if not emphatically.

For me the high point came when the morning walkthrough paid a big dividend, one underscored in Justin Simon's scout. With a little over a minute to go and stouthearted Bryant still fighting back, Yale stole an inbounds pass off one of Bryant's favorite set plays practiced against that morning. The thief, of course, was Reggie.

Yale had won five straight.

CHAPTER EIGHT

Holiday Heartbreak

ELEVEN DAYS LATER found us at the Ryan Center on the Rhode Island University campus for a Sunday afternoon game against the Rams exactly one week before Christmas. Rhode Island played in the Atlantic 10 Conference, the best mid-major conference in the country. A few years earlier, with their star Lamar Odom, the Rams had made a deep postseason run in the NCAA tournament. But so far this season the team had struggled, rumors of dissension abounded, and Coach Baron found himself on the hot seat, his team having won only one of its first ten games.

During Yale's ten-day finals hiatus I had enjoyed that memorable lunch with coaches Jones, Snyder-Fair, and Simon at which Justin told me Coach Jones, next to his father, had been the greatest influence in his life. During that lunch James rebuked me for asking him to project how his team would fare over the remainder of the season now that we had rocketed out to a 7-2 start: "Never ask a coach how his team will do down the road. It's one game at a time, at all times, to a coach." My escalating enthusiasm had been properly tamped down, my bubble of wild expectations punctured. Still, when it came to the Yale basketball team I was bullish to the point of snorting and pawing the ground.

Walking back from that lunch I asked about Rhode Island and James remarked that they "had better athletes but were a troubled team not playing together." He then declined my invitation to make a prediction on the game's outcome, frowning at me as a slow learner in light of his recent rebuke about projecting upcoming results. Yet I was already wary of Rhode Island. I feared troubled teams as I feared troubled individuals. Both had a tendency to lash out, making them dangerous. And Rhode Island played big-time basketball and had produced other NBA stars besides Lamar Odom.

That December Sunday was mild and clear. I left my upstate house early and drove straight across the Mass Pike and down into Rhode Island with clear sailing until I hit the wholesale outlets and malls crowding the corridor between Boston and Providence. Traffic there slowed sometimes to a crawl to accommodate last-minute holiday shoppers. But I had allowed so much time that I reached the campus in Kingston an hour and a half before game time anyway. When I entered the building I ran smack into James in the tunnel leading from the visitors' locker room to the arena. He was talking to another coach, a buddy who had coached with him years earlier at Ohio University.

After greeting them I walked into the arena and was immediately impressed. Only a few years old, the Ryan Center is the ideal modern mid-sized basketball venue, with a nice oval on the ground floor, a modestly raked balcony, and a narrow third tier above. From my undergraduate days working in the box office at the Theatre of the Living Arts in Philly, I could estimate house capacities and audience sizes. I guessed Ryan right on the nose at seven and a half thousand. All the seats were a padded blue and offset the clean and functional lines of the poured concrete. The openwork heating and air-conditioning pipes reminded me of the Pompidou Center in Paris.

The place also had big-time accommodations. A long, raised counter and padded seats ran the length of one side of the court for press, radio, and TV. When I sat down I noticed to the side nameplates for NBA scouts. They were there no doubt to look over Greg Mangano. I was lucky enough to be seated next to Mike Anthony of the *Hartford Courant* on one side, and, on the other, to Prosper Karangwa. Prosper was a tall, strikingly handsome, and enterprising young man from Africa who had played guard a few years back for the Siena College Saints in Albany. Since then he had set himself up as the CEO of a basketball talent evaluation company he had founded called Global Scouting Service. He and I had great exchanges during the game, and at halftime I got to chat with him. His observations and comments were

Team photo. *Left to Right, Back Row*: Brandon Sherrod, Will Bartlett, Jeremiah Kreisberg, Will Childs-Klein, Greg Mangano, Greg Kelley, Rhett Anderson, Matt Townsend, Armani Cotton. *Middle Row*: Javier Duren, Chris Fee, strength coach, Will Manville, student manager, Jamie Snyder-Fair, assistant coach, Head Coach James Jones, Matt Kingsley, assistant coach, Justin Simon, assistant coach, Zan Tanner, student statistician, Austin Morgan. *Front Row*: Isaiah Salafia, Brian Katz, Sam Martin, Captain Reggie Willhite, Mike Grace, Jesse Pritchard. *(Photo credit: David Silverman/DSPics)*

Head coach James Jones analyzes play. *(Photo credit: Ron Waite)*

The coaches huddle during a time-out. *(Photo credit: Ron Waite)*

Senior leaders. *Left to Right*: Brian Katz, Captain Reggie Willhite, Head Coach James Jones, Rhett Anderson, Greg Mangano. *(Photo credit: David Silverman/DSPics)*

Point forward and Captain Reggie Willhite directs play. *(Photo credit: Ron Waite)*

Greg Mangano dominates the low post for an easy lay-up. *(Photo credit: Ron Waite)*

JLA during the Harvard sell-out. *(Photo credit: Ron Waite)*

Raucous Yale fans cheer the Bulldogs on. (*Photo credit: Ron Waite*)

Team forms the pyramid for "Yale on three." (*Photo credit: Ron Waite*)

Austin Morgan drives in for a lay-up. *(Photo credit: Ron Waite)*

Point guard Mike Grace starts the offense. *(Photo credit: Sam Rubin)*

Jeremiah Kreisberg poised to grab a rebound. *(Photo credit: Sam Rubin)*

Sam Martin braces to throw a bounce pass into the low post. *(Photo credit: Sam Rubin)*

Brandon Sherrod drives for the basket against Columbia. *(Photo credit: Sam Rubin)*

Jesse Pritchard looking for an entry pass opening. *(Photo credit: Sam Rubin)*

Will Bartlett prepares to drive the lane. *(Photo credit: Ron Waite)*

Greg Kelley makes a play down low. *(Photo credit: Ron Waite)*

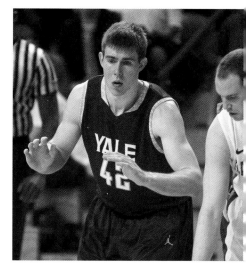

Armani Cotton defends against Harvard. *(Photo credit: Ron Waite)*

Matt Townsend positions himself to rebound a missed foul shot. *(Photo credit: Sam Rubin)*

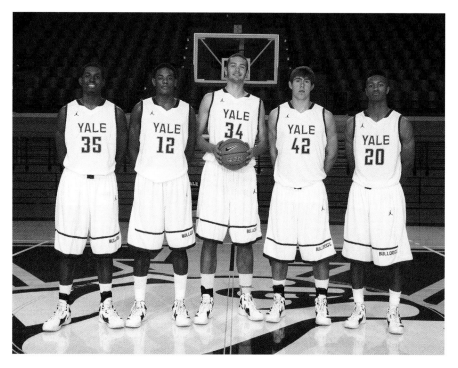

Five freshmen. *Left to Right*: Brandon Sherrod, Armani Cotton, Will Childs-Klein, Matt Townsend, and Javier Duren. *(Photo credit: David Silverman/DSPics)*

insightful and apt. Later in the season I would see him at games and get his take on things. It was always a big plus.

So too was being seated next to Mike. Though still in his early thirties, Mike is an accomplished sports reporter and a gifted writer. He and Bill Cloutier of the *New Haven Register* covered many Yale games and never failed to enlighten me on basketball and how to report it effectively. Not the least of the things Mike did that day was to teach me how to use the personal computers installed along press row, one between each set of seats. The computers featured a live statistics feed and update on the game that was immensely helpful in taking notes for later write-ups. Using these computers further cured me of my naïve amazement at how sportscasters and color commentators could have so many accurate statistics at their instant command.

Later, during the game, when I looked to my other side, Prosper was also typing rapid notes into a tiny iBook hardly bigger than a lady's makeup compact. As a hopeless techno-lout I was dazzled by all this indescribably helpful technology. Soon I too had an iBook and much of this book has been written on it impromptu at pop-up writing opportunities on the fly.

I was so early that I could watch Rhode Island's women's coach put her team through a pregame warm-up and walk-through. They were scheduled to play New Hampshire after the men's game. The Rhody women were good ballhandlers, especially two short guards, very quick and agile. Executing crossover dribbles, between-the-legs dribbles, and no-look passes whipped at warp speed, these two were impressive. As small as they were, they won my heart and that old expression "PT-boats" used by TV color commentator and analyst Al McGuire popped into my head. Watching college basketball these days I missed McGuire's naval analogies like "PT-boats" for small and quick guards and "aircraft carriers" for large and looming centers.

As a former player and coach, McGuire knew the game cold and could never contain his excitement enough to be an impartial media type. He would always start coaching one team or the other, or sometimes both, alternately or simultaneously, like a chess grandmaster working both sides of the board. For this and many other reasons I loved him though I'm told that, like Bob Knight, McGuire could often be less than lovable. In defense of them I say again: name the scandal or the exploitation of a young man attributed to either. You'll find none. The stories of these two great coaches dragging kids to class are inspiring in light of what is happening today. And few moments in sports were as amusing and informative as McGuire arguing with his broadcast partner, the affable and knowledgeable Billy Packer, on open mikes. Packer in his All-American days I saw play in the Palestra for Bones McKinney and the Demon Deacons of Wake Forest. The thrill remains vivid and enduring.

Yale was sluggish when the game started. This was understandable given the ten-day layoff for exams. With slightly more than three minutes left in the first half we were down thirteen, 32-19. Then the guys ripped off an 11-4 run to trail by only six at the break, 36-30. Watching, even when we had fallen behind, I felt the game was ours to win. The way Yale came out at the start of the second half confirmed my instinct. We were hot from beyond the three-point arc and were making nearly every foul shot. With 6:13 left to play Greg Mangano hit a lay-up to make it a ten-point Yale lead, 61-51.

Then the wheels came off. The Rams surged back with a wicked press, full-court, and we disintegrated. They turned us over several times and we fouled trying to recover the ball. Rhode Island forward Nicola Malesevic went wild, scoring point after point. He ended as the game's high scorer at twenty-five points. Over the last quarter of the game he accounted for fifteen points, hitting nine of ten free throws and adding two driving lay-ups and a short jumper in the lane. For him Yale had no answer. Nor for the full-court press.

Out of a Yale time-out with 1:08 left Jones called a play down low for Greg. When the Rams collapsed on him, anticipating Yale's reliance on Greg in the clutch, Reggie Willhite kicked the ball out to a waiting Austin Morgan beyond the arc at the top of the key. Austin nailed the three, his fifth of the game, and while he did Jeremiah Kreisberg set a monster screen. Fighting to get past the screen and block Austin's shot, defender Rayvon Harris fouled Kreisberg. Fundamentally sound as usual, Jerry hit both shots.

This five-point play converted us from two down to three up. The Rams' Mike Powell hit a driving lay-up to reduce our lead to one, 66-65. After a Rhody time-out Mike Grace was immediately fouled. He hit both, putting Yale back up by three. The Rams hurried down court but Jonathan Holton missed a desperation three as time expired. The miss was aided by great defense. Greg Mangano came out high, fronted and harassed Holton, and caused his shot to veer off course.

Yale had survived more than triumphed. Our finish was sloppy. Even though we had responded well, for the first time, to a zone defense forcing us to shoot from outside, we had mishandled the Rhode Island pressure defense twice: midway through the first half, when we fell behind by thirteen before rallying, and then inside the last six minutes, when we squandered the ten-point lead by losing our composure. Those last six minutes had given me heart palpitations.

As I left the arena I didn't feel good about the weaknesses we had shown in the first ten games. Delighted though I was for James, the assistant coaches, and the players to be 8-2 and sitting on a six-game winning streak, the longest for Yale in a decade, I knew we had to get better. We had to learn to handle pressure defense and the press. Ahead of us, after the ten-day Christmas break, lay the ACC's Wake Forest and the SEC's Florida. To win we had to play much better, especially on the road in hostile, big-time environments.

These were my thoughts as I streaked down I-95 behind the Yale bus before conceding that driver Raoul was simply too much of a speed merchant for me to keep up. I was in my fifth hour of driving that day, facing three more, and fearful of getting a ticket.

* * * * *

Wake Forest was a revelation, a beautiful school with serenely integrated architecture, Neocolonial and utterly without pretense, as plain, strong, and American as a Shaker chair. As I strolled around the campus I had the extra benefit of seeing it all backlit by an early winter sunset. In North Carolina the late December twilight lingered an hour longer than it did in New York, with a pronounced orange and gold afterglow, and I reveled in every minute of it.

Each year Coach Jones takes his team on a distant road trip over the break for the holidays. John J. Lee provided the endowment funding these trips. He is the fabled guard from Brooklyn who led Yale to its first Ivy League basketball championship in 1957. For this he found his handsome mug on the cover of *Sports Illustrated* and also had Yale's nonpareil gym named in his honor. To give you an idea of how talented he was, he still ranks third on Yale's all-time scoring list. He did this despite having played in the era of freshmen ineligibility, meaning he had only three years to accumulate his points total. Despite being a high draft choice of his hometown Knicks, Lee shunned the NBA to pursue his master's degree in chemical engineering and wound up the CEO of a major petroleum company. Besides endowing the university in general, he endowed the basketball program specifically so that the annual holiday trip could be underwritten without in any way taxing the school's athletic budget.

Coach Jones plots these road trips so that his players, where possible, get the chance to play before a hometown crowd. For the New England and Northeast recruits getting to play in front of a hometown crowd is easy. But it's difficult for the guys from the more distant sections of the country. That's where the holiday road trip proves to be a double bonus. All the players get to travel around the country and see the sights, and James makes sure the locales visited match up for some players and their hometowns.

Winston-Salem is the hometown of junior guard Michael Grace. Two of Wake's stars had played alongside Mike in high school. Wake's starter and shooting guard, C.J. Harris, was still Mike's best friend; they spoke by phone almost daily. And Mike maintained a solid friendship with Wake's walk-on reserve forward Brooks Godwin. The three had won high-school championships together. Mike had grown up watching Wake games because his dad was a graduate of the law school and his stepmother still taught there. Mike had nearly a hundred friends and family at the game. This accounted for his rousing ovation during player introductions.

So the Joel Coliseum was old hat to Mike. The second biggest arena Yale would play in all season, it had over eight thousand people in the stands for the game. There was a festive, even a giddy, feel to the night. North Carolina is a first-rate, attractive state with some of the friendliest people in the country and with a basketball mania second to none. When the arena went dark before the introduction of the Wake players, I laughed when the Demon Deacon mascot roared onto the court on a black Harley-Davidson. Cheerleaders surrounded the bike and bounced around large inflated Wake Forest balloons towering over the court's baseline next to the team's bench. I had never gotten over the shenanigans of the Demon Deacon mascot half a century earlier in the Palestra and he came through right on time again with a spectacular display of frantic energy, humor, and enthusiasm. Earlier during warm-ups I smiled to see ball boys dressed in black-and-yellow striped Wake Forest polo shirts collecting the balls under the baskets from missed shots. These youngsters were roughly the same age I'd been as a ball boy wearing a blue and white Big Brothers' T-Shirt in the Palestra at about ages eleven and twelve. Few things rival the innocent ecstasy of pregame college basketball hoopla, and Wake Forest practically owns the patent on it as far as I've been able to see.

When the game started, Wake roared out of the blocks and scored the first nine points. Instantly I feared an ACC blowout. But I tempered this angst because Yale again had ring rust from another ten-day layoff. We would get rolling, I told myself, and we did. After falling behind early and trailing by eleven points with 6:51 to go, we hit a flurry of shots and cut the lead to 34-28 at the half. I thought we were in good shape and poised to go off in the second half.

Instead Wake went off and led by nineteen with 11:34 left in the game when C.J. Harris hit a three to make the score 56-37. Isaiah Salafia then answered with a three that ignited a frenetic Yale rally supercharged when James put on a full-court press and Wake mishandled it, despite having good guards. As Yale roared back the big partisan crowd went quiet. Over the remainder of the game Yale outscored Wake 34-16 and played as well as it would all year. Reggie had a steal, Austin had a steal, and Mike had a steal (off best friend C.J. Harris, of all people). Mike scored ten of his twelve points down the stretch as he played furiously before the hometown crowd.

Greg Mangano hit a timely lay-up and a much needed jumper in the paint. Mike hit a three and Austin hit two foul shots and a three. At the 1:05 mark Yale trailed, 68-66. Forty seconds earlier Greg had launched a three that will haunt me this side of the grave. The ball whirled on the rim for ninety degrees, seemingly in the basket, before centrifugal force propelled it to dance off the rim, rising like a hopping fastball from the vacuum its spin created. Had it fallen we would have been up one instead of down two. I know, I know: had the hound not stopped to crap he'd have caught the rabbit.

We trailed by two when Wake called a time-out with fifty-six seconds left. Five seconds after play resumed Wake captain Tony Chennault hit a lay-up to make it 70-66. Reggie lost the handle on the ensuing Yale possession and Wake stole the ball. Jeremiah, trying to compensate with a payback steal, fouled C.J. Harris. Jerry fouled out and, after a Yale time-out, Harris hit both shots, making it 72-66. Greg hit a jumper in the lane and Yale trailed by four with sixteen seconds left. Tony Chennault uncharacteristically missed two free throws. Greg grabbed the rebound on the second miss and whipped the ball down court, where Austin narrowly missed a three. Reggie snared the rebound and whipped the ball back to Austin, who hit a three with three seconds left. Intelligently coached, Wake inbounded the ball immediately before Yale could foul and, when the horn sounded, we fell short by a single point against a premiere ACC program. The sigh of relief from the Wake fans was audible. Over the last quarter of the game Yale had been scary good.

After the game I chatted with Tony Chennault, who had played his high-school ball at Neumann-Goretti, a rival high school to mine and the major Catholic high school serving South Philly. He was charming and polite and

I knew again why I always liked to connect with Philly guys. Before I left the arena I shook hands with James as he stood talking in the corridor with well-dressed Wake assistant coach Walt Corbean, a man with an effortless million-watt smile who was even happier now that his team had won.

Deflated as a Yale fan, I was nevertheless elated as a Yale "coach." Over the last ten minutes I thought we had played our best quarter of basketball so far. Ringing in my ears were the postgame words of Wake coach Jeff Bzdelik: "I think the Ivy League is a great league…The Ivy League does it the right way."

Touring the campus earlier I had been much taken with the beauty of Wait Chapel, the epicenter of the main quad. Traditional yet modernist, the chapel is all clean lines, good taste, and sturdy plainness. I had sat in the first row aisle seat and sent up prayers and good karma for friends, especially for my friend George Williamson, a theologian and civil rights and peace activist from the sixties who had gone to Wake and then to Yale Divinity School. When I told him I was going down to cover the game, he said he wouldn't know who to root for with both his alma maters in a clash. I did know. Trivial to the core I had doubled back to the chapel right before I drove to Joel Coliseum for the game. Sitting in the same seat, I had the impertinence to ask God for a Yale victory, pointing out that Wake had a glittering record as a basketball powerhouse and wouldn't suffer from one tiny upset. Southern graciousness, confronted with northern aggression, still has its limits, I suppose, even with God.

* * * * *

Two days later on New Year's Eve we ran right into a gaggle of angry Gators in Gainesville. Florida is an elite program, having won two recent national titles. The game was televised on ESPNU, adding to the big-time feel of the event. The day before, a quiet Friday, Yale had practiced in the O'Connell Center for a few hours, acclimating itself to the arena. The O'Center, as it's called, seats nearly twelve thousand and is intelligently arranged in a ground floor oval with two staggered tiers above, and with not a lousy sightline in the place. During the entire practice the team had seemed up and sharp, probably the aftermath of having made such a brilliant run at Wake Forest over the last quarter of that game. Florida, on the other hand, was seething from a loss to Rutgers in double overtime two nights earlier in New Jersey. Nationally ranked in the Top Ten, having lost on the road only to Ohio State and Syracuse, both ranked higher, Florida was expected to contend for the national title. The Rutgers upset didn't help. This season Florida had won all six home games and had a streak of thirteen home victories stretching back to the previous year.

From the opening whistle Yale picked up where it had left off at Wake, scoring the first nine points as Austin hit a three from the left wing, Reggie matched it from the right wing, and Greg tripled it from the top of the key. Florida answered with a quick 8-0 run before Greg hit another three to make it 12-8, Yale. Ominously, the Gators then pressed full-court. James substituted Isaiah Salafia for Michael Grace, adding three inches to our point guard and considerable quickness and athleticism, if a dangerous tendency to be careless with the ball. Florida knocked out a 9-0 run, followed, after Brandon Sherrod made an old-fashioned three-point play, by a 10-0 run. With 9:29 left in the half Yale trailed by 29-15. All my hopes for a shattering upset of the Gators and their blue-chip players seemed like pipe dreams. At the 3:49 media time-out Yale had cut the lead to 33-23. Out of the time-out Isaiah hit a three and we were down only seven points. But Florida rallied to lead at halftime, 46-35.

I was pumped: we were playing good ball, if breaking up too much under the pressure of the full-court press. We had eight turnovers to Florida's four. The stat sheet told the tale. Florida had thirteen points off turnovers, Yale none. Florida had seven second-chance points, Yale only three. Florida had eleven points off the fast break, Yale none. And Florida had twenty-nine points in the paint to Yale's six. Florida was in charge but Yale wasn't out of contention. Yale's bench had scored fifteen points to Florida's six. We were in the game.

At the start of the second half Yale scored the first four points. Austin Morgan and Jerry Kreisberg hit quick baskets. Then Florida's undersized senior point guard Erving Walker dropped a three. Greg Mangano countered with a three. Down seven again, 49-42, Yale would get no closer. Erik Murphy and Kenny Boynton demonstrated over the next eight minutes why Florida was the leading three-point shooting team in the country. Between them they hit six treys, four by Murphy and two by Boynton for a total of eighteen quick points. That put Yale behind by seventeen with 10:42 to go. Strength shows. Next Patric Young, a brawny center, reeled off nine straight points in the paint. The game was over, Yale down by twenty-six. Yet for a long stretch it had been a contest and the final score did not indicate how competitively it had been played.

During the second half one thing scared me and two things thrilled me. At about the eight-minute mark Michael Grace got whacked hard contesting a ball being stolen from him. He thumped his head off the hardwood right in front of me. At first I feared he was knocked out, but he wasn't, only stunned and disoriented. Like the great kid he is, Greg Mangano, the nearest teammate to Mike, rushed over hollering to Mike, "Are you all right?" I had jumped up and was staring down at Mike and repeating, "Take all the time you need, Mike, take all the time you need," as Yale trainer Dave DiNapoli hurried across court. The TV guys took a media time-out and Mike, a really tough kid, shook it off and got to his feet. James substituted Isaiah, to give Mike a breather on the bench. Later in the game when Mike returned I was much relieved. Injuries terrify you once you become attached to the players. You hate to see injuries happen and hold your breath the instant one does, just as I had when Matt Townsend went down so hard in the Stony Brook scrimmage and when Javier Duren got concussed on a header in practice.

The two things that thrilled me were arguably meaningless. With forty-seven seconds left, senior Rhett Anderson hit two foul shots to draw Yale within twenty on the final score, 90-70. Rhett and fellow senior reserve Brian Katz were always exhorting and adjusting their teammates during practice in an inspirational way. My heart had cracked when we lost Brian for the season. His mature acceptance of this medical setback was uplifting, as was Rhett's acceptance of diminished playing time because Yale acquired outstanding underclassmen Jeremiah Kreisberg and Brandon Sherrod. No matter. At the start of every game Rhett ran onto the court before player introductions and manned the top of the aisle formed by the nonstarters. There he would cheer and clap at the introduction of each Yale starter and chest-bump each with enthusiasm when he reached him. That Rhett hit these two foul shots on national television thrilled me, as did the gesture that followed when James substituted five guys so they'd get to play on ESPN too. It chagrined me, as I'm sure it chagrined James, that the horn sounded before he could insert every Yale player.

* * * * *

Billy Donovan was the most fun of any coach all year in a postgame interview. Natural and complimentary, animated and articulate, he was a total New York Irishman in his element, talking basketball and radiating enthusiasm. Keenly perceptive, he noted right away how well coached and, most especially, how enthusiastic all the Yale players were, including the guys cheering on the bench. The installation of this kind of contagious enthusiasm was a hallmark of Coach Jones. I had noted it at each practice, where he insisted every time that his players "Clap it up, boys," using his signature expression. I liked this expression and will remember it always as this book's lasting auditory memory. Even when James got testy and frustrated with his "boys" he would never leave them with the impression he was permanently angry with them. Like the folk wisdom imparted to married couples never to go to bed angry at each other, James always rallied the guys before dismissing them. He always gathered them at center court on the painted bulldog emblem of Handsome Dan, the Yale mascot, and led them in a team cheer: "Okay, on three, 'Yale;' okay, on three, 'team.'" During games he taught his players to vocalize their enthusiasm from the bench, jumping to their feet and clapping at time-outs and calling out encouragement to their teammates during play.

The observant Donovan had missed none of this. He also singled out Mangano for praise and said that Greg was "terrific and unique" and also "awkward, and I mean that in a complimentary way." He said that Florida all year would not see another guy like Greg, whose unorthodox style and unpredictability "created space," meaning Greg could work his way free to get his shots off. I thought of Greg's post moves as "angular" in the same way Thelonious Monk's piano playing was, totally unpredictable and always improvised. Donovan also praised Reggie and Austin for forming with Greg a potent triumvirate on offense that made it harder to shut down any one of them. Jerry Kreisberg also drew a Donovan compliment.

When asked by *Yale Daily News* reporter Charles Condro to evaluate the Ivy League, Donovan responded that Yale was one of the best teams they'd played so far except for powerhouses Ohio State and Syracuse. He said that he didn't like giving up eleven threes to Yale, only one fewer than his team had scored. He added that he didn't mind Mangano getting his threes, as a great outside shooting big man, but he didn't like the way his guys had let the other shorter Yale players pop with impunity and accuracy from beyond the arc. With a twinkle in his eye he then quizzed Charles on how he had come down to the game, saying he knew Charles was a Yalie the moment he spotted him wearing a bowtie, a white dress shirt, and pressed khakis.

If you sent to central casting for the nicest college kid in America, Charles Condro would be sent. My own mother would have told his parents he was "a beautifully turned out young man who made a good impression at all times." Working with him was a joy, his knowledge of the game deep and his enthusiasm infectious. When Donovan learned that Charles had ridden trains from his parents' house in Richmond to Winston-Salem for the Wake game, and then all the previous night and day to arrive in Gainesville in time for today's game, he asked Charles if he would wear "Florida gear" on the Yale campus if he sent him some. Shyly Charles agreed that he would and Billy promised to send him some.

I asked Billy if he ever spoke to his former Providence backcourt mate Carlton Screen. This got his attention and he said that they had spoken just recently. I told him what a thrill it was to watch Carlton hit the crucial foul shots that put their Providence team in the 1987 Final Four under coach Rick Pitino. In parting I told him I thought he had another Final Four team on his hands. He said he hoped I was right. Two and a half months later in the Elite Eight, his Gators were solidly up in the second half against Pitino's Louisville team when Rick switched from his signature pressing man-to-man to a zone, a tactic he rarely used. Florida's outside shooting faltered, and the wily mentor won, putting Louisville in the Final Four and fracturing my prediction.

CHAPTER NINE

Auld Lang Syne and a Whole New Streak

AFTER THE GAME, I drove to Bradenton to spend two days with friends who'd taken a house for the holidays to get in some golf and swimming. On the subject of Yale basketball I blanked my mind. Coaching *is* all consuming, as I had found out. Enjoying my friends, I put aside my obsession with the team and its fate and concentrated instead on staying in the moment. By doing so I had a thousand laughs and a marvelous time.

Yet as soon as I boarded the plane back to LaGuardia on Monday night my thoughts all centered on Coach Jones and his "boys." We had played twelve games and our record stood at 8-4. James felt we should have won against Seton Hall and Quinnipiac. Not wishing to be a typical critic, yet unable to help myself, I wished we had pressed earlier against Wake Forest because I believed that game had been ours to take. This belief stemmed from my contention that nothing is harder to handle in basketball than pressure defense properly played, and nothing disrupts a team, forces it out of its rhythms, and shatters its composure more quickly or thoroughly than a well-timed and savagely sustained full-court press. Ours against Wake had accomplished all these things, yet we fell short. On the other hand, James knew the players better than I did and we had pressed for minutes on end, so maybe we were at our maximum with the number of minutes we did press. If I had learned anything in life it was the futility and danger of woulda-coulda-shoulda as a thought pattern, and James counseled me wisely not to indulge it and to concentrate instead on the next game on the schedule. Still, by James's assessment and my own, we might well have been 11-1, with only the superior athletes of Florida having bested us.

So why had we lost when we should have won? Where were the weaknesses? The things to be avoided? The things to be worked on? The things to improve before launching ourselves into the rigors of the Ivy League season, that compact tournament with scant margin for error? On the plane these thoughts chewed into me and I reviewed where we'd gone wrong.

We didn't adjust when Quinnipiac went to a zone to pack the lane and double-down on Greg Mangano, hacking away at him without fouls being called. With the middle shut down we started to freelance from the outside, taking ill-advised shots too far from the basket, missing most. Reggie, in response to Greg being doubled, tried to take up the slack. He shot too often from the perimeter, from where he was not accurate, and he compounded this error by driving the clogged lane and tossing up floaters and teardrops that didn't fall.

As a team we weren't patient and we didn't work the Flex options fully until an open shot developed; instead, guys took shots when they got their hands on the ball, even if the shot taken was contested or simply out of their effective range. For the entire game Yale shot only 27 percent; for the second half, when Quinnipiac took control, Yale shot only 22 percent, missing four out of every five shots.

Three other factors worsened this sorry state. First, like the star he was, Greg Mangano believed, much like an overconfident rookie NFL quarterback with a big arm and a string of collegiate triumphs behind him, that he could beat even double coverage and score. He couldn't. Instead he was too often called for walking, or settled for lousy shots, or incurred steals when he put the ball on the floor against multiple defenders. The smart move would have been to whip the ball out of the post to the perimeter and try for an open shot from there; failing that, the perimeter players could have simply recycled the Flex offense by reversing the ball and restarting from scratch on the opposite side of the court. Second, our low-post turnovers were augmented by open court turnovers when Quinnipiac pressed and our guys failed to handle the pressure: We lost nine stolen balls, and suffered seventeen turnovers. The third factor was Reggie getting in foul trouble and having to sit out a long stretch of the second half. When he went out, Quinnipiac's outstanding senior point guard, James Johnson, took charge, reeling off score after score and putting the game out of reach.

The unblended ego is the enemy of teamwork. After no game all year did James look angrier than he did after the Quinnipiac game. Our guys unraveled. Their egos came to the fore unchecked and wheeled out of control. Players at the Division I level are all good athletes, and good athletes have healthy egos and firm confidence developed at lower levels of the game, where success validated both traits. When these athletes step up in competitive levels, especially to Division I ball, some have to accede to those who are more talented. And collectively, all players on any single team must blend selflessly, without disfiguring ego, to form the best unit they can possibly be. So it's understandable in any one game that the wheels can come off, that ego can take precedence over cooperation, and that overconfidence can dictate foolish choices.

That's what happened to us against Quinnipiac. Our guys all got silly and stupid at the same time. The cohesion shattered and the teamwork fractured. So we lost, ignominiously, a game that was winnable had we kept our heads, subdued our egos, and adjusted to the zone and its collapsing low-post shutdown. All we had to do instead was recycle the Flex options patiently from a fresh start on the opposite side of the floor until we found the open man.

One week later Coach Kevin Willard of Seton Hall took a page from Coach Tom Moore of Quinnipiac. Willard switched to zone after our inside game with Greg Mangano and Jerry Kreisberg proved effective against their man-to-man defense. Our Flex sets were working on the first option, and Greg and Jerry were scoring quickly beneath the basket. So Seton Hall switched tactics. Besides clogging the lane with a packed zone, they also pressed us. Again Yale suffered, although we did not quite unravel and go individualistic and "freelance" as we had against Quinnipiac. The truth was that Seton Hall had a possible future NBAer in Herb Pope at power forward. He was complemented on the front line with a handful of other tall, talented, and hefty post players. With fouls to give, they all crowded and muscled Greg and Jerry for most of the game once the zone was applied.

The Seton Hall guards were also quick, tall, and gifted, especially senior point guard Jordan Theodore, another NBA possibility. He thwarted our press when we applied full-court defensive pressure in the second half in an effort to get back into the game after a 15-0 Seton Hall run. Our cause wasn't helped by their sophomore swingman Edwin Fuqua scoring twenty points off an incredibly hot hand. Still, it seemed to me, if not to James, that Seton Hall had more depth and better athletes. On the other hand, in the postseason National Invitational Tournament, Seton Hall barely nipped Stony Brook by two, and we had scrimmaged well against the Seahawks back in November. So I defer to James that we should have beaten the Pirates, and might have had we not turned the ball over twenty-two times.

Clearly we had trouble with a collapsing zone and with half- and full-court pressure. In the Wake Forest loss these liabilities didn't seem crucial, but another liability did: we completely lost focus for the first ten minutes of the second half. When this happened we drifted, rudderless, neither executing our offense nor applying our defense. Had we avoided this mental shutdown, a kind of brain freeze and muscle memory amnesia, and had we applied the full-court press sooner, that game had been ours to win.

Florida was another story. Once they got rolling in the second half we were overwhelmed by superior athletes, yet the pressure from their full-court press had a lot to do with that. When I asked Coach Donovan after the game if he had studied film of our chaotic collapse in the last five minutes against Rhode Island, he denied he had. But I discounted his denial and wrote it off to the Whistle Wall, the collegiality among coaches, like that among cops and doctors. It prevents their casting colleagues in a critical light. With coaches it's a sporting tradition, a gentleman's tradition I like. It was also true, as Donovan pointed out, that his teams routinely applied a murderous full-court press, a legacy from his mentor Rick Pitino.

* * * * *

The night after landing at LaGuardia I was in JLA for our game with Holy Cross. We got out fast against the Crusaders and led by twenty, 33-13, with a little over six minutes left in the half. As ever, when things were going our way, the key was our ability to get the entry pass into the low post, where Greg Mangano was going wild and where Jerry Kreisberg was putting on a low-post passing clinic. I could never decide, when watching Jerry's fundamentally sound game, whether his footwork, choreographed beautifully, was more impressive than his thread-the-needle passing, or whether it was the other way round. When he was drawing coverage and dishing off to Greg whenever he was open or in single coverage, it was a thing of beauty to watch, and it almost always led to Greg scoring easy baskets. Jerry also knew how to whip the ball back out to the open man on the perimeter without hesitation, a hard move for any defense to thwart when executed at lightning speed. The open man outside usually had a clear shot. Jerry knew this and played with unselfish intelligence at all times. Another impressive thing this night was his loss of a tooth in a scrum under the boards early on. He shook it off and went on playing while I fretted like a parent that his smile would be impaired.

In the second half we showed brain float again and let Holy Cross close the gap to 61-57. Our lapses in concentration, the thing James said was so hard to coach away, struck again. Yet we recovered when Jerry Kreisberg tipped in a Greg Mangano miss at the 8:25 mark to put us back up by six. We also regained our concentration and, though Holy Cross played hard, we re-established control from there on out, winning by fifteen, 82-67.

Greg Mangano had blazed the way again, scoring twenty-seven points and grabbing thirteen rebounds. Reggie Willhite added ten points and Isaiah Selafia matched them off the bench. Isaiah had his best game but marred it with a backfired three-sixty dunk off a steal that left him fifteen feet in front of the nearest defender. All he had to do was kiss the ball off the glass for a simple lay-up and two points. Instead he went all hotdog and clanked the blown dunk off the rim. In my seat I was furious. Isaiah had picked up too many street values and I saw myself in him. I feared for him. I feared that all his athleticism and potential in life would go to waste. Proof of this was his throwing a haymaker at Mike Grace back in October at practice (deftly, Mike slipped the punch). Isaiah needed to work on self-control, self-discipline, and self-possession. He was a terrific kid and I was praying that he'd lose the street antics and grow up.

In the postgame interview Bob Ryan of the *Boston Globe* and ESPN's *The Sports Reporters* asked James how he dealt with that kind of exasperation, watching Isaiah sacrifice a sure two points to failed highlight-reel acrobatics. James calmly said that he had talked to Isaiah about his "loose" handling of the ball and had urged him to stop it. In response to another question James said he felt we always had "the game in hand," even when Holy Cross made its second-half run. I had felt that way too, but I still wished we would maintain focus and finish teams off.

* * * * *

The following Sunday we played St. Joseph's of Long Island in our final non-conference game. From my seat in the press section, the January sunshine steaming through the south windows backlit the wrought iron lacing the lancet windows in the corridor behind the opposite stands. I thought again what a magnificent job architect Pope had done in designing this beautiful gym. My spirits spiked when I spotted Brian Katz walk on court with the coaches and, in a business suit, take up a place on our bench. For the remainder of the season Brian would function as an unofficial graduate assistant, encouraging and instructing his teammates, especially the underclassmen. Like fellow reserve senior Rhett Anderson, he was a classy kid.

When I had first got to the gym I watched the Yale women mop up a rout of Baruch College, 81-47, a good omen, I thought, for the men. As soon as the Golden Eagles of St. Joseph's came onto the floor for warmups I noticed they had no tall players. In the parlance of today they had no "length," meaning height. I thought Greg and Jerry in the post would feast on them. They did, with Jerry passing and Greg popping. With the perimeter guys hitting too we were up 16-2 after four minutes and 29-4 two and a half minutes later. Then the Golden Eagles caught fire, like the 10-1 team they were. They scorched the nets from the outside, knocking down threes and closing the gap at halftime to 46-43. The game would have been tied had not a three in the final seconds just missed.

My father always taught me to root for the underdog so I was pleased for St. Joseph's but piqued at Yale. In the locker room James was more than piqued. Our defense was lackadaisical, porous, a joke. We had let a badly undersized team, even if they were scrappy sharpshooters with hot hands, back into the game. He wanted his team off the snide and on the march to open the second half.

Our players responded and pushed the lead back to 65-52 after seven minutes. At that point, after executing a masterful block and steal, Brandon Sherrod snapped an outlet pass to Isaiah Salafia, who dribbled down court and hit a three from the right wing. The bench was coming through and Yale's future looked good with freshman Brandon and sophomore Isaiah sparkling. Meanwhile, Greg Mangano went ballistic. He scored thirty-five points to go with his twenty-two rebounds, both career highs, and added three blocked shots. Reggie Willhite, while scoring nineteen points, six of them in the closing minutes, notched seven assists for the game, one shy of his career high. Michael Grace scored ten points and Austin Morgan and Isaiah each had nine, meaning the three top guards accounted for twenty-eight points. Jerry Kreisberg played his usual steady game and chipped in seven points and eight rebounds while being spelled by Brandon, who added four points and two rebounds. In the end our offensive performance was strong and balanced, but when you factor in our 57-22 edge in rebounds, that's as it should be. Postgame, James was still irked about the lax defense that allowed the second highest point total of the year, 86. Only Florida, at 90, had scored more. We did top the century mark by a point for the second time when Will Childs-Klein capped matters again with a dunk, just as he had against Lyndon State. The final was 101-86.

The game was a great credit to St. Joseph's, a Division III team that eventually made the NCAA postseason tournament and finished with a record of 21-5.

* * * * *

Leaving the gym I felt good, but ambivalent. Again we hadn't closed an opponent out hard, yet we had another solid win. St. Joseph's had nailed eleven of twenty-seven three-pointers and twenty-nine of sixty-five shots, for a blistering 44.6 percentage. No question our defense should have been stouter and we should have been more convincing and assertive in every phase of the game.

Yet with a 10-4 record Yale had matched the great start of the 2001–2002 Ivy League co-champions. We could challenge for the title again if, on offense, we played heady and cooperative ball, recycling the Flex and moving the ball rapidly at all times; and if we learned to handle zone defenses and full-court pressure. We also had to avoid "dead zones" caused by loss of concentration on both ends of the floor. On defense this meant no loss of focus and energy, and no languid periods of relaxation and drift. All of this, fueled by desire and application, was doable. We were in good shape.

Meanwhile, as a faux coach, my fantasy life was thriving. While loving every minute of shadowing James and bird-dogging his team, I was also enjoying getting to know the sportswriters like Bill Cloutier of the *New Haven Register*, whose observations were as astute as his wit was dry.

Example: today the ball had bounced high over the shot clock and lodged, about fifteen feet up, in the stanchion supporting the backboard, halting all action. The referees looked at one another dumbfounded. Then swingman Jesse Pritchard sauntered over to the back wall, picked up a wide broom with a long handle, and poked the ball loose. The crowd applauded. When the applause died down, Bill turned to me and said, "There's the real Yale Man."

"I've always felt that as a basketball coach I had two ultimate objectives. One was to provide my players with the best background possible toward success in their future lives. I wanted to be the best teacher each one of them felt they'd had anywhere in their educational experience. The second objective was to win games. I've never been ashamed that winning was always important to me—and not only to me. I also considered it extremely important that our players learned how to win and all that went into it."

Knight: My Story
Bob Knight with Bob Hammel

PART THREE:

THE IVY LEAGUE SEASON

CHAPTER TEN

Travel Partners

THE FOLLOWING SATURDAY, January 14, Brown invaded JLA to launch the Ivy League season. For me the excitement had built to a crescendo all week. On Monday, Scottie Rodgers, the sports information director for the Ivy League, conducted a roundtable phone conference interviewing all eight coaches. Reporters patched in to ask questions and take notes. The comments the coaches made were insightful, the enthusiasm palpable. The feeling among them was identical to the unlimited hope and optimism so many sportswriters had memorialized as the hallmark of baseball managers in spring training before the major league baseball season opened and reality set in. Each Ivy coach thought he had a chance for a good season. Jerome Allen of Penn got off a funny line when a reporter asked him if he replayed games in his mind when he got in bed at night. He said he tossed and turned so much after close games that his wife was in a better position to answer that question.

My Ivy League season had actually started the Friday night before our first game against Brown. In talking with James after practice on Thursday evening I noted that I had a quick turnaround between the end of Friday's practice and my arrival for Saturday's afternoon game. Hotel bills in New Haven I had to keep to a minimum. He had a great suggestion. Since Friday's practice would be light and I already knew the strategy and game plan, why didn't I take in the game Friday night at Levien between Columbia and Penn and let him know what I thought. I had told him about Coach Allen's joke on the radio roundtable and about Columbia coach Kyle Smith noting that Penn had played its usual "insane" nonconference schedule, including away games against nationally ranked Duke and Pitt. So I took myself up to Levien, where I saw a terrifically contested battle that Penn managed to pull out in the last few seconds. Down two, Columbia suffered as a buzzer-beater three overshot the rim.

At the half I spotted Prosper Karangwa seated at the press table. He is the former Siena College swingman by way of Montreal, where he grew up, and Burundi, where he was born. He had also distinguished himself as a member of the Canadian national team, where he played in the backcourt alongside Steve Nash. I hadn't seen him since we'd met at the Rhode Island game. At halftime he corrected my impression that Columbia was playing a tightly packed zone by pointing out that it was actually an aggressive switching man-to-man. Recognizing defenses can be hard for nonprofessionals, and a synchronized switching man-to-man is nearly indistinguishable from a completely choreographed "ball" zone, the kind Coach Jim Boeheim fine-tuned at Syracuse. If each is played to perfection, both create the mobile "seal" all defenses strive for and all offenses have major trouble beating.

With their switching man-to-man, Columbia had smothered Penn's talented All-Ivy point guard Zack Rosen, holding him to two points, denying him the driving lanes, doubling him so quickly and well that it led me to mistake the defense for a zone. In contrast Brian Barbour, Columbia's point guard, had a very hot hand and had poured in eight points in a 12-2 run to close out the first half, leaving Columbia in front, 27-23.

It was good to be back in Levien and I thought how much easier it would have been to cover Columbia, instead of trekking back and forth to New Haven. Yet the cachet of JLA would not have been there, nor the architectural glories of Payne Whitney. Then again, Columbia boasted the McKim and White majesty of the main quad. What's more, there was, as always, that unbeatable Ivy League ambiance present at no other college games. The whole Ivy League athletic experience was retro, unadulterated amateurism at its apex, intelligent and talented athletes competing in a scholarly setting where college sports were kept in proper perspective.

In the second half Zack Rosen found his touch, Penn spread the floor, and their outside shooting opened up the lanes for penetration. They jumped ahead by four points in the first two and a half minutes. Then they upped their lead to 59-50, with only two minutes to go. That's when Columbia went on a wild run. Riding the enthusiasm of the home crowd, they thundered all the way back to trail by only two with thirty seconds left. Then, as the horn sounded, Barbour's off-balance three-point attempt, with a defender crowding him, overshot the rim and Columbia fell, despite Barbour's outstanding twenty-five-point performance.

After the game I visited Book Culture a few blocks away, one of the few great bookstores left in Manhattan, and bought a remaindered copy of Joseph Mitchell's *The Bottom of the Harbor*. As I walked down Broadway in the nippy January night air my pump was fully primed for Yale's Ivy opener the next day.

* * * * *

On the train up to New Haven my stomach had butterflies, something I hadn't experienced since right before football and basketball games in my first two years in high school. That's how nervous I was. Thoughts of how we'd do over the course of the Ivy League season tortured me. I consoled myself with thoughts of Brown's poor record, 5-11; but this consolation was short-lived when I realized that three of the five victories had come against Rhode Island, Hartford, and Central Connecticut, who had all given us fierce battles before we narrowly won. On top of this, the Ivy League was predictably unpredictable.

When I got to JLA there was an air of expectancy not present for non-conference games. The stands were filling up and would eventually hold just under two thousand spectators. The Yale ensemble band was drifting in and taking up its station in the collapsible stands near the front entrance where, after practice, I often sat and talked post-mortems and future strategy with James. The Yale Chorus gathered too, at the other end of the arena, ready to sing the national anthem to launch the Ivy season properly.

When Yale came out for warm-ups I noticed that Rhett Anderson sported a new haircut, a stark Mohawk with his California area code shaved into the back of his head. I admired the sense of dedication this haircut symbolized. Then, before the game started I met the two young men who manned the Yale radio station: Joey Rosenberg and Evan Frondorf, sitting directly in front of me in the press section of the stands, their headphones on. Talking to them raised my spirits and I admired their poise and confidence to undertake a broadcast performance at their tender age. Like Charles Condro of the *Yale Daily News* they were exceptional young men and I wondered for the thousandth time what it was like to have children and have them turn out so well. It had to be one of life's great rushes. By now I felt the same about every guy on the team, and I hoped we'd jump on Brown and prove our mettle early.

We didn't. Instead we slogged through the first half like zombies in a spongy marsh. Meanwhile the Bears of Brown darted around us and dropped shot after shot, setting a torrid pace, hitting from beyond the arc with ease and rapidity. Brown was starting their three-guard offense high, and we weren't coming out far enough on defense to challenge them. This was a big mistake against guards who could shoot from distance as well as Brown's trio of Sean McGonagill, Stephen Albrecht, and Matt Sullivan. By game's end they accounted for 51 of Brown's total of 64 points, making eleven of the team's twelve triples out of twenty-three attempts. Overall Brown shot just under 50 percent for the game but nearly 60 percent in the first half; fortunately for us, they cooled off in the second half, dropping to 40 percent.

That still left them shooting nearly 50 percent for the game and they led at halftime 38-31. Part of their falloff in shooting accuracy after halftime resulted from James stepping up the defense and bringing it out higher, to challenge all three-point attempts. This helped, but slowly. With three minutes to go Yale trailed by six.

Reggie Willhite then stole the game. As McGonagill hit shot after shot in the second half, playing his hot hand to the max, Bill Cloutier, sitting beside me, kept leaning in and saying, "He's gotta put Reggie on McGonagill." I agreed. Then James did, but only after biding his time to avoid Reggie getting into foul trouble as he had in our losses against Quinnipiac and Seton Hall.

Following a Brown time-out with 2:04 left, Reggie executed his signature move. Crowding McGonagill, he flicked Sean's dribble loose behind him, bolted for it, snatched it on the bounce before McGonagill could recover, and drove the length of the floor for a dunk so forceful it shook the whole backboard and ignited the home crowd. For an encore Reggie stripped the ball from McGonagill on the ensuing possession, passed it off, sprinted down court in time to receive a return pass, and nailed a jumper from the foul line, making it Yale 62, Brown 61. That decided the issue. Yale made six free throws, four by Austin Morgan, with under a minute to go, as Brown fouled in desperation. The final was Yale 68, Brown 64.

After the game James praised his team for keeping its composure and not panicking in the face of Brown's spectacular outside shooting in the first half, for stepping up the intensity of its defense in the second half, and for making its foul shots at the very end. Postgame, Reggie encapsulated Brown's strategic mistake: going into a slowdown with the lead, running the clock down and denying Yale the possessions it needed to pull out the game. That left Yale with no alternative but to go for the steals. Brown had made the classic mistake of underdogs in the lead: they played too cautiously, milking the clock, mistaking time as the opponent instead of Yale, intending to escape with the victory more than seize it. They also lacked a bench and, exhausted, faltered physically as well as mentally in the closing minutes. McGonagill's magnificent twenty-three-point effort evaporated when Reggie picked his pocket twice because he was gassed, on rubbery legs, and had lost his lateral quickness. As for Yale's lackluster performance, Reggie's closing remark said it all: "We can't lose the ones where we feel we have the advantage."

* * * * *

Because Brown was our travel partner we played them on back-to-back weekends. The following Saturday at the Pizzitola Center in Providence the weather didn't cooperate and we started late. Yale's bus had trouble getting through the blowing snow. As a result of the storm the crowd was sparse. Overnight and up till noon about five inches of snow fell. As I trudged to the game cars skidded, swayed, and labored up the hills from the Providence River to the Brown campus overlooking downtown. On my wife's advice I had come by train the day before and checked into the Biltmore Hotel. When I got to Providence in bright sunshine that Friday there was a dusting of snow from flurries the night before, but when I awoke on Saturday snow fell steadily and accumulated over shoe-top level, making my uphill climb to the Pizzitola Center adventurous.

I didn't mind. I had explored the Brown campus the day before. After a meditative visit to the Manning Chapel, I included a trip out to the edge of campus to inspect the Pizzitola Center, a relatively new and attractive basketball facility, with a capacity of 2,800. Most of the seats are in retractable stands on either side, but above one set of stands a short balcony adds a few private boxes and some permanent seats with good views. The delay in getting the game underway gave me an opportunity to chat with Brown's Sports Information Director, Chris Humm, a sprightly character not above needling me about what I was up to. I told him I liked to watch Ivy League basketball games featuring great athletes with really good minds who had to work hard in the classroom and on the court. I also told him how underrated I thought Ivy League athletics were in general and that the intensity of the round-robin schedules preserved the throwback tournament format for regular season games in all Ivy sports. Postseason conference tournaments are cynical cash cows that devalue the regular season.

We both liked it that Harvard was currently ranked twenty-fourth nationally, and that both Harvard and Princeton had knocked off Florida State. This was the same Florida State team that had beaten North Carolina the Saturday before and would beat Duke that very Saturday. North Carolina and Duke were two highly ranked perennial powers contending for the ACC championship with aspirations to go on to win the national title. Ironically, Florida State wound up winning the ACC championship. So, as the Florida State website put it, the Seminoles had encountered "Poison Ivy" twice. Chris and I agreed that the Ivies played the only Division I college basketball at a consistently competitive level where the amateurism was unalloyed, a pristine remnant from the days before television and shoe manufacturers raised the stakes so high that semi-professionalism and other forms of cheating and corruption crept in nearly everywhere.

Talking to Chris helped dispel my nervousness. On Thursday, before the afternoon practice, James and I had gone to lunch and discussed the first Brown game. I told him I was uneasy taking on the Bears in their own gym. James said flatly he didn't believe that winning away games was as hard as it was trumped up to be, that the "home floor" advantage was overrated. He had nothing but confidence heading into the rematch. He convinced me to be bullish, but his infectious enthusiasm and boundless optimism had waned for me by now. I kept seeing Brown's guards dropping in shot after shot the week before, and I thought the whole team might be better if their post players avoided the kind of foul trouble that had plagued them in JLA. I remembered too that Yale had trailed for all but four minutes in the win the previous Saturday.

I worried that Sean McGonagill would go off again and ignite fellow guards Stephen Albrecht and Matt Sullivan. The evening before, when I inspected the Pizzitola Center, I had found Sean McGonagill sitting in the first row in practice gear as forward Andrew McCarthy, their best big man, moved around the top of the key practicing his jumper. I told Sean what a terrific game he had played the previous week and how much I admired his game and his shooting eye. Friendly and polite, he thanked me but seemed inherently shy. I was aware that the year before he had won Ivy League Rookie of the Year honors, and in reading accounts of those Brown games in the *Times* I had noted his tremendous point production even as a freshman. When a really good shooter gets red hot in basketball, all bets are off. Anything can happen. Besides, in addition to the three talented guards, Brown had a power forward in McCarthy who was an assertive rebounder and post scorer who could extend the floor with a good long-range jumper, something he confirmed as I talked to Sean and watched him hit bucket after bucket from fifteen to twenty feet as he rotated clockwise around the key.

When the game started, my fears were justified. In the first half Brown picked up with its patient and poised game right where it had left off the week before. The score was tight. The lead changed hands four times and there were five ties. Reggie and Greg powered in eleven points apiece, but McGonagill and Albrecht matched them exactly. At the half we had a one-possession lead, 38-35, and I was anything but overconfident. Brown was a well-coached and stylish team that didn't waver or lose its composure. They hadn't committed a single turnover while Yale had two.

The first five minutes of the second half were more of the same. Twenty-one seconds in, Matt Sullivan tied it up again by hitting a three. Over the next two minutes the lead went back and forth before Yale reeled off a 6-0 run to go up 52-45 at the 14:42 mark. That's when the music stopped and the magic disappeared. Brown called time and in the huddle an incident erupted between Sean McGonagill and Coach Jesse Agel when Agel pulled the starters and inserted substitutes. The result ruined the game: Agel benched McGonagill for the remainder of the game. Playing without their star, the Bears, to their credit, didn't fold. Albrecht asserted himself beautifully, taking up the slack, and senior guard Jean Harris, who had replaced McGonagill, hit two three-pointers and two foul shots, for eight points. What killed them was a series of four inexcusably sloppy turnovers in the middle of the half that enabled Yale to pull away, mounting a lead of seven and then stretching it to eleven.

Jesse Pritchard, the swingman who played behind Reggie and also spelled the starting guards, was a major factor. He came off the bench to rebound like a man possessed, snaring eight while pouring in a decisive nine points in a scorching ten-minute span. The difference maker, Jesse was an emblematically nice young man from Iowa, a witty English major who played flat-out at all times. Both his points and rebounds were career highs.

I couldn't have been happier for Jesse, but the fate of Sean McGonagill upset me. Though stocky, the kid was nevertheless balletic in his movements, sneaky quick, and blessed with that great shooting touch. I loved his game and wanted to watch him longer. I also wanted him to galvanize his Brown teammates to push Yale, to toughen us. When McGonagill went out we got off easy. And it didn't feel good.

I also felt terrible for Coach Agel, especially after the season when he was dismissed. Even during and after the first game, I had noticed how uptight he was. Being overly intense, and the liabilities this carries, I can relate to firsthand. I knew only that I hadn't seen a better coached team than Brown all season, and I wished fervently, when I learned that he'd been fired, that some athletic director would give him a second chance at a head coaching job some day. As an assistant for years at Vermont he had been a dynamo. Like Patriots coach Bill Belichick's false showing in his failed head coaching debut with the Browns, Jesse Agel, I felt sure, once he regained perspective and learned to modulate his passion, would turn out to be a fantastic head coach for a team smart enough to hire him.

In talking to James after the game and learning that McGonagill had been distraught over the incident, I felt even worse. So did James, who said to me sotto voce in the corridor outside our locker room, "You hate to hear a kid was in tears like that."

* * * * *

Yale junior guard Sam Martin grew up in West Warwick, a suburb about a fifteen-minute ride from downtown Providence, and his mother Carol had invited the entire team back to her house for a party after the game. James had invited me and I was delighted to climb aboard the team bus and ride out to Sam's house amid all the chatter and tomfoolery common after a victory. The guys liked to pop a tape into the bus's video system and watch a movie as they rode along. So they put *Blue Chips* on. I had never seen it. Within two minutes it was clear that Nick Nolte was aping Bob Knight's body language and general demeanor as a coach with anger management and self-control issues, which prompted me to say a private prayer for Coach Agel to get his act together.

In the movie Nolte's boss as athletic director was Bob Cousy, my boyhood idol before Oscar Robertson took over that role. Because the ride was so short we watched only the opening sequences before we got to Sam's house, but I was thrilled to recognize George Raveling in the cast. For years in the early sixties I had watched George muscle rebound after rebound for Villanova at the Palestra while playing under Coach Al Severance. George's chest was so expansive he looked like a pouter pigeon going up to move bodies and snare the ball. For years he had gone on to be a good college coach, most notably at USC.

When Nolte kicked a ball into the stands it was to evince Knight's infamous hurling of a chair across the court when a referee's decision upset him, one of the incidents Knight never lived down and a contributing factor to his demise at Indiana University, where he was and always will be a legend. My feelings about Knight were clear: he was the greatest coach who ever set foot on hardwood and he was a tragic hero complete with an Achilles heel and heaps of hubris. That flawed nature doesn't negate his accomplishments. Doubtless his temper was injurious to his players on occasion and his lack of self-control set a regrettable example for them and for all young people.

But against these flaws you have to set out his outstanding dedication, his unshakable integrity, his admirable character, and his colossal knowledge, of both basketball and of many of life's most meaningful values. As I mentioned, no scandal ever tarnished a program he ran. He never exploited a player. He pushed kids to attend class. He urged his players to get their degrees. And he quietly took care of Landon Turner, the great post player at Indiana rendered a paraplegic in an auto accident. Also, for many inner-city kids, a strong male disciplinarian is not necessarily a negative factor in their formative years, especially if, on the streets and sometimes even at home, they've been exposed to violent, chaotic, and destructive behavior portrayed as assertive or, worse, glamorous.

When I watched Knight's teams from Army onward through Indiana and Texas Tech, the massive effort his players put out would not be generated without admiration and even affection for their coach spurring them on. Anyone who ever played sports knows that. And the unimpeachable excellence of the 1976 Indiana team is beyond debate. I rank that team without hesitation as the greatest college team ever. And, unlike the great teams of UCLA that preceded it, that team left no booster scandal in its wake. No players were paid under the table or with no-show jobs and fancy cars. I've also been told reliably that coach John Wooden could curse every bit as vividly as Knight.

All these thoughts tumbled in on me as I watched *Blue Chips* and mulled the benching of Sean McGonagill and the fate of Jesse Agel. Like Nolte in the movie, like Knight in real life, Agel's overstated intensity and his quick anger were serious liabilities. As I was experiencing firsthand, coaching was loaded with frustration. Like any form of teaching, it took patience and tolerance. It also demanded restraint. Even as a faux coach my nerves were tested week after week. I imagined all the time what it must be like to really be at the controls and under crushing pressure to win or be canned. When you can't get your players to do what you want, coaching so closely paralleled the trials and tribulations of parenting. Through my own character flaws I had learned that you couldn't control other people. You could only hope to guide and influence them. Parental control is over once a child goes out the door. The same with coaching. Once the players go out on the court, the coach's control ends. They are free agents, and to err is human. A coach has to be able to absorb mistakes and tolerate the best-laid plans gone haywire. James Jones, like his brother Joe, though in no way lackadaisical, seemed to have the temperamental maturity and stability to handle the unpredictability and the built-in disappointments and frustrations inherent in coaching young people.

I worried that Coach Agel, despite his obvious gifts as a teacher, tactician, and strategist of basketball, had become too frayed. From what I could see before the game-ruining incident, McGonagill had suffered a defensive lapse on the play preceding the time-out, the argument, and the benching. Mike Grace had driven hard and scored a lay-up. But you could rebuke a kid without embarrassing a kid. I'd seen James Jones do it time after time and have the kid remain intact and under control. Benching a kid for the rest of the game is extreme, even if he gave you the sex and travel directive. Sitting him down for five minutes is enough to get the message through. McGonagill deserved a second chance to try to beat Yale.

* * * * *

At the party Sam's mother Carol was a joy. When we got to their handsome split-level she had the whole feast laid out in a rich buffet. The guys dug in while I tried to make myself inconspicuously observant. The thing that amused me the most was the abandoned pile of sneakers in the vestibule; they seemed to be waiting to be claimed by Brobdingnagians; some were the size of small skateboards. The players did not know yet what exactly I was doing by following them so closely, and so ignored me, to my delight. While they chowed down I took up a place on the sofa in the living room and talked to Matt Kingsley, the senior of James's trio of assistant coaches I thought of privately as the Three Wise Men. Later in the season I referred to them once in earshot of the players as the Three Wise Men and was later amused to hear the players refer to them that way.

That week at practice I had overheard James and Matt discussing a recruiting trip to look over a prospect. I now asked Matt about Yale's approach to recruiting and he explained that occasionally during the season he or one of the other assistants would get away to check out a prospect. Sometimes even James would come along. But Matt told me most of the recruiting was concentrated in the summer, at James's Yale Basketball Bulldog Elite Camp in June and at the AAU competitions around the country in July. Then Matt and I discussed the game and he mentioned that we should have pulled away more rapidly and won more decisively once McGonagill exited the game. I agreed with him. Jesse Pritchard had been galvanic off the bench but we should have keelhauled them the minute McGonagill went into dry dock. McGonagill not only piled up points but he saw the court well and fed the open man relentlessly, clocking up a pile of assists while propelling his team. With him on the bench we let them hang around too long. Once again we didn't finish properly.

By now the buffet line had dwindled and I filled a plate and retreated to the downstairs den. There I walked into a shrine of trophies, all won by Sam and cherished by his mom, who proudly displayed them. Most of the trophies were for victories in karate tournaments, but many others were for basketball triumphs. They overflowed the room. Some were huge, the size of department store mannequins for showcasing children's wear. One or two were monumental, about five feet high. Looking at them I knew instantly that Sam was a compulsive, obsessive competitor, a man striving for mastery of self, for a oneness, a merging of self with a difficult task; he strove constantly for a total mastery of a challenging skill set, a melding of mind and muscle memory into an amalgamated unit. I loved him for it.

When James announced that the bus was leaving I drifted back upstairs to say goodbye. Austin's dad, Jay, mentioned he was driving back to Providence with his wife Sherry. He said they'd be glad to drop me at the station. When they did, I had a two-hour layover so I went across the street to the giant mall, Providence Place, and made notes and mulled the game. We had displayed balanced scoring for the second straight game against Brown and had made a good team effort: Greg dropped in eighteen points and snared eleven rebounds, Reggie powered in thirteen points and three assists, Austin added five assists and tallied ten points. Jerry and Mike, the other two starters, scored eight points apiece and Jerry matched that total in rebounds. Off the bench Brandon Sherrod and Matt Townsend each scored two points, Isaiah nailed a three, and Jesse banged in his quick and deadly nine points. Even better, we had recovered our winning ways, notching four in a row and ten of our last twelve. Still, as James told me several times after practices, we hadn't "put it all together, we hadn't played at our highest level yet."

I got into my New York apartment right before four a.m., weary but warmed by memories of Providence in the snow, how beautiful it was, how it reminded me of Society Hill in Philly, and how it put me in mind also of a vest pocket version of Boston, especially in its colonial splendor and academic prowess. Roaming the bookstores of Thayer Avenue in the heart of the Brown campus with snow crunching underfoot had been memorable, especially since real bookstores were vanishing from Manhattan at an alarming rate. It had been especially gratifying in the Brown bookstore to spot a book of scholarly criticism devoted to the work of John Edgar Wideman, the talented guard for Penn I had watched in the Palestra half a century ago who had gone on to be a Rhodes Scholar and a prominent writer. I could kick myself for lending my copy of his first novel, *A Glance Away*, to someone who never gave it back.

CHAPTER ELEVEN

The Crimson Clinic

ALL WEEK EXCITEMENT ran high. In basketball Harvard and Yale play "The Game" twice a year, home-and-home. Round one this year was at Yale. Harvard was still nationally ranked and had the better overall record, but Yale at 2-0 in league play was tied with them for a share of the Ivy lead, as was Penn. This added a sweetener to the mix for whoever came out on top tonight: the loser would fall from a tie for the lead.

JLA was rocking when I got there. The game had been sold out for weeks and the air of expectancy was thick. When Harvard last visited JLA to play Yale—on February 26 the previous winter—the game had been the barnburner I witnessed after intuiting that Yale was going to upset the then front-running Crimson. They did, winning a thriller by a single point, 70-69. Both teams had played brilliantly and I expected to see that same savage competition and admirable proficiency reprised. So did the crowd and the large complement of media, three or four times larger than usual.

Special refreshment stands had been set up in the corridors behind the stands, and on the gallery the stand selling Yale gear was doing a brisk business. Yale's ensemble band was warming up under the blared rap music of the PA system: "The Motto" by Drake, "Power" by Kanye West, "Dynamite" by Taio Cruz, "We Found Love" by Rihanna, "F.A.M.E." by Young Jeezy, and others. Music at sporting events was de rigueur these days but in a more contemplative age you could attend a sporting event and discuss the game with fellow spectators: the strengths and weaknesses of the players, the strategy of the coaches, the smart counter move, the lax or rigid officiating, and so on. That kind of single attention to anything was on the wane in the age of multitasking, where many things were done simultaneously in an ambiance of raucous and chaotic audio and visual stimulation, with only the one drawback: usually, nothing was done well.

Seeking an audio respite, I went down to the locker room to stand in the back and hear James address the guys before the game. Like all the other coaches tonight, James was wearing sneakers with his suit, a sartorial eyesore but one for a worthy cause: High-school and college coaches across the country were wearing sneakers this weekend to emphasize the Coaches Versus Cancer campaign designed to find a cure for cancer and increase the number of birthdays celebrated worldwide in the future. James was such a sharp dresser that the sneakers did look comical, despite their emblematic seriousness.

As always, he had bulleted his main points on the whiteboard along the far wall. There he also diagrammed key plays alongside the bulleted points. This was a last-minute review. All week long James had drilled the guys on these key plays. They illustrated Harvard's favorite moves on offense and how Yale should defend them. First, we needed to watch for high picks that would break their dangerous long-range shooters loose. Second, James demanded that: "Five stays on the blocks at all times—no cheap baskets," meaning that center Greg Mangano was not to be lured away from the basket but to patrol there in the event Harvard got a man loose on penetration, especially on drives for easy lay-ups or on backdoor plays on the weak side.

We also couldn't let Harvard get points off their sets. They were patient on offense. We had to thwart them repeatedly no matter how long and patiently they tried to penetrate the lane or find the open perimeter man. We needed to stay alert on the cross-screens and on the down-screens, both designed to break a man loose for dribble penetration and an easy bucket underneath. Harvard ran a lot of ball-screens and Yale had to stay alert to switch and break them up. This might involve hedging or taking charges. Hedging meant coming out nearly parallel to the screener and forcing the dribbler to drive wider, allowing time for his defender to recover. The recovering defender had to be willing to plant and take a charge from the dribble penetrator. If either technique worked well the screen was negated.

When we were on offense we had to stick to our basic strategy and handle their unstinting defensive pressure. All week James had emphasized that Harvard's defense was much more intense and effective this year than last; it was "stepped up," as he put it. They played mostly man-to-man with a little zone mixed in "for a few possessions." Midweek, James told me he was "very curious to see how they guard us in the post." The reason was easy to know. We were both the tallest and the highest-scoring team in the league.

In our big upset of Harvard at the tail end of the previous season our low post game had worked beautifully: Mangano scored eleven points, hauled down thirteen rebounds, and blocked an astonishing five shots; Kreisberg added thirteen points; and Willhite scored fifteen to go along with eight assists, two steals, and one block. The front line accounted for 39 of 70 points. That kind of proficiency in the low post had freed up the perimeter guys so well that the starting backcourt totaled twenty-five points. Shooting guard Austin Morgan scored sixteen points by hitting four of six threes and going five for eight overall, with a perfect two for two from the foul line. The point guard then, now graduated senior Porter Braswell, had scored nine points. Reserves Mike Grace, Jesse Pritchard, and Rhett Anderson each added two.

That's why in tonight's rematch James wanted the guys "to look to get a lob," meaning to work the ball down low on the blocks to get the front line scoring again. When this happened it would open up the inside-out game as Harvard overcompensated defending the low post, which would leave the guards on the perimeter loose for open shots. In cases where the first option into the post, the lob, was not there, James wanted everyone to whip the ball back out and look to "hand off on the wing," thereby spreading the floor. If the guys on the wing started to pop their outside shots, Harvard's defense would have to come out farther, thus opening the dribble penetration lanes and, reciprocally, facilitating the low post game. That's how Yale's offense had worked the last time these two archrivals had clashed eleven months before.

Naturally Coach Jones wanted a repeat. In closing he said, deadpan but emphatic, "I would suspect you guys marked this date in your calendars." He then fell silent, arms crossed, one hand on his chin, staring at his players, one by one, making eye contact with each. For a long moment he scanned the room before acknowledging that this was what we had worked for, a big game, as evidenced by the big crowd, the noise, the excitement, the media hoopla. Then he added, in a sharp voice: "Don't be a spectator out there. Be a player. Remember you're a player."

* * * * *

Both teams came out uptight, feeling each other out, stomping sideways like two wary sumo wrestlers, reluctant to risk grappling but determined not to retreat and risk forfeiting the match by stepping outside the circle. Each squad wanted to show that its collective will was equal to the stress of this challenge. The scoring started slowly, nerves biting deep. Nearly three minutes went by before Harvard's Laurent Rivard hit a lay-up. A few seconds later Jerry Kreisberg matched it with a jumper in the lane, a good omen, I thought, superstitious as ever, because Jerry had hit the last and deciding basket in the upset last season. At the first media time-out with 15:16 left it was 4-2 Harvard, Brandyn Curry having popped a short jumper in the lane. Right after the second media time-out at 10:49 Yale led when Jesse Pritchard canned a three from the left corner to make it 12-11. With a quarter of the game gone it looked like another thriller in the making.

That's when Harvard reeled off a 12-2 run and extended it to a 19-7 run to go up by eleven, 30-19 at intermission. Despite Harvard's swarming, aggressive, relentless defense, we were in the game. But their balance scared me: their starters had scored fifteen points and their bench had matched it. Harvard coach Tommy Amaker, a former All-American guard at Duke, was running fresh players in every few minutes. Harvard was going to have fresher legs and more energy in the second half. To stay in the game we would have to redouble our efforts; as Reggie Willhite liked to say, it would be "an energy thing," with our guys reaching inside themselves for everything they had.

We had also fallen into the usual trap in the first half. Greg Mangano had taken nine of the team's twenty shot attempts. When the ball went into him in the low post he was retaining it even as the Harvard defense collapsed around him, double-teaming him. Instead of working the inside-out game and getting the ball to an open man on the perimeter, Greg was trying to do too much himself. Yet, in truth, Greg was having trouble getting the ball to his usual perimeter outlet man on the strong side, shooting guard Austin Morgan. Harvard was covering Austin maniacally close, especially rugged defender Oliver McNally, a savvy senior guard who at six-three had four inches in height on Austin and a big edge in wing span. Austin had attempted only one shot, a miss. When covered hard our offense was making the same old mistake. Lacking patience, we did not reset and rework the Flex until it opened an opportunity. Instead we settled for low-percentage shots and too often went freelance instead of ramping up our teamwork. Open on the weak side, as he was for most of the season, Jerry Kreisberg was not getting the ball.

Yet we were very much still in the game, down by only eleven with a whole half to play. James pointed this out and succinctly reviewed what the guys were doing wrong. He told them how to correct it to get back in the game and win it. Then, with his unfailing enthusiasm, he huddled the team, hands clasped in a pyramid above their heads, and told them "Yale on three." In unison they counted aloud to three and yelled "Yale" before filing back out. At the portal into the gym they paused and huddled again before charging onto the floor to loud applause.

* * * * *

Harvard played like a team possessed. At the first media time-out at 15:48 we trailed by fifteen, 38-23. At the second media time-out five minutes later we were down nineteen, 48-29. They were ginning points on us at will. Harvard's balanced attack on offense was a thing of beauty to watch, the ball movement blistering and the sharing total, every man looking for the open man, everyone working the offense patiently until the scoring opportunity for the open man developed organically. Keith Wright, Harvard's senior power forward and the Ivy's Player of the Year the previous season, worked the low post to perfection in concert with junior small forward Kyle Casey. Point guard Brandyn Curry penetrated for lay-ups, or dished off to shooting guards Oliver McNally or Laurant Rivard. They each canned a three while Rivard went three for three again on the foul line, just as he had in the first half.

The Harvard bench continued to deliver. Steve Moundou-Missi, a graceful, speedy, and athletic small forward from Cameroon, added two more points, two more rebounds, and yet another spectacular steal to give him ten points, five rebounds and three steals for the game. He played only seventeen minutes. Fellow freshman Corbin Miller, a shooting guard, hit two free throws to go with his first-half three, giving him five points for the game, also in seventeen minutes. Junior guard Christian Webster, who'd been injured recently, costing him his starting job, came off the bench to score four quick points in nine minutes, all in the second half. This matched the first-half total chipped in by reserve freshman guard Wesley Saunders. To climax the whole ensemble scoring effort, junior guard Dee Giger, rangy and quick, executed a deft steal in the waning seconds, dribbled the length of the floor, and slammed home a dunk. Less the fabled dagger shot than the final nail in Yale's coffin, it raised the final margin of victory to thirty points.

Many in the sellout crowd had left midway through the half when Harvard's lead ballooned to over twenty points. Bill Cloutier and I had exchanged hushed whispers about what a clinic Harvard was putting on. I thought back to the Rhode Island game when, while eating lunch in the media room, I overheard a reporter say to sportswriter Bill Reynolds of the *Providence Journal*, a friend: "Harvard is a middle of the pack Big East team." I asked and learned that he was Kevin McNamara, a colleague of Bill's on the *Journal*. At that point Harvard had already toppled Utah and Florida State and given Connecticut a close game. About Harvard I remembered thinking there in the media room, laughable now in hindsight, "Wait till we get 'em in JLA."

I never dreamed their defense would hold us forty points below our season average, turn us over ten times in the first half and twelve in the second, for a crippling total of twenty-two, and limit us to sixteen second-half points. My heart ached for James and his three assistants. All week at practice they had prepped the guys physically and psychologically. All for naught it turned out. As I started down to the media room, adjacent to the Yale locker room, I was stunned to the point of mild shock.

Yet my hat was off to Coach Amaker. He really had run a clinic, evoking his coaching bloodline: Coach Krzyzewski at Duke, begotten by Coach Knight at Army, begotten by Coach Taylor at Ohio State. Into the mix via Knight came the ball movement genius of Coach Hank Iba at Oklahoma State and, also, Iba's famous "swinging gate" defense, a swarming and ever shifting man-to-man. Going even farther back Knight brought forward the wicked wizardry of Coach Branch McCracken's smothering man-to-man at Indiana. Finally, drizzled into the incomparable Knight coaching confection were his cagey borrowings from Clair Bee at LIU and Joe Lapchick at St. John's.

In forty minutes of scintillating excellence, Tommy Amaker had evoked the entire legacy. Even though he had thrashed my team, my admiration for what he'd accomplished was infinite. It had been a drop-dead beautiful demonstration of perfectly played basketball.

* * * * *

In the media room Amaker was up first. Without an ounce of gloating he answered questions and recapped what his team had done. After saying, "Defense is the number one identity of our team," he lauded the two things he next prized the most: "those B words for us—bench and balance." He was pleased with "the ball movement" on offense, and with Keith Wright's play in the low post, where he was "light on his feet." Laurant Rivard he singled out as "a tough kid and great shooter, with great endurance and real savvy." About holding Austin Morgan to three points he said simply: "McNally was outstanding." Freshman Steve Moundou-Missi off the bench had also been "outstanding tonight." About the entire team effort he remarked, "On the road it's impressive."

A reporter asked if he got a special thrill from winning in JLA, where Yale had upset his team eleven months earlier and forced them into that one-game playoff loss here to Princeton by a single point on a buzzer-beater. He said, "Yes."

Harvard rightly blamed Yale for their loss of the title and the NCAA bid, and tonight had been pure payback. As reported by Mark Blaudschun in the *Boston Globe* the next day, Laurant Rivard said after the game: "They cost us a bid to the NCAA Tournament last year. Coach made sure we came into this one motivated. We thought a little about Princeton and we thought a lot about Yale that we lost that close one. We made that the focus of what we did." The Crimson had their revenge. The top cardiologist at Mass General could not have been more clinical at cutting our heart out.

Coach Jones and Greg Mangano were up next. Gracious and fully composed, but obviously stung, James, after stating "we didn't run a good offense tonight," added, "I'm not sure who we were tonight. We made mistakes I'd never seen before." Without whining, and giving full credit to Harvard's defense, he noted that Austin had been "smothered" and that, on some of our turnovers, he was "still not sure how we lost the ball." Mercifully the reporters kept this interview short.

Greg followed. He and Reggie were good postgame interviewees and Greg did not disappoint this night, putting his finger right on the problem. After calling the game "disappointing," he said: "Embarrassing. I think that's the right word for it. We got embarrassed on our own court. They're a solid defensive team. Too often we weren't ready for the ball, and they were getting to the ball faster than us." He concluded, like the competitor he is, by saying, "We have an opportunity to play tomorrow before sitting on this bad feeling for a week."

When the reporters turned to James again, he emphasized Harvard's depth and added: "It's hard for me to digest this until I see film."

Earlier Tommy Amaker had pointed out that the Ivy League is "a great league with great history and great tradition," mentioning tonight's sellout crowd and the influx of media, including regional television, before concluding: "This is a great time in the Ivy League." At least for Harvard it was, who had just beaten Yale in basketball by its largest margin of victory.

* * * * *

On the train I feared a letdown against Dartmouth the next night. At home this fear made it hard to sleep. Plus, looping scenes from the Harvard game in my head as I stretched out in bed supplied my own personal horror movie, and I admired James because I suspected he was most likely already looping the actual game films at home in his den into the wee hours of the morning. He was compulsive about winning, try as he might to keep perspective and balance in his life. And he had to be upset about tonight's game, since I certainly was, even in my much lesser capacity. Watching a game like that for a coach who has prepared his team for everything the opposition would likely do and then watching the opposition do it with impunity is hard to handle. This is where coaching approaches the frustration levels of parenting a feral child. You instruct, you warn, you counsel, and then you get to watch the whole horrible scenario you instructed, warned, and counseled against unfold right in front of your eyes. Your instinct to blame is strong and your ability to resist is a measure of your character and your maturity.

Still, it's hard to get to sleep after a rout. There was so much I wanted to say to the players but it wasn't my place to say it. I almost got back out of bed and emailed James to tell the guys what a great Scottish buddy of mine always said in situations like this: the shopworn but always effective Rudyard Kipling line about adversity introducing a man to himself. So you can imagine my surprise and delight the next night before the Dartmouth game when James used exactly that quote, skipping the literary citation that I, as an English major, would have redundantly and foolishly included.

This was in the locker room during the Dartmouth pregame speech. James also warned the guys not to "get caught sleeping on the perimeter," meaning to stay alert and contest the outside shots; not to "get caught in No Man's Land," meaning not to lose your man and end up wandering around alone on the empty weak side; and, finally, not to "help guys who don't need help," meaning not to double-team Dartmouth players who were not serious scoring threats. James was at pains to describe how their big men were ineffective other than at short range. He didn't want the defense spread unnecessarily by trailing these "bigs" outside, far from the basket, and thereby opening the gaps and driving lanes and rendering our defense porous and vulnerable to dribble penetration by their able guards.

On defense he reviewed what to do against their better outside shooters, the guards again, and said to be wary of a veteran guard, Jabari Trotter, a former starter and an explosive scorer now coming off the bench. Trotter was not so much demoted to the bench as sacrificed to Coach Paul Cormier's youth movement. There were offensively potent freshmen forwards to contend with as well: Jvonte Brooks and Gabas Maldunas, a six-foot-eight Lithuanian. Both were starters, as was a tall freshman guard, a swingman really, named John Golden, a long-range marksman. The other two starters were junior guard R.J. Griffin, a streak shooter who could pile up the points, and sophomore Tyler Melville, a tremendous ballhandler and quick penetrator who, if the outside shot was not there, liked to break his defender down off the dribble and blow by him for easy lay-ups.

Earlier in the week at practice James had enumerated the keys to victory: offensive execution with good ball movement exploiting the inside/out game when the low post was jammed; aggressive defense that contested the outside shooters and contained the penetrators; domination of the boards by blocking out and grabbing rebounds; and a demonstration of team toughness at all times, winning the battle for 50/50 loose balls even if it meant diving on the floor after them.

Looking right at the players again, slowly and sequentially, James said with deliberation: "We don't want to lose in our own building." When he called for the pyramidal handclasp and the collective cheer of "Yale on three," I looked above the lockers at the inscription on the wall: "Protect this house," and hoped we wouldn't lose twice in a row at home. The night before Harvard had shattered our perfect 6-0 home record.

Sleepless the previous night, I had gone on the Brown website and read an account of their win over Dartmouth. It had been a seesaw game that Dartmouth led at halftime before Andrew McCarthy and Sean McGonagill took over in the second half to secure the win. McCarthy had scored nineteen points and grabbed eleven rebounds to complement his school record seven blocks in one game. McGonagill had dished off ten assists and scored eleven points, seven in the late second-half surge that sealed Dartmouth's winless fate in three Ivy games. James had pointed out that Dartmouth and Brown ran similar offenses, using a lot of sideline triangle action. Like all coaches, I distrusted playing winless underdogs, knowing that the old saw about every dog having his day could jump up at any time and bite you.

* * * * *

The game was lackluster, Yale listless. Dartmouth jumped out fast. When James had seen enough and called a time-out with 8:43 to go we were down eight, 23-15. Before the time-out Isaiah Salafia and Sam Martin each hit a three, and out of the time-out Greg Mangano and Michael Grace matched threes from the top of the key, making it four triples in a row. Then Greg executed a pretty spin and lay-up in the lane and Matt Townsend followed on the next possession with one of his butterfly baby hooks in the low post. After a 10-0 run Yale had its first lead of the weekend, 25-23, at the 5:20 mark. From there to the half, Austin scored three, Reggie three, and Greg two, for an 8-3 run and a halftime lead of 33-26.

We seemed, despite a lack of spark, to have the game under control. In the locker room James said we should never have spotted them an eight-point lead but since then we had done a good job of guarding them. He singled out classy Matt Townsend for guarding extremely well. He cautioned the guys to stay alert for the backdoor play, reminded them that Dartmouth was mixing in a good three-two zone, and goosed them to watch for guard Tyler Melville to penetrate even deeper after breaking his man down off the dribble. Containing Melville would be a good idea, he suggested, with a hint of sarcasm. Melville had burned us for eight points, two on dribble drives and easy lay-ups. Alert as ever, James had noted this: it wasn't in the stats.

James always shared the floor at halftime with his assistants, letting them add comments, usually in sequence by seniority. Matt went first and elaborated on what James had said as it applied to the guards. Then Jamie exhorted the post players to stay alert on defense for "a lot of trickery" and, on offense, to "share the ball, move the ball around." He emphasized our height advantage and how we had to cash in on it, then ended by saying, "We have too many weapons." Justin followed and underscored our height advantage. We weren't capitalizing on it. He urged the post guys when facing Dartmouth's zone "to force them to make one-on-one plays on us" and "to look for your teammate at the basket." If we did this, our height would get us easy buckets. After a short pause he concluded: "Bigs, the onus is on you."

* * * * *

At the start of the second half we were not only listless again but again spotted Dartmouth a lead. Six and a half minutes in, reserve senior swingman David Rufful hit a jump hook in the lane and Dartmouth went up, 36-35. When Jabari Trotter dropped in a three on their next possession they went up four. We couldn't recapture the lead until Reggie hit the second of two foul shots to make it 45-44. Two possessions later John Golden made a lay-up in the paint and Dartmouth was back on top, but for the last time. Reggie answered with a jumper and we never trailed again because he took the game over.

Back at the 12:16 point James had pulled Reggie for a breather right after he stole the ball from Jabari Trotter and tied the game at 39 apiece off a lay-up. On the bench James spoke to him animatedly. When Reggie went back in the game with ten minutes left he went wild. In nine and a half minutes he scored Yale's next nine points, putting us up 50-46 off a lightning quick reverse lay-up with four minutes to go. He wasn't finished. After Jeremiah Kreisberg hit a free throw, Reggie fed him down low for a lay-up.

On our next possession, out of a Yale time-out with 1:11 left, Reggie found Mike Grace behind the arc at the top of the key. Mike made his second three of the game, putting us up 56-48. From there Austin Morgan hit four foul shots sandwiched around two more by—who else?—Reggie. In that same stretch Tyler Melville got another lay-up off a drive and, at the buzzer, David Ruffel hit a meaningless jumper from the foul line to make the final score Yale 62, Dartmouth 52.

Team captain Reggie had willed his Bulldogs to victory yet again. This was the fourth game he had taken over and won: Hartford, Sacred Heart, Brown at home, and now Dartmouth. He had also sealed victories with two late steals against Central Connecticut and a single late steal against Bryant. Tonight his team had come out for the second half flat and had committed seven turnovers in the first eight and a half minutes, four of them in the first six minutes. I knew now viscerally why coaches always lamented turnovers in postgame interviews, sometimes even maundering about them. In the early minutes of the second half my stomach had hurt the whole time we imitated the Washington Generals against the Globetrotters, and I ended up white-knuckling my ballpoint for most of the second half. I could only imagine how James and his three assistants felt watching this sideshow. We had twelve second-half turnovers to go with our seven in the first half. That meant nineteen more on top of our twenty-two against Harvard the night before: forty-one for the weekend. At practice when James got frustrated with sloppiness he meted out push-ups and wind sprints. I had a feeling that practice this week might look like boot camp.

At the postgame press conference James said simply: "We have to get better. It wasn't a ten-point game. It'll only look like that in the papers." He did say accurately: "Defensively we did a good job. They run an offense much like Brown's. We were ready."

When Reggie came in, I asked a rare question. Usually I didn't feel like taking up time the real reporters needed, but I was so impressed by what Austin Morgan had done with four minutes gone in the second half that I asked Reggie for his opinion, saying I admired the play so much. Jabari Trotter had stolen the ball from Austin at midcourt. Immediately, sprinting all out, Austin ran Trotter down and slapped the ball out of his hands and out of bounds as he went up for an easy two. Like the leader he is, Austin had set an electrifying and serious example at the right moment among all the buffoonery of our clownish turnovers. Reggie said in response: "Austin's great snuff is an energy thing." Then added: "We won. It doesn't necessarily feel that good. There's a lot of work to do. We can go one of two ways. We can splitter or come together."

Before I left I asked James if sophomore guard and super athlete Isaiah Salafia was okay. Right before the midway point in the second half he drove the lane and was clothes-lined and clobbered. Seconds later James took him out and he didn't reappear. James told me he would be okay but had suffered whiplash. This fear of injuries was a constant, ever looming liability.

As I walked to the train station I was relieved that we won, and I especially grinned at the thought of James shooting Jeremiah the "thumbs up" sign from the bench in the waning minutes after Jerry, who had played a really solid second half, took a hard charge with textbook aplomb. Always stressing in practice the proper way to take a charge, James called the drill "Rome," even on the agenda. You either got a thumbs-up for doing it right or a thumbs-down for doing it wrong, just like the gladiators in the Coliseum. This was serious: if you planned to have a family it was important to learn the right protective technique because taking a charge involves serious exposure of the gonads. At practice when the guys got into the Rome drill, it was usually comical, and James always made sure, while serious about teaching the right cover-up technique, to let them get in some laughs as, one-on-one, they sent each other sprawling on the floor, knocked ass over tin cups.

CHAPTER TWELVE

Penn/Princeton Weekend

PENN/PRINCETON WEEKEND IN the Ivy League is a big deal. I first heard the expression "Penn/Princeton weekend" at a Columbia game several years ago. Until then I had never been aware of the significance this weekend held for the other six teams in the Ivy League. Growing up in Philly I had been aware of Penn and Princeton as archrivals, and as the two superior basketball programs in the Ivy League, one or the other winning the title nearly every year. I had not been aware of them as travel partners making the rounds of the other six schools once a year in tandem on consecutive nights. Since living in New York City I had gone up to see them at Levien against Columbia on consecutive Friday and Saturday nights but I had never heard the phrase "Penn/Princeton weekend" until then. So I was unaware of the awe and dread the phrase evoked.

We would next host the Penn/Princeton weekend. But, before that, on Monday night Penn would play Princeton in the Palestra. These two traditionally played their home-and-home travel partner games on weekday nights, usually Tuesdays, and for years they played the final game of the Ivy season on the Tuesday following the last weekend. That would be the case again this year on March 6 when Princeton hosted Penn. For many years these two games determined the Ivy basketball champ, and usually the last and often deciding game was televised, as it would be this season in five and a half weeks.

My Palestra nostalgia was acting up and I thought I'd go down and take a look at round one between the archrivals, so Monday afternoon I hopped the train. The last time I'd been there was for the March 8 game the previous spring when I was pulling for Penn to upset Princeton and send Harvard to the NCAA tournament as sole champion. Instead, though Princeton trailed at halftime, they got hot and pulled away from Penn in the second half to win by a dozen, 70-58. That's how Douglas Davis happened to hit the buzzer-beater in JLA four days later that cost co-champion Harvard the NCAA bid.

This night it was Penn's turn for payback. Princeton was coming off a sixteen-day layoff—for reading week and final exams—and never got in rhythm. In all phases of the game Penn senior Zack Rosen was magnificent. From the start he took charge of the game and never relinquished it, scoring five points as Penn surged to an 11-2 lead. Rosen was spreading the floor and starting his offense high, far from the basket. Time and again Penn's forwards, Henry Brooks and Rob Belcore, would set ball-screens for Rosen a step beyond the elbow, near the arc; then, after running his man into the screener, Rosen would step back and pop a quick three before the Princeton defenders could switch or hedge. Alternately, Rosen would pick and roll with the screener or find a teammate open in the near corner or streaking along the baseline for a backdoor lay-up.

Princeton fought back, shooting well, but they could not close the gap to fewer than five points the rest of the way, despite a good game from All-Ivy forward Ian Hummer, whose father and uncle had played for Princeton, making him a kind of legacy athlete. Unlike Columbia in Levien two weeks earlier, Princeton gave Rosen too much leeway and he surgically dissected them. If you wanted to stop Penn, a team of streak shooters, you had to deny the ball to Rosen and challenge him from the minute he crossed half-court, as Columbia coach Kyle Smith had demonstrated in his team's two-point loss three weeks earlier.

On the train back to New York I felt confident that if we played together on offense and put up an aggressive defense, we could beat both Penn and Princeton.

* * * * *

There was no need for anything special to enhance the Penn/Princeton weekend but thanks to my friend Elizabeth Beier, a comely, articulate, and charming editor, there *was* something. It's called Louis' Lunch and I had no clue it existed until Elizabeth, a Yalie, told me not to miss it. She said the hamburger had been invented there over a century ago and immediately I knew, as a hamburger freak, that I had to try it. She was right. Louis' burgers are held in place by steel wire gridirons while cooking simultaneously on both sides in vertical cast iron gas stoves over eight decades old. Then the burgers are served between two slices of toast, no ketchup or relish allowed. The meat is lean and delicious and the condiments would only spoil the taste. I had two.

When I walked into JLA the excitement was palpable and the place was filling up fast. Eventually over two thousand spectators filed in. The Yale band and the Yale cheerleaders were in place. The atmosphere was charged, the place thumping to blaring rap music. As I watched Penn warm up, it felt funny to see the players again so soon. It also seemed odd as a Philly guy myself to root against Penn, but I had committed to Yale heart and soul and I devoutly hoped Penn would not reprise tonight the shooting touch they had displayed against Princeton on Monday when, in the first half, they hit nearly two-thirds of their shots, including a dazzling seven out of ten three-pointers. In the second half they had again shot well enough to hold off a Princeton rally as Princeton too shot well. My fervent hope was that both would cool off their hot shooting this weekend.

Penn did. After winning four straight games, they came out flat. Our defense had a lot to do with this. All week James had preached swarming defense to the guys, and they attacked with vigor, moving and switching and hedging on side ball-screens quicker than jack-in-the-boxes, and fighting through ball-screens out high on the elbows and on the perimeter. Nothing in basketball is more exciting than lockdown defense played aerobically except precision passing that leads to easy buckets. All week James had preached that the only way to beat Penn was ever vigilant, ever energetic defense. His scouting report was brilliant on this point, and the guys were applying it like it was the blueprint to heavenly bliss and eternal happiness. Watching them play this way was exciting, and as a coach it was gratifying to see strategy and tactics unsparingly applied. I could only imagine how good James and Matt, Jamie and Justin felt.

Yet at halftime, thanks in large part to our nine turnovers, the score was knotted at 29 apiece. Penn was known for its physical play on defense, and had been for the half century I'd watched them. So far they had two steals, one by sophomore guard Miles Cartwright and the other by Rob Belcore, a rugged six-six forward who sometimes mistook the battle under the boards for a rugby scrum and was not averse, farther out on the court, to running someone over or tomahawking the dribbler's arm from behind while obscuring the official's view with his other arm. In a crowded lane he would sometimes ring the ballhandler's waist in front with one arm, thrust his chest into the guy's back, and punch the ball loose with his other, semi-camouflaged arm. In my mind I called him Roughhouse Rob and simultaneously loved and loathed his game. He played like a huge lumberjack on crystal meth. The North Philly street kid in me issued promptings to don a uniform, trot out onto the court, front him on the low blocks, then wheel and elbow his nuts halfway back to his native Chicago the first time the refs were looking elsewhere. Ivy League kids, bless them, were too polite for this sort of thing.

* * * * *

In the locker room at the half James was cool and analytical. Always, before he spoke to the players, he huddled in the corridor outside with his assistants. After a brief but animated conversation, all four would enter the locker room as James went to the front and addressed the team. He started with his signature "Clap it up, boys," and then delivered crisp praise for the overall defense but excoriated the defensive rebounding, which he characterized as "awful." He lamented that Penn got seven offensive rebounds on us, even though we were the best rebounding team in the league. As an aside he reminded Greg Mangano, who otherwise was playing well, to "throw the ball out of the defended post." Then he said we couldn't live with Penn's Mike Hewlett, a six-eight senior center, and the rambunctious Belcore getting "put-back rebounds." After a pause he roared: "Second chance points like that can kill you."

Jamie was next and wanted our "X5"—meaning our center on defense, Greg Mangano—to get "on top" of screens. Greg already had one block and it was obvious that Jamie wanted more. When Penn went to its two-three zone, alternating it sparingly with their teeth-in-your-throat man-to-man, Jamie wanted his "Bigs" to "duck in, up-fake, and bounce pass." Matt followed Jamie and told his guards to "get lower and clear more space." When Penn defenders pushed the guards in their back, trying to jar the ball loose, he wanted the ball protected better. He also wanted the offense to rotate the ball faster side to side: the classic mandate on ball movement. Then Justin reminded everyone "there was little difference between losers and winners." As the scouting report had emphasized, he urged the guys "to stay with

Rosen and keep the pressure on him and on Bernardini," Penn's two deadliest shooters. In closing he pointed out that "Penn had thirty shots in the half and we had only twenty-two."

That was true. Penn had taken more shots, but Greg Mangano had ten points on 50 percent shooting, Austin Morgan had six points on two three-pointers, and Mike Grace had seven points on a solo three and a pair of two-pointers. Among them they had scored twenty-three of our twenty-nine points. Except for some sloppy ball handling we could have been up a few points instead of tied. That we led the league in turnovers pained me, as I'm sure it did the coaches. Fearing Penn, I nevertheless felt that the game was ours to win provided Penn's four seniors didn't take over, especially high scorers Rosen and the quick and graceful Tyler Bernardini, who had a textbook-perfect outside jumper, with good range, as well as a tendency to drive the baseline backdoor and deposit a two-handed dunk as delicately as if the ball were a gigantic Fabergé egg.

* * * * *

As I retook my seat for the second half I told myself to stay positive. We did jump out front with an 8-0 run: Austin hit a three, Mike Grace drove and flipped an alley-oop to Reggie for a dunk, then Greg dropped in a picture-perfect three from the top of the key. When Greg went up for his jump shot he had an over-the-head cocking motion that reminded me of the great Oscar Robertson. Greg's shot was beautiful to watch, especially since he made his jumper often, even from far out, a rarity in a man two inches shy of seven feet. His long-range accuracy put me in mind of Dirk Nowitzki and Larry Bird. We were up a quick eight but, before the first media time-out at 15:49, Rosen hit a jumper shortly after Fran Dougherty, a lanky sophomore forward with good post moves, scored on a put-back, which no doubt pained James after his halftime injunction against allowing any.

When the media time-out ended, Penn worked the ball around with three crisp passes before Bernardini scored on a lay-up, reducing the lead to two. Greg answered, nailing a three from the left wing after a drive and kickout by Austin. When Rosen and Belcore responded with matching lay-ups, James called a time-out with 12:47 left. Out of the time-out, Greg tipped in a missed jumper by Austin just before the shot clock expired. We were up three, briefly. Then Rosen canned a foul-line jumper, leaving us up one, 42-41, at the second media time-out with 10:55 to go.

When play resumed, Greg fouled Dougherty in the low post and he sank one of two free throws, tying the score again. From there Reggie fed Brandon Sherrod for a lay-up in the low post, then Greg scored on a short bank shot in the paint. Meanwhile, Rosen, after feeding Belcore for an assist, hit a pull-up jumper in the lane. That meant we were tied at 44 and then again at 46. This game was ridiculously tight. Greg nailed a short jumper from the left baseline, giving him four straight Yale points and putting us up by two. Steve Rennard, a reserve sophomore guard with a nice shooting touch, countered with a three off an in-bounds play. Penn was up a point.

The media time-out at 7:36 gave the coaches a chance to adjust their strategy. When the time-out ended, Reggie reversed the lead by hitting a jump shot, making it Yale 50, Penn 49. A touch-and-go game like this is great for the fans but hard on the coaches. For nearly two minutes, as the teams matched defensive intensity, the score held. Then Belcore stripped the ball from Michael Grace, drove the length of the floor and dropped in a lay-up, restoring Penn's one-point lead. On Yale's next possession Austin Morgan suffered a rare turnover. With 4:47 left Rosen hit a midrange jumper from the right side, stretching Penn's lead to 53-50.

From then on Yale played spirited defense. First Reggie stripped the ball from the sure-handed Bernardini at the 3:45 mark. Again, fierce defense by both teams eliminated any scoring for over a minute. Then with two and a half minutes left Penn's Miles Cartwright, who had sealed Columbia's doom three weeks earlier by hitting threes repeatedly on rapid ball-reverses to the weak side, missed a three on that same play.

Five seconds later Reggie drove hard and kicked the ball out to Greg at the top of the key. He rose, cocked the ball over his head, and swished a three for the game's last tie, 53-53. It was Rosen's turn to miss a three. Then on Penn's next possession Reggie struck again, flicking the ball away from Rosen for a game-deciding steal. When Reggie drove the length of the floor and missed a lay-up, the ever alert and always hustling Austin, trailing the play, seized the rebound and laid it in, giving Yale the lead again at 55-53. To use Reggie's own phrase, the two fastest starters and best team leaders had combined for an "energy thing."

Penn went cold. In the closing minutes Bernardini missed a jumper, Rennard missed a three, Rosen missed a three, then followed it, off Rennard's rebound and feed, with another missed jumper. Bernardini, Rennard, and Rosen were all good shooters. The gods had clearly smiled on us. Granted that our smothering defense had something to do with this dry spell, Penn's premier shooters rarely missed like this. And Cartwright's earlier missed open three on the weak side had given momentum back to Yale just when Penn could have gone back up by three.

In contrast to Penn's cold shooting, Yale hit five fouls in the last twenty-three seconds to clinch the game. After Brandon Sherrod hit one free throw but missed the second, Greg Mangano made his own spectacular energy play. As soon as Greg snared the rebound off Brandon's miss, Mike Howlett fouled him. Greg missed his single free throw but snared his own rebound, only to be fouled again by Howlett. Greg sank both shots. Seconds later, contesting a rebound under Penn's basket, Howlett fouled Reggie, who canned both shots at the opposite end of the floor to make the final score Yale 60, Penn 53. Howlett's three fouls in eleven seconds netted Yale four points.

* * * * *

Despite giving up nine points off turnovers in the first half and eight more in the second half, Yale had won through diligent application of James's detailed strategy, playing monster defense and, on offense, moving the ball rapidly to the open man. We had won a typical tooth and nail Ivy League battle, tense right to the end despite Penn's inexplicable tailspin. We had played our best game of the year, heady and tenacious on defense, smart and selfless on offense.

In the postgame interview, Jerome Allen was all class, making no excuses but pointing out that expecting to win a game where you gave up fifteen offensive rebounds was ridiculous. Acknowledging that his team did not yet have "what it takes to win a championship in this league," he stated that the opportunity to reach their team goals was still before them. Then, chagrined, he added that it was very hard to lose and that "we didn't look hungry tonight."

When his turn at the mike came, James, obviously pleased but not gloating, remarked that Reggie "should wear a cape." Then he praised Bernardini and Rosen as "two of the top players in this conference." When Bill Cloutier mentioned that turnovers and offensive rebounds were still giving Yale problems, James agreed but added that "tonight we had overcome our bad plays," and that "this was a sign of a good team." He emphasized that "we wanted to take care of the ball down the stretch" and "not hurt our chances with more mistakes on turnovers." Then he lauded Rosen for his excellence on shooting off ball-screens and said: "You pick your poison with

Rosen," meaning he'd drive by you for a lay-up if your defender powered through the screen to contest the outside shot. Bill asked if James agreed that Greg Mangano's tying three-pointer was "the biggest shot of the year so far" and also whether Yale "got the biggest rebounds of the night." James agreed. Bill closed by saying how impressive Greg Mangano had been.

Greg followed, lavishing praise on Brandon Sherrod, emphasizing that Brandon had cleared two defenders out of the lane on Greg's crucial rebound at the end, the one off his own miss that led to the two new free throws he made. He also pointed out that "it was hard to win any game in this league" and so put his finger on the Ivy League's most appealing attribute. In earlier interviews after starring in games, Greg had generously lauded his guards and, in one instance, had gone out of his way to heap kudos on sophomore Isaiah Salafia for hitting crucial threes.

Earlier during the game I had been depressed that Isaiah had dropped off the team because of "personal problems." James had told me this sad fact midweek and I was still shaken by the news. I didn't want to see a kid as gifted and bright as Isaiah make a mistake that would haunt him, as my not trying out for Drexel's team haunted me. There had been an outside chance I might have made it. There was an inside chance that Isaiah, so naturally talented, would eventually star at Yale.

In parting, James mentioned that there wouldn't be many nights when a major wing player like Bernardini shot two-for-thirteen, or when a superior point guard like Rosen went oh-for-five from beyond the arc. That was exactly what had happened: Fate truly had smiled on us. Earlier, minutes after the game ended, in the locker room Matt Kingsley had made the most memorable remark of the night: "I love you guys right now but tomorrow I won't." Like the great coach he is and will be when he gets his own team, Matt then went on to say how focused we'd have to be to beat Princeton in less than twenty-four hours. That's pure coach-think: the need to jettison the radiant glow of victory and get back down to business.

Giddy on the train home, I was reined in by the sudden thought of seventeen turnovers. No wonder, voicing more coach-think, James said to me all the time: "We're a work in progress."

* * * * *

The next afternoon I saw Coach Jones in all his well-deserved glory. I caught a morning train and arrived at JLA well before the two o'clock start time for the annual Alumni Game. We didn't play Princeton that night until seven but James had mentioned the Alumni Game as something I might enjoy. As usual he was right. More than the game itself I enjoyed seeing him photographed at midcourt before the tipoff surrounded by his former players. He was beaming and they were joshing. Then, when the game began, Bruce Rossini worked the clock and kept score, sometimes erratically, prompting corrections from either bench. Bruce is a local guy, disabled and dependent on a wheelchair, who came to all the games, including riding to the Yale Bowl for football games in the van for the band. Yale had a real feel for the New Haven community, and a devoted local fan base, because it extended hospitality to neighboring high-school and CYO teams, allowing them to use the facilities. After the photo op, the veteran players divided into the White team and the Blue team, the first wearing Yale's home uni's and the second wearing the away uni's. The game, quite competitive, was a hoot, with the guys on both benches catcalling and hollering, bantering and bashing away at one another.

It was a lively family affair. Natalie Gonzalez, Associate Athletic Director for varsity sports, was there looking after things. A graduate of the University of Florida, she had been an invaluable help at the Florida game in Gainesville back on New York's Eve sitting next to me at the press table, working the computer and updating the stats constantly. Like Bruce Rossini working the clock at the scorer's table, another local guy named Bucky attended most Yale sporting events and refused to give me his last name no matter how many times I asked. A walking encyclopedia about Yale sports, Bucky ID'ed all the veteran players in the alumni game, extolling their best moments as undergraduates whenever they made good moves or hit difficult shots. He shouted out greetings to the players, who all knew him, just as they all knew Bruce. Bruce and Bucky were like twin mascots and good luck charms. Coach Agel of Brown had shown his generous and japing side by giving Bruce a Brown jacket as a gift, knowing full well that Bruce would wear it in JLA and irritate the Yale faithful. Every time I saw Bruce sporting the jacket, I laughed.

James sat with a group of his current players in the retractable wooden stands at the lobby end of the court. It was fun to watch the current guys relate to their former teammates, now graduated, out on the floor. Before the game Reggie had been the most effusive and animated to see his old buddies, followed closely by Rhett Anderson. As seniors they had known the veterans for the three previous years. Joining Reggie and Rhett were Jesse Pritchard, Will Bartlett, Mike Grace, and Greg Kelley. Team manager Will Manville also sat in the group. Along with James they were all having a high old time of it, booing, catcalling, and insulting the alumni players.

Before the game I had been happy to recognize Porter Braswell, the quick little point guard who the year before had engineered the brilliant upset of Harvard on this very court. I leaned down from the stands, introduced myself, and told him how much I liked the way he played basketball. A week after orchestrating the upset of Harvard he had guided his team to that double-overtime win in Levien against Columbia, handling the ball deftly against the press and dishing off to the open man brilliantly, often after partial dribble penetration. He had a good shot and could score when needed. These attributes were missed, as well as his high basketball IQ, his senior leadership, and his deep savvy.

For what it matters the Blue team won in a two-minute overtime, scoring eight points to the White team's three, making the final 89-84 following the 81-all deadlock after regulation. It was especially nice to see assistant coach Justin Simon playing with several of his former teammates. After the game I talked with Matt Minoff, a member of James's first recruiting class and a former team captain who had gone on to play professionally in Israel. A South Jersey guy, Matt and Justin Simon had been classmates. I also spoke to Casey Hughes, a classy guy from New Haven whose dad had played for Central High School in Philly. Having grown up within walking distance of the campus, as a kid Casey used to sneak into JLA to play basketball before he ever became a Yalie. He too had played four years for James, but two years later than Matt and Justin. Matt and Casey were so entertaining that when I looked up from my notebook, all the other alumni players had scattered. Feeling hungry, I hurried out to get something to eat only to discover that Louis' Lunch, still family-run by the fourth generation, closed on Saturdays and Sundays. I went instead to the Educated Burgher and scurried back to Payne Whitney in time to watch the warm-ups for the Princeton game.

* * * * *

Against Princeton we picked up where we left off against Penn, playing wicked defense that was exciting to watch and, on offense, moving the ball around against Princeton's aggressive defense. They alternated a clawing man-to-man with a little bit of zone, principally a one-three-one designed to eliminate our dribble penetration, choke off our low post game, prevent easy lay-ups, and force us to beat them "over the top" with low percentage, long-range shots. Like Penn, Princeton was famous for playing defense with relentless vigor. Under legendary coach Pete Carril, pressurized defense was a Princeton staple, but one outshone by his famous "Princeton Offense," with its breathtaking backdoor baskets, weaving ball-screens on the perimeter, its give-and-go's, and its pick-and-rolls. The Princeton Offense was pure team basketball elevated to perfect synchronized excellence, spotlighting choreographed intelligence over raw, chaotic talent, and making Princeton ever dangerous against teams with better athletes but lower IQs. This explains why Coach Carril titled his monumentally sound and instructive book *The Smart Take From the Strong*, one of the best books ever written on coaching basketball.

The first half had only one tie, at 10 apiece, then the lead shuttled back and forth before we pulled away, mainly because Reggie, Greg, and Jeremiah were clicking. Our front line guys were going off: Reggie scored thirteen points, Greg nine, Jerry six, for a first-half total of 28. Austin added four to make our halftime lead 32-23. In the second half we jumped out fast and then Reggie took a pass on the perimeter, drove to the basket, and slammed down a gargantuan dunk, bringing the nearly sold-out crowd to its feet and putting us up by eleven, 44-33, with a little over eleven minutes to go. I thought we might be home free, with the game completely ours, but this was the Ivy League, and this was Princeton, the team that had beaten ACC champion Florida State in Tallahassee in three overtimes on December 30 while we practiced late that night in the O'Connell Center for our game the next day against Florida. I remember after that practice how James lingered on the court, checking his cell for ESPN updates on the score in Tallahassee.

Unfortunately for us, Reggie's dunk galvanized Princeton as well as the Yale crowd. Always and ever Princeton, they launched a comeback. When Ian Hummer hit a foul-line jumper with 2:41 left to play, the blood rushed to my head as our lead dwindled to three, 50-47. Greg answered, hitting one of his classic top-of-the key threes to put us back up by six. Princeton forward Mark Darrow then followed his own missed three with a put-back, and, a minute later, added a low-post lay-up to pull Princeton within two, 53-51. Jeremiah Kreisberg dropped in two free throws and Reggie canned another, putting us up 56-51 with nineteen seconds left.

Seven seconds later Reggie missed a three and fouled Hummer battling for the rebound. Twelve seconds remained. Hummer hit the first foul shot and intentionally missed the second, hoping to get the rebound. Instead, contesting the rebound, Hummer fouled Mangano. Because Princeton was over the team limit of eight fouls in one half, Greg shot twice, missing the first and making the second, giving us a five-point lead, 57-52, and placing Princeton in a deep hole, needing two possessions for a possible tie. Darrow responded with a drive and a stylish left-handed lay-up.

With 6.9 seconds left Princeton called time-out, needing only one possession and a made three to tie the game and send it into overtime. But when play resumed, Douglas Davis immediately fouled Austin Morgan, ranked among the best foul shooters in the country and deliberately designated by James to receive the in-bounds pass, on which Princeton had no choice: foul immediately or watch Austin dribble out the clock.

With a sense of drama, Austin missed the first shot but made the second, putting Yale up 58-54. James instantly called time-out to remind the guys to press hard on defense but not to foul, especially on a three-point attempt that would award the Princeton shooter, if he made the shot, a possibly tying free throw on top of the three-points, jeopardizing the Yale victory. No doubt James flashed back on the five-point play we made at the end of the Rhode Island game that ensured our win.

Douglas Davis, put back in the game by Princeton coach Mitch Henderson specifically to take the crucial three-point shot, missed. There would be no reprise of Davis's NCAA-clinching buzzer-beater against Harvard the last time Princeton played in JLA.

* * * * *

We were 5-1 in the Ivies and trailed 6-0 Harvard by a single game. All during the train ride home I was ecstatic. Winners of fifteen games, we had played back-to-back games according to James's plan and had won while moving the ball rapidly on offense, recycling the Flex until we found the open man, and, on defense, mixing a clawing man-to-man with a clinging zone as mobile and shifty as floodwater. Tonight we had mixed our 23-T zone in well, with two men out front and three men back, the middle man in back being a rover, cheating up toward the two defenders out front, and we had made Princeton shoot poorly. Their strategy had been similar, mixing the one-three-one zone with a two-three zone while playing mostly swarming man-to-man. As payback, Princeton had made us shoot poorly, too. The game was cookie-cutter similar: to their 19-57 field goal shooting percentage of 33.3, we had shot 20-57 for 35.1. They hit four three-pointers out of twenty-one attempts to our three out of twenty attempts, but we made three more foul shots than they did, and that made all the difference, especially since we won the rebound battle 45-34 and held our turnovers down to ten, roughly half our average in the previous three games.

In two straight games we had handled pressurized defense, including the full-court press. We had recycled the offense when the low-post first option was not there, sharing the ball, and we had defended like dervishes on both nights. In his closing halftime remarks, Justin Simon echoed what James had been preaching since October: "Take good shots, hold on to the ball, and defend with all your hearts."

At an inky hour of the night, before going to bed, having been too excited for hours to do so, I emailed James my congratulations, telling him truthfully that when I got to the train station I felt so good they could have uncoupled the locomotive and let me push the train, running behind it, all the way to New York.

Emotionally, coaching basketball was like a rollicking bull ride, continually bucking you up and down and all around. When you were up the feeling was incredible. Basketball's ability to wrap individual ecstasy in collective exultation was one of the hallmarks of its divine nature.

CHAPTER THIRTEEN

The Miracle of Morningside

My HIGH FROM the sweep of Penn and Princeton didn't last through Sunday afternoon. I thought instead how Cornell had beaten Princeton already in Ithaca, by eight points, and how, that same January weekend a month back, I had watched Columbia nearly topple Penn in Levien, falling only two points short. So I worried. We had to travel the long bus ride on Thursday for Friday night's game in Ithaca against Cornell; then, after the game, we faced a nearly five-hour bus ride down to Manhattan to play Columbia Saturday night. I had learned that Rhett Anderson, the reserve senior forward with the great leadership skills and the inspiring team spirit, had written sports columns for the *Yale Daily News*, so I asked him to give me his impressions of the long junket.

Rhett wrote a lively report detailing the horrors of long bus trips for tall young men. Buses are designed to accommodate persons with roughly my dimensions, five feet seven inches tall and 175 pounds. But Rhett, for instance, is six feet, eight inches tall and 230 pounds. Greg Mangano is two inches taller, as is Jeremiah Kreisberg. Jerry is the same weight as Rhett but Greg has ten pounds on him. Buses are not designed for the comfort of such men. On the Yale team only guards Michael Grace at six feet even and backcourt mate Austin Morgan, an inch shorter, have any comfort on a bus. This discomfort factor applies to the Yale coaches as well, except for Matt Kingsley, but especially for Jamie Snyder-Fair and Justin Simon at six feet nine inches each. The trip from New Haven to Ithaca is roughly five hours, as is the second leg from Ithaca to Manhattan, which pulls in at three in the morning. Mercifully, the trip back to New Haven from Manhattan is under two hours.

This accounts for the rigors of the Ivy League schedule: fourteen round-robin games, every game a rivalry game, some arch-rivalry games, many involving long bus rides in between, partially overnight, every game back-to-back on weekend nights except for the two travel partner games. This is why coaches speak of the "second night in the Ivy League" and its fatigue factor that accounts for so many upsets. In fact, at halftime of the Princeton game the preceding Saturday night, even though it was a home game for us, Coach Snyder-Fair had reminded the guys in the locker room not to succumb to the "second night" syndrome and to fight through fatigue with energy. The junket to Cornell is especially tough, lying as Cornell does in the center of New York State, in Natty Bumpo country, far from all other Ivy schools, and requiring a long bus ride.

In the Princeton game I saw a graphic instance of this second-night syndrome when Michael Grace dribbled into the shallow front court and the Princeton defender, reserve sophomore guard Ben Hazel, who had five inches on Mike, challenged him for the ball. Hazel stole it successfully when Mike, on jellied legs, tried to cut hard to his right and slipped, exposing the ball to Hazel's longer reach. With a flick of the hand Hazel knocked the ball loose. Only a block by the ever-alert Reggie prevented Hazel from getting an easy lay-up. This occurred in the endgame where Ian Hummer snared the loose blocked ball at the foul line and, in one motion, went up and nailed a jumper that brought Princeton within three points with two minutes to go. Greg Mangano answered with his vital three, but the turnover off the steal, due to Mike's fatigue, had made things dicier.

* * * * *

After four minutes we were up on Cornell 12-2 and then 32-18 with about six minutes left in the half. We were playing to our potential: distributing the ball, feeding the low post, and hitting from outside. Greg Mangano continued the shooting and rebounding that had won him Ivy League Player of the Week honors for averaging 21.5 points and 11.0 rebounds against Penn and Princeton. This marked the eighth time Greg had won the honor, one shy of former Brown great Earl Hunt, the record holder who had been interviewed between halves at our game in snowy Providence two weeks earlier.

By this point in the game all five Yale starters had scored and, off the bench, Jesse Pritchard and Brandon Sherrod had executed two perfect plays, Jesse driving and dishing twice in a row to Brandon in the low post, first for a dunk, then for a lay-up. Matt Townsend, also off the bench, had hit two shots in the low post back-to-back, the first a lay-up off a feed by Reggie, the second on one of his fluttery little jump hooks. We were playing the basketball bible according to James to near perfection.

Yet one thing niggled. Sporadically, like a man stepping into the surf to test the water temperature, Cornell coach Bill Courtney put on a press, then called it off. Cornell had scored its first two points off a trapping backcourt steal from Mike Grace and a driving lay-up by guard Johnathan Gray. Near the midway point in the half Cornell also trapped Austin Morgan on the right sideline, but he alertly called a time-out to retain possession of the ball.

With about five minutes left in the half, Courtney put on a frantically energetic full-court press. James's scouting report had warned about this, but Cornell was so quick and energetic applying it that it sparked a 15-2 run, making the halftime score Yale 34, Cornell 33. In the last three minutes Johnathan Gray hit a three from the left corner and dropped in a lay-up on a drive, giving him seven points in the half, which was two-tenths of a point short of his season average for a whole game. Considered a "utility" guard behind All-Ivy senior point guard Chris Wroblewski and another senior, deadeye shooting guard Drew Ferry, Gray, a junior, was not usually a high scorer. Yet in his scouting report James noted that Gray, a walk-on, had averaged 12.8 points in Cornell's last four games while shooting 40 percent on threes.

Despite these ominous developments, at intermission I felt that the game was ours to take, despite the fact that we had lost seven straight in Ithaca, a notoriously hard place to win and the only place where Bill Bradley's championship team had lost in league play his senior year. Before the game James had been more than usually uptight, and had told the team in his closing pregame remarks that they had traveled a day early and gotten a proper rest, unlike the last game of the previous season when they had made the long bus ride up from Manhattan after beating Columbia in that exhausting double-overtime game, playing fifty instead of forty minutes. Tonight Coach Jones really wanted this win and was determined to push his team to get it.

* * * * *

The second half was tumultuous, a treat for spectators and a torment for coaches. There were five lead changes and six ties. The Cornell crowd really got into it. The final minute of regulation was, as Yale SID Tim Bennett put it in his press release, "wild." With fifty-seven seconds left we went up 67-66 on Reggie's two free throws. Wroblewski struck right back, after a drive, with a jumper in the lane. Reggie then missed a jumper and, after a mad scrum under the boards, Austin somehow snared the rebound, drove the lane and hit a lay-up, putting us back up, 69-68. Johnathan Gray countered with a long three from the left wing with twelve seconds left, putting us down two, 71-69. But Austin was not out of heroics, nor Greg Mangano. Austin took the in-bounds pass, raced the length of the floor, and drove in for another lay-up, knotting the score at 71. When Cornell attempted to answer, Greg made the most spectacular block of the season after Wroblewski retreated along the baseline into the left corner and went up for the potentially winning basket. With the ball airborne Greg took a giant stride from the left lane, leaped like an eight-point buck, and snuffed the ball midair as the horn sounded ending regulation.

The overtime was every bit as exciting. Dwight Tarwater scored a putback in the low post for Cornell, and Greg Mangano matched it seconds later with a low-post lay-up off a feed from Austin Morgan. Eitan Chemerinski hit one of two foul shots before Cornell jumped out front by four on Gray's fifth three-pointer, 77-73. We responded with two made free throws by Jerry Kreisberg. Then sophomore forward Dwight Tarwater canned a jumper at the top of the key to restore Cornell's lead to four, 79-75. Austin Morgan retaliated with a three—only to have Gray hit his sixth and final three, making it 82-78. Reggie countered with a three from the top of the key: 82-81, Yale down a point. Seconds later Wroblewski stepped back along the baseline and hit a jumper. Cornell 84, Yale 81. After Austin's missed three on Yale's next possession, Gray made one free throw, missed a second, but nevertheless sealed Yale's doom with only six seconds left by stretching Cornell's lead to four and making it a two-possession game, absent a dumb foul by Cornell. Mike Grace sprinted down the floor and hit a three but it meant nothing. Final: Cornell 85, Yale 84.

Our odyssey to Ithaca had ended in heartbreak and Johnathan Gray had a career night, dropping twenty-nine points on us, helped by hitting six of eight threes. Overall he shot nearly 60 percent for the game, making ten of eighteen shots from the floor and adding three of four foul shots. His overheated shooting hand practically glowed. Repeatedly he made threes from far behind the arc, long arching rainbows, what legendary Palestra broadcaster Les Keiter called "ring-tailed howitzers." Wroblewski came through as well, scoring eighteen points to complement ten assists and adding eight rebounds—a team high, and by a guard yet!—and only two more rebounds than fellow guard Gray.

Their bench also outscored our bench by five, sixteen to eleven. To our two fast break points they had eight, mainly off the press; to our fifteen turnovers, again mainly off the press, they had only eleven. Off turnovers they scored twenty-three points to our four. In the paint we each scored twenty-six. We had two more second-chance points, eighteen to their sixteen. We outrebounded them by two. Each team had twenty assists. So we lost by a single point, 85-84, after an overtime brilliantly played by both teams. Like most sports, basketball can be cruel.

We didn't deserve to lose after playing such a sound game. Neither team did. Cornell probably played their best game all year. We walked head-on into a fatwa from fate. The box score told the story; each team outscored the other by one point in each half and in the overtime: Yale in the first half, Cornell in the second half and in the overtime. Yale played a balanced game: forty points from our guards (Austin Morgan twenty-two, Michael Grace fifteen, Jesse Pritchard three), and forty-four points from our front line (Greg Mangano fourteen, Jeremiah Kreisberg thirteen, Reggie Willhite nine, and Brandon Sherrod and Matt Townsend four each). We worked the Flex, cutting, slashing, and scoring in the post, and also hitting from the perimeter: Austin and Mike notched seven of fifteen from beyond the three-point arc, with Jesse adding one of two and Reggie one of three.

Newman Arena is a handsome, brightly lighted gym and, traumatized, I can see the game clearly in my mind's eye half a year later. Such is the price of coaching.

* * * * *

Second-night syndrome got very real that weekend. After the game I drove home in blowing snow at reduced speeds for the first three and a half hours of the nearly five hour trip. When I got into my house I was too wired to sleep. I was also deflated in a more painful way than I had been after our rout by Harvard. The combination of shock and disorientation from an upset, compounded by a sense of what might have been, haunts you for hours. Our outstanding freshman forward Brandon Sherrod had gone oh-for-five at the foul line. What if he had made two? What if Greg Mangano had not sat out crucial stretches in foul trouble from playing great defense, but too aggressively?

What if we hadn't walked into what might turn out to be the greatest game of Johnathan Gray's life? After the season he would be good enough to play for the Virgin Islands national team. As a walk-on he was an underdog, and, despite resenting what he'd done to us tonight, I always liked to see "the blind squirrel get the nut." For the rest of the season he distinguished himself enough to earn Honorable Mention, All-Ivy, and that's no mean feat. Leaving the arena after the game I had watched him beaming his way through a joyous radio interview on the sideline. Happy for the kid, I was nevertheless annoyed that he hadn't saved his super game for Harvard on the last night of the season, when I was aware Harvard had to visit Newman Arena; a few weeks earlier in their gym, Harvard had barely edged Cornell. Plying these futile mind games, I heard my inner ear echo James's great line: "Ed, you gotta coach going forward."

Still, I couldn't fall asleep once I got into bed and had only a few hours rest before getting up early and catching the train in Hudson for the always spectacular ride downriver to New York. Usually the majestic riverside ride raised my spirits, but that didn't happen this Saturday. Spotting the players four decades in age, I felt as if my blood had been drained. I hoped to nod off from the train's rhythmic glide and the metronomic clicking of the wheels; usually this provides a nap for me. But that never happened. Every time my eyes closed I saw a sold-out Levien rocking with Columbia crazies just dying to see their young and talented team dash our championship hopes. To allow for delays I had taken an early train and so got into my Upper West Side apartment in time for a brief nap that saved but didn't restore me. No matter how much caffeine I poured down my throat my energy didn't spike.

Dawdling in my apartment caused me to arrive uncharacteristically late, only fifty minutes before game time. My greatest fear was that our team would play as deflated and flat as I felt. Making things worse, Columbia would be pumped, having combined torrid shooting and shutdown defense the previous night to rout Brown, 86-60.

I hurried down to our locker room, where James was magnificent in his pregame remarks, isolating again the challenges we would face, warning not to let Brian Barbour penetrate and dish, and not to fail to fight through the many ball-screens Columbia would use. We also had to be watchful of Mark Cisco getting his game in high gear off feeds into the post. Standing and listening, the thing I feared was Columbia coach Kyle Smith's defensive acumen. He knew how to isolate a team's offensive strengths and choke them off. He favored a frantic man-to-man, switching and moving at maximum speed all over the floor, and he also mixed in a two-three zone designed to clog the lane and cripple the inside game. To add to our woes, Columbia had a good press. These were the very three things that gave our offense trouble when we didn't play smart.

In closing, James said: "Bring the fight tonight. We got 'em five times in a row. It was difficult for me when my brother coached here but not anymore. They're up from winning by 26 last night. They want us. Let's win and end the weekend on a positive note." This was not "Win one for the Gipper!" but Ivy League kids don't feed on corn. James had said the exact right things for a team to hear that had got in from a five-hour bus trip minutes before three a.m. after a shattering overtime loss a few hours earlier.

James had already bounced back, his ebullient self. The night before he had sat outside the locker room staring with glazed eyes at the stat sheet and saying to Tim Bennett, over and over, how close and balanced the game had been and how we had played well enough to win. Those stats mesmerized me too. Cornell shot 65% overall in the overtime, 70% from the field, and an astounding 66.7% on threes. Missing two of four free throws prevented them from shooting just under 70% for the entire overtime. That's how hard Lady Luck had sideswiped us. My final thought as the teams lined up for their intros in raucous Levien was that we couldn't be unlucky enough to face that kind of torrid shooting two nights in a row. Yet Columbia's players, when introduced, especially stars Barbour and Cisco, dashed onto the court sky high, hopping and chest bumping, high-fiving and slapping backs and butts, obviously pumped and primed to get us on their home floor.

* * * * *

Meiko Lyles hit two early threes for Columbia and Cisco scored twice down low, first on a lay-up, then on a hook. Reggie, who had scored our first points on a driving lay-up, then scored six straight points after Jeremiah Kreisberg had hit a short hook in the lane off a pretty feed from Mike Grace. Reggie's last two points of six straight tied the game at ten with 12:49 left in the half. Three ties followed over the next four minutes, each team quickly matching the other's two-point lead. Then Columbia jumped out front to lead by seven, 30-23, at the half. By scoring four quick points in the last minute and a half,

Reggie held us in the game. Of our twenty-three points he had fourteen. Jeremiah had six, Brandon Sherrod two, and Greg one. Only Reggie of our Big Three was hitting his shots; Greg and Austin were cold. Scoreless Austin was so cold he had blown a breakaway lay-up and Greg, for the second night in a row, was flirting with foul trouble that had already cost him time on the bench. So far he had logged only nine minutes of playing time.

In the locker room James calmly enumerated the adjustments to be made, reemphasizing the points cited before the game, stressing again to shut Barbour down on dribble penetration so he couldn't dish the ball down low or kick it out to the perimeter. On offense James restated the need to work the ball side to side. Then Matt Kingsley sharply pointed out that four of their threes came off our mistakes. He said not to slough off outside shooters and instead to "stay at home," crowding them to prevent open shots. Next, in a loud voice, Jamie, annoyed, told the Bigs to toughen up; this was Division I basketball and entailed a lot of "pushing and shoving," so "strong up." Justin encouraged everyone, concluding: "Guys, it's about character in the second half." Before calling the hands-clasped huddle, James snapped, "Our half, let's go."

At first James looked to be all wrong. At the first media time-out, Columbia was up ten and, by the second at 11:39, they led 49-30. When play resumed, Cisco hit a baseline jumper to make the lead 51-30. Seconds later Mike Grace hit the floor clutching his left ankle in pain. Time-out was called and trainer Dave DiNapoli rushed out to help. James followed and stood over Mike and Dave, joined by his son Quincy. Fear-ridden and in despair, seeing our championship aspirations and my hopes for my book dashed, I nevertheless took heart, spotting Q for the first time. Young James Quincy Jones really did bring us luck.

Yet thoughts of us making a championship run seemed remote with Columbia up "only eighteen" after Brandon Sherrod scored an old-fashioned three off a low-post lay-up and a plus-one foul shot right as Mike went down. When time was in, Columbia's Chris Crockett restored the lead to twenty with a lay-up. With under ten minutes left we were down twenty. Austin responded with five straight points, his first of the night, hitting a short jumper followed by a corner three. Columbia called time-out with 8:21 to go. Forty seconds later, at the media time-out, we still trailed by fifteen, 53-38.

Out of the break Jeremiah canned a turnaround jumper in the lane but Barbour answered with a driving lay-up off an inbounds play to make it

55-40. Greg tapped in a put-back before Austin scored three with a driving lay-up and a plus-one foul. Then Greg tapped in Austin's missed lay-up off a drive and had a chance for a plus-one free throw, but missed. For an encore Greg popped in one of his signature threes from behind the arc atop the key. Down five, James immediately called time-out with 4:26 to go.

Lyles hit a three from the right wing to restore Columbia's lead to eight with 4:20 to go. After the final media time-out at 3:36, Jeremiah and Reggie executed the prettiest feed of the season. Standing under the outer rim of the basket, Jerry wheeled and handed off to Reggie cutting along the baseline for a reverse lay-up, while simultaneously screening Reggie's defender. So fast and smooth was this play there was no time for a defensive switch.

On Columbia's in-bounds play, James immediately put us in a full-court press. After Austin stole the ball from Barbour, Reggie hit a baseline jumper. Both teams then failed to score until only thirty-six seconds remained. That's when Jesse Pritchard, lurking on the weak-side wing, took a reverse pass and hit the biggest three of the year to save Yale's title chances. Following a forced turnover in the backcourt caused by our full-court press, Reggie drove for another lay-up, giving us the lead 59-58, the first time we'd been up since halfway through the first period.

Columbia had a chance to regain the lead when Greg fouled senior forward Blaise Staab. But Staab clanked both free throws. On our next possession, Greg missed a one-and-one foul shot with 2.1 seconds left. Columbia seized the rebound and scrambled up-court, only to watch a desperation heave go far wide of the mark. Yale had played shutdown defense and Reggie had scored six of our last nine points, all except for Jesse's monumental three, a shot I'll be able to visualize on my deathbed. One night later, cruel basketball had turned kind.

* * * * *

In the locker room afterward, though totally wrung out, I was lightheaded and wanted to linger. The coaches were ecstatic, the guys wild. James told the team he had only been involved before with two such astonishing comebacks. He cautioned the team not to "party too hard. Don't go crazy celebrating tonight." When word arrived that Harvard trailed Princeton by six in Jadwin, the players started to chant, "Harvard sucks!"

We had escaped with Ivy win number six even though Penn had faltered on my upset prediction the night before against Harvard in the Palestra.

As we learned minutes later, Princeton made up for Penn's power outage by upending Harvard, 70-62, preserving my other prediction that Harvard couldn't beat both Penn and Princeton on consecutive nights on their home courts. Thanks to Princeton, we were again only one loss off the pace and back in the hunt.

Thanks also to seniors Greg Mangano and Reggie Willhite, who each scored ten second-half points. With twenty-four points, Reggie was the game's high scorer and added an amazing seven steals and five assists. Playing smart, we had made only fourteen turnovers but had turned Columbia over twenty-one times. Our defense had been outstanding, our full-court press devastating. For a team trailing late in the game, a smothering press was always the right gambit, always the smart option.

Still stunned, standing outside the downstairs locker room I asked trainer Dave DiNapoli if he had a resuscitator in his kit. Laughing, he assured me that he did. Another weekend like this and I would need one, I told him. When James came out holding son Q by the hand, I was still standing in the corridor, trying to get my bearings back. After greeting a grinning Brian Katz, James looked at me, smiled, and said, "Ed, my Ed, how we doin'?" By way of response I could only laugh.

Minutes later, when I got upstairs and looked back at the Yale bench, James stood with son Quincy, daughter Rachel and wife Rebecka, as happy as a man could be. In the crowd clustered around him were some of his former players I had met the week before at the Alumni Game, including a beaming Porter Braswell, who, the last time I had seen him in this building, had directed the stirring double-overtime win at the tail end of the previous season.

The only downer was walking home with my great buddy Ed Carpenter, a Columbia man whose heartbreak was palpable. I bled for him, having experienced the same thing twenty-four hours earlier. This coaching profession banished you to the pits only to propel you onto the heights with frightening speed and with total disregard for your health—and for your sanity, especially in the topsy-turvy Ivy League. The miracle of Morningside had just proved that.

Miracles though, by definition, defy explanation. Despite this, postgame, Columbia coach Kyle Smith supplied one: "Yale is a good team and Willhite wasn't going to let them lose."

CHAPTER FOURTEEN

On the Road Again

PRACTICES WERE NOW shorter but I still liked dropping in and checking on James's procedures, drills, and exercises. With all our basic systems in place, both on defense and offense, more time was devoted to the "scout" on each upcoming opponent: on their offensive sets and their defensive alignments. Our second and third team players would simulate our upcoming opponent's sets, the offensive plays likely to be used. Our first team players would practice foiling these plays in our defensive alignments. Then our second and third team players would line up in the upcoming opponent's favorite defensive alignments, and our first team guys would run our sets, our offensive plays, against these alignments. All the while James and the Three Wise Men would make adjustments, corrections, and refinements.

Also, in the locker room there would be whiteboard skull sessions about what we were likely to confront in our next two weekend games. James would draw the opponent's offensive sets on the board and detail how he wanted the defense played against them, exhorting certain players to be aware of this and alert for that. Then he'd do the same thing with defensive alignments and gambits we were likely to encounter. James would diagram them and then diagram how he wanted them attacked.

Facing two different opponents on successive nights posed a coaching challenge. It was hard enough to prep for one opponent but to prep for two on back-to-back nights posed time management and differentiation problems. James and his assistants would prepare game plans several pages long on each team, listing their strengths and weaknesses and spelling out their tendencies and predilections on both offense and defense. The guys would be expected to study these plans carefully and commit them to memory, with special focus on what their individual responsibilities would be during the two upcoming games. Important in these game plans would be James's section titled "Keys to Win." He would list three or four points crucial to secure the win. For instance, for our most recent game, the miracle of Morningside against Columbia, the "Keys to Win" were:

1. Contain Penetration
2. Blockout/Rebound
3. Offensive Execution
4. Contest Shooters.

These translate as: First, choke off drives in the lane and especially don't let point guard Brian Barbour penetrate and dish. Second: crash the boards and deny second chance baskets to a team that really knew how to score. As a corollary, their front line players were rugged inside, especially Mark Cisco, who knew how to block out and to clear out to get the rebound. Third: move the ball on offense and recycle the Flex until we found the open man with the best high percentage shot. That meant no forcing the ball into the defended post or forcing shots once the ball did get in there. Fourth: defend all over the floor and challenge every shot and every shooter. We had won that game by a single digit by unstintingly executing all four tasks in full sync over the last quarter of the game.

What those closing ten minutes against Columbia had demonstrated was great coaching in action.

* * * * *

In a nice way I had lobbied James for months to see if Yale would let me ride the team bus on a road trip. I wanted to make the trip to Hanover for Dartmouth and down to Boston for Harvard. The last thing I wanted in the face of Yale's continuing generosity was to put them in any way on a liability hook. So I offered to sign a letter absolving the university of any responsibility for me while riding the bus with the team. They accepted and all was set. I also wanted to attend a dawn practice and skull session at least once, and I managed to combine the two. We left for Dartmouth late afternoon Thursday, so I took the train up to New Haven Wednesday for afternoon practice, stayed overnight at the Marriott a block from Payne Whitney, and got up at dawn on Thursday and attended early practice in JLA following a locker room skull session on the Dartmouth scout. After the scout I especially liked the tranquility of JLA bathed in early morning sunlight, the polyurethaned hardwood gleaming with highlights.

The bus left at quarter past four and I was there early. I liked it immensely that James made me shift back one row of seats, saying that he needed SID Tim Bennett in his "usual" seat. As always, at practice the afternoon before, I had sat in my usual seat in the permanent south stands. Because I'm superstitious I sat there for luck. When I first started playing Little League baseball my grandmother, Julia Drakeley Kelly, told me that professional baseball players never washed their uniforms when on a hitting streak. They were afraid to "wash the hits out." Ever since, about sports, I've been superstitious. I was happy to know that James apparently was too. My grandmother also told me that major leaguers in the early days raised their caps whenever they passed a beer wagon full of empty barrels. That kind of respect for alcohol had got me in trouble, and lay behind my foolish decision, once rejected by organized school sports, not to redouble my efforts and try again. Every time I read that as a sophomore Michael Jordan was cut from his high-school team only to make the team as a junior and go on be a superstar it pains me how easily discouraged I am. In all my early efforts at writing I followed the same dumb pattern until I remembered my boyhood lessons on dribbling instilled by my father. Persistence, will power, and practice are the keys, as Michael Jordan explains in his short primer, *I Can't Accept Not Trying*.

On the bus ride Rhett Anderson's brilliant report on the previous week's junket to Ithaca and then down to Manhattan came alive for me. Wanting to be as unobtrusive as I promised James I would be, I sat quietly the whole nearly three-hour trip up Interstate 91 through lashing rain and poor visibility. But I did keep turning and looking back at the players and realizing their discomfort. Many stretched their long legs across the aisle and reclined as only the young can without arising and, as a result of sustained contortions, doing an imitation of a cat with rickets. Their long legs formed an obstacle course to the john in the back and I was glad that I'd had the foresight not to drink my usual allotment of diet soda and decaffeinated coffee.

Reserve swingman Armani Cotton saved the day for many by having in his carry-on bag the DVD of *The Bourne Supremacy*. Jaime Snyder-Fair had insisted we put a movie on. This occasioned banter between James and Justin Simon about the relative merits of Will Ferrell movies, on which James was negative and Justin positive. Having never seen one I had no opinion but from the trailers I had seen I would have been firmly in James's camp. Snatches of conversation from the back of the bus revolved around the relative merits of NBA stars, just as they had at the Florida practice in Gainesville. This time a controversy arose over "Who was better? Allen Iverson or Kevin Garnett?" For me the answer was obvious since Iverson, indescribably gifted, never learned the secret to winning championships: practice and teamwork. I kept quiet of course. So did James, quietly reading newspapers as nearly everyone watched the movie or grooved to their headsets or thumbed away at their cells. A few simply dozed. I made notes and read work I had taken along.

One snatch of conversation excited me. Sitting directly behind me our team statistician Zan Tanner and Jeremiah Kreisberg discussed the upcoming game with Harvard. Jerry mentioned that tickets on the Net were being scalped for a hundred bucks. If the genie had popped out of his bottle and asked the one thing I wanted more than anything else, more than this book to work, I would have said, "For Yale to beat Harvard."

* * * * *

But Dartmouth came first, and it was a potentially disastrous game. All winless teams are dangerous; in the Ivy League, doubly so. While interviewing some of the players later that night at the Fireside Inn in West Lebanon, where we were staying, I had mentioned to be careful not to overlook Dartmouth by over-anticipating the Saturday night showdown with Harvard. James had emphasized this point to the team at practice both Wednesday and Thursday, reminding them that Dartmouth had lost the previous Saturday to Penn on the road only because Zack Rosen, on an otherwise cold shooting night for him, had stepped up with 3.2 seconds left and dropped in a three to unknot a tie and give Penn the win, 58-55. Dartmouth had lost narrowly in other league games to boot, and they had played us tough in JLA three weeks back, losing only when Reggie took the game over in the closing minutes with a big assist from Austin's four straight foul shots and from Greg's timely three. Back then, coming off the Harvard debacle, we had trailed most of the game and been torpid but for the last five minutes. In Dartmouth's small but cozy Leede Arena we couldn't afford to repeat that lapse.

Thankfully, we didn't. The game was pretty much ours from start to finish except for a late spurt in the second half, when Dartmouth pulled to within four at 60-56. We responded and won the game in the waning minutes by hitting our foul shots, making one after the other—in fact, for the game we made thirty of thirty-three, an astonishing 90 percent. Our height advantage helped too; we outrebounded them thirty-nine to thirty-one. Four starters shared the ball and the result was balanced scoring, inside and out: Austin had game honors for us with seventeen points, including twelve of twelve foul shots; Greg added sixteen, Reggie thirteen, and Jeremiah eleven. Off the bench our two talented freshmen post players, Brandon Sherrod and Matt Townsend, had eleven points between them, Brandon with six, Matt with five. They also combined for five rebounds.

Significantly, Jesse Pritchard made his first career start at shooting guard when Austin moved out of position to play the point. Starting point guard Mike Grace's ankle injury from the Columbia game had not come around, despite trainer Dave DiNapoli working on it hard all week and even that morning in Leede during our shoot-around and walk-through. Now that the talented Isaiah Salafia was gone and Mike was hurt, we had only one true point guard left, Javier Duren. Javy's upside was unbelievable but he had never fully recovered from his crash to the floor during practice right before Thanksgiving. He had suffered a severe concussion and James, rightly, refused to expose him to further injury. Concussions are nothing to sneeze at, as the NFL is learning.

As a result James played Javy sparingly the rest of the season. This hurt us, though it was clearly the right thing to do ethically. At six feet four inches Javy had height and he had a basketball IQ in the Mensa range. Because I would rather see a great pass than a hotdog dunk, I couldn't take my eyes off Javy when he was on the floor. After the season I told him he had that preternatural gift some players have—Magic Johnson, Maurice Cheeks, Bill Bradley, John Stockton, Bob Cousy, Oscar Robertson, Chris Webber—of seeing 220 or 230 degrees while looking straight ahead, what is often called "eyes in the back of your head." Javy could read the floor the way Einstein could interpret celestial movement. When he comes into his own, watching him will be a joy.

In Leede Arena this night we won, 70-61, and swept the season series. After the game Austin summed it up: "This was a trap game. Dartmouth is much better than their record shows." Austin knew his stuff. The next night Dartmouth and coach Paul Cormier's youth movement cashed in as they upset Brown for their first league win, 58-53.

* * * * *

After the game I lingered near our locker room, waiting for the team so we could board the bus for the trip down to Boston. As I sat in the stands I noticed a distinguished man, rather tall, lingering there as well. He had a quick smile and a kind face and I pegged him instantly for a coach. Right after the game he had spoken along the near baseline with Dartmouth senior Jabari Trotter, the gifted guard with a good shooting touch whose playing time had suffered under Coach Cormier's youth movement. The way Jabari handled his reduced minutes was admirable, the same way our senior Rhett Anderson had handled his reduced minutes with the advent of talented freshman forwards Brandon Sherrod and Matt Townsend. Both Jabari and Rhett were mature beyond their years and each handled his setback with equanimity, remaining enthusiastic team players, not disgruntled benchwarmers. They understood that a coach sometimes had to teach going forward, for the future, and that meant seasoning rookies for their upperclass years as soon as possible for the good of the program.

When Reggie emerged from postgame media interviews he too talked to the tall gentleman. After Reggie went into the locker room I walked over and introduced myself. The man was Malcolm Wesselink, and he had coached basketball for twenty-six years at Phillips Exeter Academy in the New England Prep School Athletic Conference. Before his retirement, he had coached former schoolboy teammates Jabari and Reggie. Coach Wesselink's pride in having sent so many of his players on to play at top-flight colleges was heartwarming. Just from his eyes and his caring manner it was apparent that he was a fine man and a great influence on young players.

When the guys came out of the locker room we were ready to roll down Interstate 91 and work our way toward Cambridge for the Harvard rematch.

* * * * *

About two and a half hours later we pulled into the forecourt of the Newton Marriott. It was shortly after midnight. Excitement was running high and Tim Bennett said we should have breakfast in the morning. I thought that was an excellent idea. Sitting across the aisle from Tim on the bus ride I had watched him tapping keys on his laptop as he completed his write-up of the Dartmouth game and posted it to the Yale website, having spent just under an hour on it. I was impressed, and made a mental note to read it. When I did, it was—not surprisingly—concise, accurate, and well-written. This was a good thing for me, then and now. After the game I liked to compare impressions with Tim, though as a Yale guy he had to use a certain hometown slant. Yet he never distorted the facts. And now, half a year later as I finish this book, his accounts are helpful when I browse my notebooks, check my running score notations, and brood over my commentary.

In my room I was excited and unable to hop straight into bed, knowing I would only toss and turn. Instead I reviewed my notes from three scintillating player interviews the night before at the Fireside Inn. I had spoken first to Reggie and discovered that he was fluent in German, having learned it from his Croatian mother. His dad had been a career serviceman stationed in Germany, and Reggie had been born there. He and his two younger brothers had spent time abroad while growing up. Because his family had moved around like most military families, Reggie had attended three different high schools, the last one in California run by Benedictine Brothers. As a basketball player in high school he had drawn interest from several colleges in the University of California system and from the very eager Air Force Academy. But he elected to do an additional year of college prep and attended Exeter for a year. There he caught the eye of Matt Kingsley and Yale recruited him.

A political science major keeping his options open for a career in business or law, Reggie concentrated hard on his studies. For now he told me that basketball didn't interfere much with them, though every once in a while he would be forced to miss a lecture. Whenever this happened he would get hold of all the assigned material and catch up to the class. There were no tutors for him. Because he was always modest he didn't tell me he had a high academic standing, but at year's end he made the National Association of Basketball Coaches' honors list for academic achievement. This is an award restricted to juniors and seniors who have maintained a high grade point average at the same institution for their last two years of eligibility. At year's end Yale would place three others besides Reggie on this NABC's honors list: fellow senior Brian Katz and juniors Sam Martin and Austin Morgan. In closing the interview Reggie mentioned he was happy that his younger brother attending Tufts would be at the Harvard rematch. Though understated and humble, Reggie proved as articulate as he was athletic.

Jeremiah Kreisberg was next. Watching Jerry from Day One I had wondered where he had learned his outstanding footwork in the pivot—low or high post—and how he had come by his unselfish and intelligent approach to basketball, underscored by his excellent passing ability. I suspected early schooling from people who knew what they were doing. Imagine my delight to discover that his dad, his uncle, and his cousin had all played at Wesleyan, where Matt Kingsley had starred. In fact Matt recruited Jeremiah. What gratified me even more than learning that Jerry's dad had played college ball was learning that his mom had too. His height came from their genes, of course, his dad being six-six and his mom five-nine. You don't come by being six-ten by accident. I had been impressed that Jeremiah had been good enough, while still a teen, to play in international competition for the Israeli national team.

Near the end of our talk Jerry added something that electrified me. His grandfather Barrett G. Kreisberg, before becoming a distinguished Manhattan lawyer, had played college ball at George Washington University in the thirties, the era my own dad had played starting guard for Roman Catholic High School in Philly, before I showed up there twenty-three years later. When Jerry added that grandfather Barry had also played professional basketball in the pre-NBA barnstorming days, I wondered if he had ever crossed paths at GW with Red Auerbach, the fabled coach of the Celtics dynasty, and, while barnstorming, with Dolph Schayes and Red Holzman, the thirties stars of NYU and CCNY. At CCNY Holzman had played under legendary coach Nat Holman before becoming legendary himself as the coach of the seventies Knicks, the greatest icons of teamwork in professional basketball history, winners of the NBA title in '70 and '73. Grandfather Barrett eventually married Jerry's grandmother Luisa, who for years served as director of the Harkness Foundation for Dance. Barrett himself sat for years on the board of the Brooklyn Academy of Music, famous for its avant-garde offerings in dance, music, and drama.

Jerry didn't mention his grandparents' cultural credits, but discovering them went a long way in explaining his quiet sophistication and his princely manners and comportment. Unflappable, he has a bemused and charming personality. Exposure to it raises your spirits. As the first option in the low-post this upcoming season he will be spectacular.

The last player cornered in the Fireside Inn was Sam Martin, busy at his studies on the computer in the soundproofed, glass-enclosed business center just off the lobby. Fascinated by him ever since I'd seen his textbook shooting form in our snowy October scrimmage against the New Jersey Institute of Technology, I asked him immediately about his prowess in karate, mindful of that trophy-filled den in his suburban house outside Providence. He told me how, at an early age, he'd lost his dad to a heart attack caused by lung disease and how his mother Carol had insisted he build himself up physically in order not to suffer the same fate as his dad. She got him into every sport to build up his lungs. In prep school he ran low- and high-hurdles to thwart asthma. But his favorite sport was always basketball, and Carol saw to it that the hoop and backboard went up at the foot of the driveway, where Sam practiced devoutly: "I was a little obsessive/compulsive. I always worked hard. I wasn't the most natural athlete."

Carol was the most natural mother, working as a professor of business administration at Bristol Community College and at two part-time jobs in order to put Sam through the best prep schools, including the highly regarded Worcester Academy. There Sam came to the attention of master recruiter Matt Kingsley and ended up at Yale. In high school Sam had played in the NEPSAC against Yale roommate Reggie Willhite, whom he would succeed as team captain for the upcoming 2012–2013 season. Sam's prep school coach, Ed Reilly, had been a big influence. Reilly was a man who never cursed and disallowed any gossip about teammates, two traits Sam admired. Their relationship was close and Sam was happy to find the same kind of closeness with Coach Jones, a man he considers, like Ed Reilly, a good mentor.

I always sensed a kinship with Sam, though, as an athlete, I wouldn't have amounted to a pimple on his duff. He seemed, like me, to have a confidence problem when things didn't go well right from the start. If his first shots didn't fall he had a tendency, when next open for a shot, to lapse into hesitation that wasn't justified in light of his sharpshooting ability. I kept telling him that, when open, a skilled shooter, to help his team, shoots. When Sam was on, he was dangerous, but opposing teams seemed to know this. Like Austin on the wings, Sam too was hounded there, and in the corners, where he was also deadly, especially on three pointers.

A political science major like Reggie, Sam had worked the previous summer in Washington as an intern for Rhode Island Democratic senator Jack Reed. This was a boon for a young man with Sam's people skills and his ambition to attend law school and possibly enter politics. Know this about Sam: by the age of ten he was a black belt in karate. He's not a fellow to underestimate.

When I finished checking these notes on player interviews, I glanced at my entries from an interview I'd conducted with Matt Kingsley that afternoon, again in the lobby of the Fireside Inn. This was after our morning practice in Leede, as the players rested for the game against Dartmouth. I had intuited since talking to Matt at the team party at Sam's house that he was a topflight recruiter. The fact that he had recruited all three players I'd interviewed the night before confirmed this. With a grin Matt told me it was true he had ranked as the second leading scorer at Wesleyan when he graduated in 1998, but that in the intervening years he had fallen in the rankings to four or five. He mentioned that he might still be the school's top three-point scorer.

When I asked about recruiting, he told me how important Yale Basketball Bulldog Elite Camp was every June, and how important the "open" recruiting period that followed in July was. Coaches during this open period could roam the country, scouting players at AAU events, mostly regional tournaments. Matt had surprised me back at Sam's party when he said that recruiting during the high-school basketball season was restricted by the obligations of coaching the current Yale team. Coaches could only "get away" to take in high-school games on a catch-as-catch-can basis.

Since the "scouts" I'd sat in on fascinated me, I asked Matt about what went into putting one together. The videos were elaborate, highly selective, and intensely detailed. Matt said he usually watched fifteen hours of video to put one scout together, based typically on four or five minutely studied games. Considering how illustrative the final result was, this made sense. Just looking at the finished product I knew it had to be a time-intensive task. Matt explained that there was a computer program available for this purpose, called DV Sport, similar to the programs available to filmmakers and to theatrical directors. Then there was the written game plan put together by the assigned assistant coach before being polished and finalized by James after an in-depth discussion among all the coaches, since James and the other assistants would have studied many of the same game films of the scouted team. It was an involved process, time-consuming and demanding.

In winding up the interview, I asked about Matt's family. I had seen his kids after home games. He had a daughter five, Amelia, and a son two and a half, Eli. Thirty-six years old, Matt had been at Yale for seven years. Then I hit gold when I asked if he had jumped straight into coaching after graduation. He confessed he had first tried a job in finance in Boston, but it had bored him. So he left to become a coach, first in high school, then in college.

I thanked him and then got even luckier. I mentioned that I'd noticed how uneven the officiating could be in Ivy League games compared to our non-conference games. Matt said, "Because we have no conference tournament, the referees don't realize the intensity of the Ivy games will be at such a high pitch. So they're not prepared for it."

* * * * *

The intensity of our next Ivy game, the Saturday night rematch with Harvard, was going to be at a high pitch, so high that Tim and I were subdued in talking about it over breakfast Saturday morning in a glass-enclosed conservatory overlooking the Newton River at the back of the hotel lobby. The tension I felt, personally, surprised me. On the surface I had no skin in the game, other than hoping my book would be dramatic, whatever happened. But that was just the surface. At a much deeper level I was fully identified with the coaches and the players. This had happened in a kind of transference similar to what takes place in psychotherapy, where the thinking of the therapist replaces the thinking of the patient. In this instance coach-think had replaced writer-think and all I could do was run strategy in my head coupled with probable game scenarios. Like Sam Martin I was obsessive and this was all I could manage mentally in the run-up to the game.

Waiting in a hotel room on the road for a night game is draining. Time crawls. Clocks and watches seem to have stopped as surely as they did for Dickens' jilted Miss Havisham in *Great Expectations*. I frittered time by studying, but not really absorbing, my game notes. Early in the morning the coaches had walked through the Harvard sets in an event room off the lobby. James had been brilliant, covering every set and thumb-nailing the strengths and weaknesses of every Harvard player likely to be used against us that night. He arranged our guys like life-sized pieces on a chessboard and moved them around the room, weaving in and out between them, adjusting them, snapping sharp rebukes if their attention seemed less than laser-like in intensity. As he ran through the Harvard roster, I realized he had cited about ten players capable of stinging us. Usually a coach has only three or four to concentrate on. I recalled Coach Amaker's comment after his team routed us three weekends earlier: "Balance and bench."

After the run-through we broke for a few hours for lunch and a rest. Then in the afternoon Jamie Snyder-Fair, who had the "scout" this time, gathered the guys back in the event room and gave them what he jokingly referred to as a rousing "Knute Rockne" speech. He was bullish and I loved him for it. When I asked him how he felt, he said, "Ed, what do you think? This late in the season, we're one game behind the leader and playing the leader tonight in what amounts to a championship game! How much better can it get?"

I acknowledged his point but I worried. Bill Cloutier had described the Harvard defense after the first game as "smothering." Bill knew basketball. He had come to Wednesday afternoon's practice and sat beside me watching. I told him a TV crew had earlier interviewed James on the sideline under the watchful eye of Tim Bennett. Bill commented that despite the lopsided result of the first game the rematch this weekend would draw lots of media attention. When I asked him what he thought of our chances in the rematch, he cited Harvard's defense and said he thought we were "up against it." Being the great guy he is, he hastened to add that he hoped he was wrong.

When the team boarded the bus for the ride into Cambridge about an hour later I hoped he was wrong too.

* * * * *

Lavities Pavilion is the oldest and smallest gym in the Ivy League, opened in 1923. Like frayed seersucker, it's emblematic of shabby gentility. Capacity is only fifty people over two thousand, smaller than many high-school gyms. But for tonight's game the old barn was rocking. Bill Cloutier's prediction about the media overflow was accurate. Extra seats had been crammed into every available nook and a special structure for the overflow media had been built above the permanent stands, just under the roof, on the side of the court opposite the team benches and the permanent press row. Constructed of wooden scaffolding, this crow's nest for the overflow media was something akin to a gallows or a guillotine stand.

To that, of course, I was banished. So were my buddies Bill Cloutier and Mike Anthony, as well as the incomparable Charles Condro of the *Yale Daily News*, and so too was yet another engaging and affable young sports journalist named Naveen Reddy, representing *rush the court. net*, described on his business card as "the ubiquitous college basketblog." Having him seated next to me was a masterstroke of luck because he was as deeply knowledgeable as he was unstintingly helpful. The man was a pure delight even in what I considered our makeshift crow's nest under the rafters.

Yale's locker room was on the opposite side of the gym from our crow's nest so I could not possibly get to it, hear the pregame talk from James and his assistants, and make it back to my seat without missing the opening minutes of the game. Besides the overflow crowd, which I later learned exceeded the arena's capacity by a hundred and fifty people, there were three long flights of makeshift stairs to climb to reach our loft in the rafters. When Yale came down the stairs from their locker room, which, as I assumed and later had confirmed, was far too small and cramped, the crowd got raucous and there were loud boos for the visiting archrivals. After the player introductions, right before the game started, the Yale team formed a human hive and started to jump in unison, captain Reggie in the center jumping the highest and whipping up his teammates. They were ready to go.

Harvard jumped out in front, helped by eight quick points from senior shooting guard Oliver McNally, who hit two quick threes and a two-point jumper in the lane to give Harvard a 15-9 lead after seven minutes. They pushed this lead to 23-9 and then, at the media time-out with 7:56 left, ballooned it to 27-13. With 3:54 to go the lead reached twenty at 35-15 and my sense of déjà vu dread reached critical mass. Then Yale exploded for an 11-0 run to whittle the Harvard lead at halftime to 35-26. At nine points down we were back in the game. Yale had won six games this season after trailing at halftime. Again, I couldn't get to the locker room through the Third World crowding and the obstacle course layout of the facilities. Shabby gentility has its charm but not when it entails such discomfort.

Greg Mangano had twelve of our twenty-six points, five of our thirteen rebounds, and all four of our blocks in one half of basketball. He had held us in the game. Reggie and Brandon Sherrod off the bench had four points each, and Jeremiah, Austin, and Mike Grace had two each. Once again the Harvard defense was swarming like riled wasps protecting their nest. As James pointed out after the game, for nearly all of the first half on defense we played out too high on the perimeter and they had dribble-penetrated around us for easy lay-ups, in addition to McNally's two quick threes when he scored more than half his team's points in the first seven minutes of play. Laurent Rivard, who had clobbered us from the perimeter in the first game, this time nailed a three to make Harvard three of six from beyond the arc in the first half, a handsome 50 percent. Once again Harvard's balanced scoring was eerie; seven men had scored between four and six points each, with McNally tops at eight. Each team had only two turnovers and Yale had five fouls to Harvard's nine. All told it was a good half of basketball, saved by Yale's eleven-point surge in the closing three minutes.

It was anybody's game. I remembered James's opening salvo at the morning walk-through: "It's not about them, it's about us." It truly was. We could come out and pick up where we left off and tie for the Ivy lead or we could "splinter" as Reggie had so eloquently put it after the initial Harvard rout. I prayed that we would answer the bugle call and charge.

* * * * *

Initially we did. In the first minutes of the second half Jeremiah scored four points, Greg hit a foul shot, Austin made a three and we were down only five, 39-34. Two minutes later Greg hit two fouls to make it 42-38, Harvard by four. But about a minute later Brandyn Curry popped a three from the right corner to restore Harvard's lead to nine, 47-38, because Keith Wright had snared a low-post feed for an easy lay-up on the possession before Curry struck from the corner. With ten minutes left Corbin Miller, a freshman from Utah, poured in a three from the left wing. I could hear James underscoring in a loud voice that morning during the hotel walk-through not to let Miller shoot uncontested. Right about this time Sam Martin shot a three from the left corner that rimmed out. Silently I had thought Sam might get hot tonight and give us a quick ten points off the bench and a victory. But just as in our first game, Austin Morgan was blanketed on defense once again, and Harvard for the second time was defending tight on the perimeter, up in Sam's chest and face wherever he went. Harvard shadowed Sam as tight as they stalked Austin, no matter that Austin was circulating like a berserk neuron, pinballing from strong to weak side and back, fighting through the lane and weaving along the baseline. Without the ball Austin moved as well as any player in the Ivy League, but Harvard hounded him again.

For the next five minutes Harvard's lead fluctuated between eight and ten points, which is where it stood at the time-out Harvard called with 5:43 left: 56-46. A minute and a half later Harvard took another time-out with 4:08 left and Yale down eight after Greg Mangano hit a three from his favorite place, just behind the arc at the top of the key. With time back in, Wright hit a low-post lay-up off a feed from Curry, who was killing us with dribble penetration, just the thing James had railed against all morning. Coaching was not for those short of patience. That put the Harvard lead back to 59-49 at the last media time-out with 2:52 left. With time back in, Austin fouled

Curry, who hit one of two free throws to make it 60-49. Amaker now borrowed his old Duke archrival North Carolina's clock-killing technique, not quite a four-corners stall but a long and effective weave, at the end of which Casey got loose in the low post for a cheap dunk.

The dunk, and the thirteen-point lead it gave Harvard, ignited the Harvard student section seated below us. They started to chant that Yale was a "safety school" and followed with the suggestion, "Let's play football," at which Harvard had bested Yale for five straight wins and counting. Amused, I laughed. Then Curry hit two foul shots to make it 64-49 before Wright slipped free in the low post during another time-killing perimeter weave and he too slammed down an uncontested dunk. The Harvard heckling grew louder as fans started to leave. With only seconds left Reggie hit a meaningless dunk that at least pulled us within fifteen for the final score, Harvard 66, Yale 51. The Harvard defense Bill Cloutier called "smothering" had asphyxiated us again. Greg Mangano's three with 5:07 left was Yale's last score until Reggie's meaningless dunk. Essentially for the final five minutes Harvard held us scoreless.

My hat was off to them and to coach Tommy Amaker, who mentioned again postgame that the go-to man for Harvard was the open man. With fearful symmetry, all but one of the ten Harvard players profiled by James at the morning walk-through had scored. Curry was the high man with eighteen and Christian Webster the low man with one, but in between everyone else had at least four points and Keith Wright hit double figures at ten. Coach Amaker said he and his assistants emphasized "the three Cs" to their players: "Concentration, composure, and confidence." He mentioned how important it had been, just as in game one, to stick tight to Austin, to move in sync with him on the perimeter. Again they had succeeded.

We had played a good game, with only seven turnovers to Harvard's eight. But as in our early losses at Quinnipiac and Seton Hall, Reggie got into foul trouble in the middle of the second half, when he picked up his fourth. With him on the bench, the main cog of our defense was out of commission. After the game James emphasized that we had spotted them too big a leg-up with the twenty-point lead in the first half. But the truth was simpler. On the way out of the glass-enclosed lounge overlooking the court, after Coach Amaker concluded his postgame remarks and his Q&A media session, I said to Joey Rosenberg, who had called the game for the Yale student radio station, "Harvard's got two starting teams. Ten starters, in effect."

For Thursday's practice agenda "Compete" had been "The Word of the Day" James chose. The definition read: "Try to outperform, to try and win or do better than others." I was proud that we had competed tonight.

Slumped in my assigned bus seat, waiting for the players to straggle aboard, I observed that James was still competing. Obsessively reviewing the game film on his laptop—the game not over a full half hour yet—he was parsing the action frame by frame, zooming forward and back, looking for insights for the next game. The man never quit, he never said "uncle." It was one more thing to admire about him.

When Greg Kelley and Jesse Pritchard boarded the bus to retrieve their gear, I perked up. They were staying the night in Boston, Greg's hometown. On the way down the exit stairs Jesse, with his devilish and winning insouciance and his irrepressible ebullience, looked straight back at me and said, "Ed, we have to talk. I'm thinking of writing a book about you."

CHAPTER FIFTEEN

JLA Magic

ALL WEEK THERE was a sense of letdown, of anticlimax. James was having none of it. Not for nothing was he the dean of Ivy coaches in his thirteenth season. He knew anything could happen in the ferociously competitive tournament that was the Ivy League regular season. It wasn't a case of dog eat dog, it was rat eat rat. Out in front Harvard was not home free. They were facing the always-taxing Penn/Princeton weekend while we would host Columbia and Cornell on consecutive nights in JLA, where we had lost only one game all year. At 7-3 we were off the 9-1 Harvard pace by two games. At 7-2 Penn trailed Harvard by a game and a half while 6-3 Princeton lagged behind us half a game in the win column but stood dead even with us at three losses. Of course Penn and Princeton still had to play their usual showcase game the Tuesday after the final weekend. Things were tight and nothing was settled.

That's why James was his usual self, bursting with enthusiasm and radiating positive energy. He focused the team hard all week in practice and underscored our narrow and miraculous comeback win two weeks earlier against Columbia and the narrow and freakish loss the night before to hot-handed Cornell, both away games. Now we got both teams on our home floor, and James was determined that we sweep them, blanking Columbia in the season series and paying back Cornell for playing spoiler to our championship dreams.

The difference for us this year in both Harvard losses was guard play. We missed Porter Braswell, his floor generalship, his dribble penetration ability, and his distribution talents as a spotter of the open man. At point guard this year we lacked height, quickness, and experience. For the last two games stouthearted Mike Grace had tried to rush back into action on his tender ankle but had been gimpy and impaired and only aggravated his injury. Jesse Pritchard had stepped up to start at shooting guard but that left Austin, a marvelous shooting guard, playing out of position at the point. Our guard contingent was decimated: senior shooting guard Brian Katz lost to double retina surgery, talented freshman point guard Javier Duren lost to a severe concussion, and wildly athletic sophomore point guard Isaiah Salafia lost to personal problems.

The upcoming weekend against Columbia and Cornell marked the one-year anniversary of the epic upset of Harvard that galvanized me to pursue James to do this book. Thinking back on the rapid ball movement and balanced scoring Yale had on offense that night with Porter Braswell at the controls only increased my misgivings about our guard play from here on out. When James and I spoke about the strategy for the upcoming games he was all confidence, as usual, and thought we would handle both teams well by sticking to our original strategies from the first games.

Against Columbia we needed to prevent point guard Brian Barbour from penetrating and either dishing to the open man or driving the gaps himself for easy lay-ups. The same thing held true the following night against Cornell and their All-Ivy point guard, Chris Wroblewski. Against both teams we had to control the glass and win the rebound battle. On offense we had to execute and not panic but work the multiple options of the Flex till we got an open shot, resisting forced shots taken prematurely; if we settled for low percentage shots, we'd lose. And as always we had to outwork our opponents, getting to loose balls first and preventing easy fast break baskets by hustling back on defense.

On Saturday night Cornell could not possibly play a better game than they had played to beat us on their floor: it was out of the question that Johnathan Gray would show up with his shooting hand scalding hot and drop twenty-nine points on us again. Because Cornell had pressed us so effectively, I reminded James to instruct the post guys not to abandon our ballhandlers and run up court. Cornell had twice turned over Mike Grace in the left quadrant of our own backcourt by trapping him in a lightning-quick double team by their taller guards, whether Wroblewski, Ferry, or Gray. Our "bigs" had to be reminded to check whether our guards needed help advancing the ball up the floor. If they did need help, the bigs had to station themselves near midcourt and take quick passes from the guards about to be trapped.

When James said this was a good point my head nearly soared off my shoulders and rocketed around the room. It was the same great feeling I had back in December when I asked him to tell Isaiah to stop trying to dribble between two guards, something easy to do in high school but wickedly difficult at the Division I level. When James told Isaiah at practice in the O'Connell Center before the Florida game to "stop trying to split the trap," he flashed me his thousand-yard stare. The only guard who could split the trap consistently in the Ivy League this season was Zack Rosen, whose shuffle step and slippery crab dribble was a thing of beauty.

Like James, I felt we were ready to win two.

* * * * *

One of the great pleasures of my coaching escapade was getting to know the parents of the players, and, in the case of assistant coach Justin Simon, his father. Mr. Simon, a lawyer, had that benevolence and bonhomie I find unbeatable. Justin and his dad were extremely close, his mother having died very young. Mr. Simon then raised three boys by himself. He left a high-powered Manhattan law firm and became a Mr. Mom while running a law practice locally on Long Island. Justin's dad showed up at nearly all our games. The same thing was true of Reverend Kelley, reserve forward Greg Kelley's dad, a great and knowledgeable fan in addition to being a theologian.

My seat in the auxiliary media section in the stands was right next to the family section for the Yale players that was right behind the Yale bench. During the game and especially at halftime, before or after I scrambled downstairs to the locker room to hear James and the Wise Men address the troops, I would huddle with Reverend Kelley or with Mr. Simon and compare notes. The sense of family this gave me was incredibly helpful. Sam Martin's mother Carol would usually be there, reluctant to miss any game Sam was in. I introduced myself to Greg Mangano's family too; his father, his stepmother, and his brothers often came and pulled like crazy for Greg.

During the Penn/Princeton weekend I had the good fortune to meet Isaiah Salafia's mother but I might have been awkward when I encouraged her to tell Isaiah to call me if I could be any help to him. He had left the team that very week. I told her I missed him already and felt like the two front teeth had been knocked out of the team's smile. I knew how much I regretted not trying out for the Drexel team as my Uncle Tom had advised me to do, and I had been tortured as well for four-decades-plus for storming out of the University of Virginia in a foolish snit minus my master's degree. I didn't want Isaiah to replicate my folly and incur lifelong regrets.

Whenever I mentioned to James how great the players' parents were, he would smile and say, "Ed, I'm telling you. You meet the best people here. They're just the best people." This was certainly true of Austin Morgan's mom and dad, Jay and Sherry. Jay had told me that Sherry was the daughter of Mel Nowell, the talented starting guard on Fred Taylor's early sixties Ohio State team that won the national championship in 1960 and finished runner-up to Cincinnati the following two years. That team featured future Hall of Famers Jerry Lucas and John Havlicek and two other players good enough to make the NBA, Austin's grandfather Mel and Larry Siegfried. Bob Knight was a backup guard on that team.

In 1961 that Ohio State team, on the way to losing the championship to Cincinnati in an upset, had drubbed my boyhood idols in a semifinal, the St. Joe's Hawks, 95-69. Coached by Jack Ramsay, that team featured point guard and future coach Jimmy Lynam. A few years earlier Jimmy had been a camp counselor and basketball instructor of mine at the Big Brothers' Camp Wyomissing along the Delaware River in sight of the famous Delaware Water Gap. I can still name the starters for St. Joe's that year and I still smart from the point-shaving scandal that forced St. Joe's to forfeit its third-place trophy, earned in a four-overtime endurance test with Utah. I remember the newspaper article in which Jimmy described throwing his commemorative watch in the river, my first shattering lesson in the corruption inherent in amateur collegiate athletics mixed with too much commerce, a situation that has only grown worse, except in the Ivy League.

I liked knowing that Austin had this bloodline back to grandfather Mel, the same way I liked seeing his parents Jay and Sherry at every game and knowing they had flown in from Reno, Nevada to cheer Austin on. I also liked knowing that freshman Matt Townsend descended from Harvard footballers and that sophomore Will Bartlett's father had been a multi-sport athlete at Princeton. Then again, Mike Grace's dad, now a lawyer, still held the school record for assists at UNC Asheville. This only reminded me that I had besmirched my own dad's legacy as a starting guard at Roman Catholic

High School by taking a wrong turn in attitude while I was a teenager, instead of waiting for my spurt in growth the summer before I turned sixteen and trying out again for the varsity as a better man would have.

*****

In the locker room before the Columbia game James closed his remarks by emphasizing that he did not want a repeat of the "deficit" we had imposed on ourselves two weeks back in Levien before we worked our miracle comeback. He wanted us watching Cisco in the post, especially when he popped out for quick jumpers on the "short side," meaning the side with the ball out on the perimeter, usually in point guard Brian Barbour's capable hands. We also had to hedge hard on side-ball screens for Barbour or for sharpshooting two guard Meiko Lyles. Earlier in the week James told me the big key to this game would be "denying the ball" to Cisco and Barbour when they were in position to score. That was the plan on defense.

On offense we had to set "good, hard screens," make "good, hard entry passes" to the post, and work the Flex options. While doing this we needed to set solid screens for Jesse Pritchard to "come out," meaning for him to pop out from the weak side corner to the wing for open shots. Last, we also had to set screens for Reggie to receive an "elbow pass" as he drove toward the basket for easy lay-ups, either along the baseline or down the lane.

We jumped on them early, executing all facets of the game plan. By the time Columbia called a time-out at the 13:50 mark we were up 15-5. Over the next seven minutes we pushed the lead to 23-9 while playing shutdown defense. We continued to play beautifully but Columbia rallied over the last five minutes to close the gap at halftime to 30-22. We had played well but hadn't shot for a high percentage. But, then again, neither had Columbia until their closing run.

At halftime in the locker room, James wanted us to fight harder through ball screens, "you'll see one every possession," and he wanted "hands up on Crockett," a speedy senior guard who, in eleven minutes off the bench, had given Columbia a five-point lift. James wanted us to get back quicker on transition, "You're celebrating and they're charging up the floor." Matt wanted us to get the "post touch" when our shot clock was running down, urging a pass into the low post to Greg or Jeremiah. This was good advice especially since we'd worked the inside game well and had the added bonus of pinning two personal fouls on Mark Cisco already. Jamie wanted to see us "dive for loose balls," and, on offense, to get "deep post penetration" and to "swing the ball and re-post on the opposite side." Jamie wanted ball movement by recycling the Flex and then having his bigs rotate to the opposite side of the lane and look for the entry pass there. This touched the heart of the matter for me; all year we had been deficient working the inside-out reload on the Flex. Before calling for the team huddle, James closed with an exhortation to "Move the ball, cut hard, create some motion."

We came out charged up and maintained our 8 to 10 point lead for the first seven minutes. Then Columbia struck, closing the gap to 50-49 just past the halfway mark. A team of dangerous streak shooters, Columbia was surging. At the 5:55 mark they tied the score at 56, then matched buckets and tied us again at 58. For us it was character time. The previous Saturday in the Palestra Columbia had let Penn off the upset hook when Zack Rosen served as a decoy on an inbounds play with a second and a half left in overtime. Instead of taking the last shot Rosen fed Matt Dougherty for an easy, scripted lay-up after setting a surprise screen for him, a brilliant instance of coaching by Jerome Allen. Watching Columbia shoot the ball so accurately I suddenly feared they'd upset us.

Then a prediction by Coach Gallagher of Hartford back in November came to pass. He said Brandon Sherrod would have a big night in JLA before the season was out. This was that night. Brandon sparkled off the bench, scoring six points over the last four minutes. For the game he scored ten points and grabbed six rebounds. Matt had the scout and had prepped the guys for an inbounds play he wanted executed on offense. In Brandon's late six-point binge, he cut exactly under the basket as Matt had directed, Austin found him with a quick feed, and we got an easy, and decisive, lay-up.

Then, with forty-seven seconds left, Austin stole the ball to ensure our victory, 75-67, after we made our mop-up foul shots. We had played a balanced, intelligent, energetic game and when the gut check came we had answered the character call. For the third straight year we had swept good Columbia teams, well coached the last two years by Kyle Smith and well coached the previous year by James's brother Joe. I was happy for James that a win over Columbia no longer induced ambiguous feelings about pinning a loss on his brother.

Leaving Payne Whitney I was especially happy for Brandon. On the first day of practice back in October as James and I stepped out of Tompkins House, the townhouse beside Payne Whitney that houses the athletic offices, we bumped into Brandon in street clothes. He was the first player I met and the ideal one-man welcoming committee. On his way to get a haircut, he stopped and James introduced us. For the entire season he was always glad to see me and greeted me every time with a smile and a handshake, addressing me always as "Mr. Breslin" or "sir." Not just a favorite of mine, Brandon charmed and intrigued Bill Cloutier, who profiled him in the *New Haven Register* in what will be the first of many articles written about him if his career pans out the way I think it will, with him being celebrated as one of the best power forwards ever to play in the Ivy League. A graduate of Choate, Brandon sings each Sunday in his church choir. That I never got to hear him is one of the things on a long list of good intentions I never got to fulfill during my tour with James and his team.

* * * * *

For the second time in two weeks we played an outstanding game against Cornell, only this time they didn't respond in kind and we won in a rout, 71-40. Turnabout is fair play and we got a measure of revenge for having lost in overtime in Ithaca even though we had executed our game plan at all times, and had shot a torrid 52.7 percent. We had deserved to win and hadn't. This time out, instead of shooting 45.8 percent, Cornell shot a dismal 22.6 percent, hitting only fourteen of sixty-two shots attempted. Our defense caused that. We did the things James had inculcated for five months: we had our hands up, we communicated, shouting out switches, and we "walled up," clustering together and moving laterally as tight as a chorus line to get a "seal" on all the gaps and force Cornell to beat us long-range with low percentage shots.

Cornell's flaccid performance was more than second-night-in-the-Ivies syndrome. We were clearly the better team and against the team that had put the thorn in our season we hit back hard. When a team you coach plays like this, a feeling suffuses you. I saw it in James and in the Three Wise Men and I felt it myself. This feeling is an ecstasy that far exceeds mere satisfaction and is more than the fleeting joy of victory. It's a deep sense of gratification for sweat equity endured to achieve a collective goal and it has a kind of mystical glow that lingers for days.

For Yale it couldn't have happened on a better night than on Senior Night. Before the game, the four seniors accompanied their parents onto the floor to have their picture taken at center court flanked by their parents and Coach Jones while the large crowd applauded. It was especially impressive to see Brain Katz feted with his mom and dad even though his season had been tragically curtailed. All season he and Rhett Anderson had been great senior leaders, as had Greg Mangano and Reggie Willhite. Seeing them recognized for their four years of participation and accomplishment was gratifying. An especially classy touch occurred when Reggie's parents were unexpectedly detained in California and couldn't attend. James walked from center court to the sideline and led Reggie out flanked by Matt, Jamie, and Justin.

The game itself was anticlimactic from a spectator's point of view, which is often very different from a coach's. While it was gratifying for a coach to watch all the teaching and drilling and practicing for nearly half a year pay dividends in coordinated play and symphonic execution, for a fan the game was over quickly. With about seven minutes left in the first half we exploded for a 16-2 run from an 18-18 tie to make it 34-20 before Cornell called a time-out with 1:37 left. At halftime we led 37-24. On offense we were doing it all with rapid ball movement and balanced scoring.

Greg Mangano had a hot shooting hand for the third straight game and Jesse Pritchard settled into his starter's role and scored ten first-half points. Reggie thrilled me when he snuffed Johnathan Gray. I didn't want Gray going off again; I didn't want him to gain his confidence. Neither did James because he had Reggie on him early, risking foul trouble. The previous night against Columbia, James had put Reggie on Brain Barbour, but not until late in the game, at the crucial juncture. This was a pattern James usually followed so that Reggie wouldn't get in immediate foul trouble as he had against Quinnipiac and Seton Hall. Our scoring in the first half was so balanced that, to go along with Jesse's ten points, Austin had nine and Greg eight.

In the second half we just kept it up. With about seven minutes left, Jesse Pritchard hit a three from the top of the key to put us up 53-31. When Greg dropped in a short low-post jumper half a minute later, our lead jumped to 55-31 and the game was clearly over. As he had in Florida when the game got out of reach for the wrong reason, with this game out of reach for the right reason, James inserted guys who didn't usually get much playing time. Freshman Armani Cotton executed a picturesque reverse lay-up off a classic feed from fellow freshman Will Childs-Klein, the reserve center. Sophomore Will Bartlett banked in a three from the right wing. To cap things off, as time ran out, sophomore Greg Kelley nailed a three at the top of the key. All four of these underclassmen will play much bigger roles in the future, especially Armani Cotton and Greg Kelley, who had a serious injury as a freshman and was still working his polished offensive game back to a high sheen.

The entire game I had watched rapt as Jamie Snyder-Fair's scout came vividly alive. In our afternoon skull session in the locker room and then out on the floor in JLA, Jamie had walked the guys through exactly what he wanted them to do, both on offense and defense. They had done it, with James and Matt chipping in on how to handle Cornell's brilliant side-screens and their shifty crack-back screen, a kind of quick double-reverse screen. Our team had followed instructions and executed all of the game preparation to a T, just as it had the previous night against Columbia.

For the whole second half Austin covered Cornell's star playmaker, Chris Wroblewski, super close, holding him scoreless after he had knocked in ten points in the first half. When Austin shuffled laterally and backward he was so quick he reminded me of a dragonfly skimming the surface of a lake: he was that fast, light on his feet, and shifty. He simply locked Wroblewski down, choking off all scoring possibilities for him. This was as exciting to watch as a two-minute segment had been back in the Princeton game where we had covered them to the point of total frustration. As a result, Princeton forfeited the ball to the expired shot clock on two consecutive possessions. Whenever that happened without the offensive team being able to get a shot off I always wished the crowd would burst into a standing ovation. It's one of the great feats a team on defense can pull off, like a sustained and awe-inspiring riff in jazz.

* * * * *

That afternoon in JLA after the team shoot-around, for the second day in a row I had watched from the stands as Austin dragged out a contraption whose function is similar to a pitching gun in baseball. In fact it too is called "the Gun." Roughly the size and shape of a jukebox, it has a large net funnel on the top, about eight feet high and four feet wide, to retrieve the basketball from outside shots and cycle it back to a shooter out on the perimeter practicing long shots. The ball, whether a made shot or a rebound of a miss, drifts down from the mesh funnel into the jukebox from where it is propelled out to the shooter. Austin would wheel the machine around the perimeter, starting in one corner and working to the opposite corner. I liked to watch him do this. His dedication reminded me of learning to dribble under my father's practice conditions back in our basement in North Philly. It reminded me how diligently you needed to practice any skill you wanted to be good at. For me that was especially true of writing. If you wanted good sentences and got only gobbledygook, you had to suck it up and shoot the sentences again.

But this final Saturday of the season in JLA I had an impulse. I had left the stands for the second straight afternoon to fetch wayward balls, the missed shots that rebounded out of reach of the Gun's mesh funnel. I would then pass them back out to Austin on the perimeter, and he would reshoot them. As he was about to leave, I said, "Austin, do you think it's all right for me to try to hit a shot in the most beautiful gym in the world."

Being Austin and totally noble, he said, "Why not?" Fearing my frozen and arthritic shoulders might embarrass me farther out, I stepped to the foul line and, to my shame, took four attempts to hit a free throw. But on try number four I did get nothing but net. It took nerve to do this in front of Austin, who was ranked in the top ten nationally in free throw shooting accuracy. When I was a ball boy in the Palestra, as we gathered the last remaining balls before putting them back in the rack for the game to start or, after halftime, to resume, I always hit a shot for luck. This was an extension of a practice I honored for the whole time I played basketball, even for pick-up games and solitary shooting sessions. I would never leave a court until I had hit my last shot, superstitious as ever. James shared this tick: at every practice he made his players hit a final foul shot before leaving the gym. Puffed up, I had now made a basket in the two most gorgeous gyms in the world, JLA and the Palestra. The child really is the father of the man.

After we beat Cornell later that night, I was puffed up again and had two more to go: first when news arrived that Penn had upset Harvard in Cambridge, Zack Rosen hitting the deciding shot; and, second, when I booted up Tim Bennett's website account of our game and learned that James had got his one hundredth win in the Ivy League tonight, only the fifth coach in history to do that. I remembered telling him at one of our lunches that I always wanted what was monetarily best for him and his family but I hoped he would stay and become for Yale basketball the equivalent of football's great Carm Cozza. With a hundred wins he was on his way.

And at 9-3 we were again only one game off front-running Harvard's 10-2 pace. As usual in the Ivy League nothing would be settled until the very end, Penn lurking half a game back of Harvard in the win column and Princeton hovering in mathematical contention two games behind the leader. The important thing was that we were still in the hunt and you couldn't blame a guy for hoping and believing. The amusement park ride of a lifetime was not yet over.

CHAPTER SIXTEEN

Downtime

From the outside Princeton's Jadwin Gymnasium presents itself best. The scalloped roof articulates a futuristic statement as bold and glorious as the Sydney Opera House. Inside is another story. The vast and vaulting interior looks like the set, housed on a cavernous sound stage, for a Spielberg-Lucas futuristic space odyssey that might have been titled *Multipurpose Encounters of the Worst Kind*. Watching a basketball game there is akin to sitting on the set of a *Star Trek* extravaganza or enduring a Ridley Scott space opera featuring dizzying special effects designed to permanently damage your inner ear and destroy forever your sense of balance, so that you'll reel in total disorientation through the remainder of your life, untethered in zero gravity. Watching a basketball game, especially from the poured concrete cantilevered balcony asymmetrically installed on only one side, feels like you're viewing the game from the Mirsky space station. The far reaches of the interior beyond the basketball court are large enough to accommodate spring baseball practice and its long fungoes. The interior has all the intimacy of a rocket storage facility at Cape Canaveral.

This is a tragic state of affairs because no aficionado thinking clearly could forego Princeton basketball. Only the legend stenciled boldly on the hardwood floor salvages Jadwin: "CARRIL COURT." To watch a Pete

Carril-coached Princeton basketball team was to bear witness to one of life's finest performances.

* * * * *

On the Friday morning of the Princeton rematch I took the train down from New York early to catch our noon shoot-around. Jadwin empty quintuples its horrors. Emptiness accentuates its undifferentiated spacelessness, its seemingly infinite vacuity. Watching the guys work out, I asked Matt Kingsley if he'd ever played here and how in the world a shooter did not suffer disorientation in this atmosphere as vast and cold as outer space, with no proper background in sight. After all, even outer space had the benefit of a black background. Jadwin merely had a half-shell recessed ceiling quilted with ironwork trusses in a misguided homage to Buckminster Fuller's geodesic dome. What's more, seen from behind in the parking lots, Jadwin resembled the world's largest highway salt storage igloo, with decorative flanges jutting up from the descending roof. In answer, Matt said he'd tried shooting here and it was awful.

The feeling at our shoot-around, though, was good. Having played exceptional basketball two games in a row and having won nine of twelve league games, we were a team to reckon with, especially discounting the freakish upset at Cornell. We were here for the reprise of the dreaded Penn/Princeton weekend but we had beaten both teams a month ago; of course, both would now be on their home floors, and pumped up as well for payback. But the way we had started to play lately things looked rosy if we executed our game plans.

With Princeton we had to contain their outstanding forward Ian Hummer and their deadly outside shooting wizard Douglas Davis, among the best guards in the league. The rest of the Princeton team did not lack for balanced scoring either, and the legacy of the Princeton offense, always so inventive and proficient, hung over the head of any Princeton opponent like a headman's ax. Fail to defend against the Princeton Offense correctly and it would mince you. You had to stay tight on each player and avoid breakaway pick-and-rolls off deft and lightning-quick screens, and you had to guard against quick-strike backdoor cuts for easy lay-ups. Then there was the outside shooting prowess of Davis, now compounded by a classy freshman named T.J. Bray with a stinging shot from way outside. With a nifty jumper, Hummer, too, was murder not just in the paint but up to fifteen feet out. Tonight in Jadwin we would have our hands full.

* * * * *

We quickly scored the game's first four points but Princeton went on a tear and we were down 23-8 with nine minutes left. All week we had practiced with vigor and spirit; we had been sharp. In the morning shoot-around we had recapped all the Princeton sets and walked through our own opening sets—and still we came out flat. My stomach fell. Then we caught fire and pulled back to within four points, 32-28, with a little over a minute left. But Princeton tallied a quick five points when T.J. Bray drove for a lay-up and followed it, after Greg Mangano got tied up on the baseline and lost the ball, with a closing three-pointer that put us down nine at halftime.

Yet all year we had been a good second-half team that staged many comebacks, including the colossal recovery against Columbia. So we were very much in this game and James's remarks at halftime confirmed this. He told Greg to "get the ball out from the post and sprint back when the foul is not called." Greg had a tendency to fall into moot outrage when a foul was not called against his defender; as a result he often lost concentration and momentum getting back down court to defend the paint, at which he was the best in the league, with his tremendous blocking ability. His pointless protests to the refs often cost him focus and us points surrendered.

After James concluded his remarks, Matt snapped out directives to dominate the rebounds. We had only one on offense despite being "the biggest team in the league." He said not to give Princeton so much space, not to let them penetrate and cut on us, and not to let them "dribble around us." All of these offensive attributes were signature components of the Princeton Offense.

Jamie spoke after Matt and emphatically told the guys to "wipe the long faces off. We've got twenty minutes. They're doing whatever they want. Hit somebody." After a pause he added, "We have to score off multiple reverses. We have to finish the play." Again, on offense, Jamie wanted ball movement, "reverses," not a forced shot from the well-defended, strong-side low post. He wanted the low post rotated instead to the opposite side, the weak side, of the court. When we failed to do this we bogged down and became one-dimensional and easy to defend. This tendency had plagued us all year. Too often Greg and Reggie jumped the gun, shucked the Flex options, and forced shots, ignoring the men open on the weak side, to whom we should have snappily reversed the ball and reloaded the Flex. When we made this mistake, we were like a boxer telegraphing his blows and therefore easy to foil. Ignoring the weak side we were like a sculler using only one oar and going in pointless circles. Watching it, my teeth ached and my jaw clenched. As coaches were we lax? Were we at fault for a lack of discipline?

With halftime nearly over, James added quickly: "They got twenty-two points in the paint and we got eight." He paused and frowned, hands on hips, giving that sweeping killer-eyed stare of his: "Start again with plays, like at the beginning of the game." He nodded and called for the team pyramid and the hands-raised cheer.

* * * * *

After eight minutes, we tied the game at 40 off a Greg Mangano drive and lay-up. Then Princeton cranked it up and jumped out to a 49-40 lead and maintained their nine-point edge at 51-42 with 7:35 left. After we each tallied two points, the lead remained nine with seven minutes to go at 53-44. We were battling, but Princeton seemed determined to hold serve. After Reggie drove and deposited a lay-up and then fed Greg on the right wing for a clean three, James took a time-out with 5:04 left and us down four. With time back in, Austin drove for a lay-up and we were down only two, 53-51. Princeton forward Mack Darrow then hit a foul shot. In response Reggie drove the lane, spun balletically, and hit a reverse jumper to make it Princeton 54, Yale 53.

How Reggie managed this smacks of the miraculous because Jesse Pritchard, another great defender, had collided with him while attempting to hedge a perimeter screen moments earlier. Reggie had winced in pain and gone tentative on his right leg, stepping awkwardly and putting weight on it gingerly. This was not good for the fastest and best defender in the league. From then on, with Reggie partially hobbled, Princeton tallied ten points to our four, all scored by Greg, two on a lay-up and two on foul shots. At the very end Douglas Davis nailed a pair of crucial free throws and Hummer punctuated the final score with a rim-rattling dunk, so Princeton prevailed 64-57.

Again we had played well, except for the early lapse, but Princeton, a young team jelling rapidly, had come together to dominate us at crunch time. Not to make excuses, because Princeton probably would have won anyway, but once Reggie suffered in the collision with Jesse—the equivalent of a casualty from friendly fire—any hope we had for yet another "Reggie to the Rescue" ending disappeared.

Before that, with four steals and fourteen rebounds, Reggie had set the school record for steals in a single season at sixty-three and had reached a career-high in rebounds for a single game. Austin had thirteen points, Jerry, like Reggie, had ten, and Greg had twenty points and fourteen rebounds, so we had balanced scoring. But statistics don't always tell the story. Though Reggie had five assists, Greg, as was all too often the case, had none. Because of retention of the ball in the low post, and because of aborted options on the Flex in favor of hasty or forced shots, our offense had been lopsided and star-heavy, and, being one-dimensional and predictable, easy to defend.

Moments after the game we learned that Columbia had taken Harvard into overtime at Levien only to falter at the end, as they had two weeks earlier in overtime at Penn. Columbia was luckless. Like Cornell, they were far more dangerous than their record indicated. Before they upset us in February, back in January Cornell had upset Princeton in Ithaca. This was a nasty-hard league to dominate.

The Harvard win eliminated any chance we had to win or share the title. Same for Princeton. Only Penn had a mathematical chance to tie Harvard. To do this they had to beat us the next night and, three nights later, beat Princeton.

* * * * *

Earlier that evening, before the game, my good buddy Gene Mydlowski and I had an early dinner. Gene lived one town over from Princeton in Hamilton. For years we had worked together in publishing. He loved basketball and had played small forward in high school for Notre Dame in nearby Trenton, his hometown. He had Knicks season tickets and we often took in a game at Madison Square Garden, though I preferred college basketball to the pros. This had always been the case but became more pronounced since commissioner David Stern had forsaken the rules of the game to enshrine Michael Jordan, who didn't need the help and unintentionally corrupted the pro game even more than it had been in the drug-ridden seventies. By suspending calls on Jordan for walking, for discontinuation of his dribble, for palming the ball, and for sliding his pivot foot, Stern reaped an international marketing bonanza, as did Jordan. But in the process the pro game deteriorated into an agonizing travesty showcasing rank sensationalism, degenerating to nothing but hideous and unbridled entertainment lacking the rigor of a real sport.

I was staying overnight with Gene and his wife Cathy and daughter Elizabeth. After the game, over a late-night snack of pizza in his kitchen, Gene spoke incontrovertible truth when he said our post play was too slow and retentive. Pregame I had mentioned not a word about it. I said, "I know," and left it at that. But when I went up to bed I thought back to my first lunch with James and telling him I thought Yale could surprise people and win the Ivy title. That possibility was now never going to happen. We had never achieved the requisite cohesion and the essential unselfish teamwork required.

Earlier in the afternoon I had visited old Dillon Gym. I wanted to see where Bill Bradley had played, where he had electrified college basketball and intrigued the oh-so-talented John McPhee to heed his father's heads-up and come down to his alma mater to check out a freshman sensation named Bill Bradley. Out of that excursion McPhee eventually got his basketball classic, *A Sense of Where You Are,* one of the premier sports profiles of all time.

Having absorbed Dillon's serene ambiance and stony simplicity, I browsed the bookstores along Nassau Street. There is no prettier college town on the planet than Princeton other than peerless Cambridge University, in a class by itself amid its sustained English Gothic perfection, especially as viewed while punting on the river Cam, but Princeton has a marvelous aura of its own. There are few better places for a quick breather, a restorative prayer, and an invigorating shot of spirituality than the Princeton chapel with its vaulting arches and its glorious stained-glass windows. Schools that started as seminaries have an enduring aura, like Harvard, Yale, and Princeton.

Restless now that we were out of the Ivy League race, I read a book I'd bought that afternoon in one of the stores lining Nassau Street. Based on a real murder at Columbia University in the fifties, it was the collaborative work by William Burroughs and Jack Kerouac, the noir crime novel titled *And the Hippos Were Boiled in Their Tanks.* Maybe you can figure out why not, but it seemed relevant to me. The net of the net is it eventually tired me to the point of sleep.

* * * * *

When I got to the Palestra the usual overload of emotions hit me. For many people the Parthenon is the most beautiful building in the world, but for me it's the Palestra. A classics professor at Penn gave the arena its evocative name when it opened in 1927. In Greek the word denotes an area in the forecourt of the gym where the athletes would perform. Every time I came here I remembered writing an essay in eighth grade in Sister Eileen Loretta's class at St. Francis Xavier's grade school on the Parkway, within walking distance across the river and through a sliver of Fairmount Park. This was in the winter of 1960–1961 when Jack Ramsay's St. Joe's Hawks made their NCAA tournament run and finished third after losing to Ohio State in the semifinals. So enchanted had I been with the Palestra and the raucous Big Five and Ivy League games I saw there that winter that I wrote a short essay about it, the opening line of which drew this remark from Sister Eileen Loretta: "You're a good writer, Mr. Breslin." On such tiny hinges does the huge door of fate swing.

The Immaculate Heart of Mary sisters called us by our last names in class, preceded by "mister" or "miss." Manners were emphasized daily and their tone and tenor was Victorian. You didn't call anyone by their first name until they told you to. Telemarketers drive me wild to this day when they address me by my first name, a sort of MBA smarminess fostered by the Californian habit of too-quick familiarity and over-determined informality, both loathsome to me.

Sister Eileen Loretta was so taken with the opening sentence of my schoolboy essay that she sent me to the Mother Superior's office to read it to her. She in turn liked it so much she sent me around all three floors of classrooms to read it to every student, all of whom were bored cross-eyed listening to it. More mortified than proud, I was glad when this ordeal ended. But as for mortification and writing it did set a precedent it's healthy for every writer to experience, the earlier the better, for you have to have a tough hide to survive at writing.

The opening sentence of that essay contained a description of the gleaming hardwood court with the prophetic center jump circle bearing the interlocked letters "UP," standing for the University of Pennsylvania but doubling as a witty pun on what was to be done there: the center jump that started the game and, back in those days, started the second half as well. In those interlocked letters, form and function were in perfect harmony and I had glommed onto it, at age thirteen. I had also glommed onto the thrill of writing, of putting words to your thoughts and feelings and form and sub-stance to your experience.

Four years later in Roman Catholic High School when I read Joyce and Hemingway in Mr. Winiarski's senior class in literature my fate was sealed. In

Latin class back then I learned the Roman phrase for "the itch to write" but I've forgotten it, though the itch has never left me. Introducing me to these two writers Mr. Winiarski had done me a great service. Like every teacher at Roman he had a nickname, in his case "Winnie the Pooh." For that matter even the priests had nicknames—the Rector, Father James T. Dolan, for the habit of keeping a toothpick permanently lodged in the side of his mouth, was known as "Spike." Father Walsh, the administrator who kept attendance, was known as "Knobby," for the comic strip character, and the disciplinarian, Father Maloney, was christened "Iron Mike." The "oldest free Catholic High School in America," Roman was a hoot.

The Palestra was not. It was serious, a sacred place, the epicenter of Philly basketball, a shrine to roundball and to Philly's obsession with the game, which takes a backseat to no place, not even to Indiana or Kentucky or to Tobacco Road. Not for nothing is Philly known in basketball circles as the "cradle of coaches." In my mind's eye I can see all the Big Five coaches that fateful winter of 1960–61: Harry Litwack at Temple, Jack Ramsay at St. Joe's, Al Severance at Villanova, Donald "Dudey" Moore at La Salle, and Jack McCloskey at Penn. Each could coach like a demon conjurer, especially Ramsay. The good feeling of being in the Palestra as a boy, often as a Big Brothers' ball boy, is unmatched for me except for the rush I feel in the Grand Concourse in Grand Central Terminal or in Matisse's Rosary Chapel in Vence, the beautiful town perched above the French Riviera.

Bottom line: being back in the Palestra anticipating an oversized soft pretzel and a cup of Bassett's vanilla ice cream reinforces for me what Freud called the feeling of oceanic well-being. The world may be all wrong but being back in the Palestra is all right. Especially under the delusion you are a college basketball coach, my best nonsexual fantasy ever.

* * * * *

When I came down the ramp to the court an hour before the game, Greg Mangano sprawled on the floor doing his stretching exercises with enormous elastic bands he slung under his sneakers and stretched by pushing each leg in turn to full extension against the bands' severe resistance. Before every game and before every practice he did this. I walked over and told him to have a great game and get our twentieth win. For James, I badly wanted us to win twenty games for only the sixth time in school history. James already owned one of those times with his co-champions of 2001–2002. It would be nice to see him get another.

When I settled into my seat behind the Yale bench at the opposite end of the floor, Mike Grace come out of our locker room hobbling on a pair of crutches. Trying to come back too soon the night before against Princeton, he had done in his injured ankle. Our point guard was out of commission for good. The way Jesse Pritchard had come on in the four games since replacing Mike in the starting lineup had been exciting to watch. Against Cornell he had achieved a career high with thirteen points to go along with two steals, three rebounds, and a nifty assist. But the truth was that Jesse in the lineup at shooting guard moved Austin out of his natural position and forced him to man the point, not Austin's forte.

When I went into our locker room to hear James's final remarks I was struck by how small the room was and how old. What did I expect? The gym had opened in 1927. I listened to James's final remarks but my mind wandered thinking of all the great players who might have used this locker room before playing in the Palestra: Don Nelson of Iowa; Nate Thurmond of Bowling Green; Jerry West and Rod Thorn of West Virginia; Bill Bradley, Jeff Petrie and Brian Taylor of Princeton; Cotton Nash of Kentucky; Tom Gola, Billy Raftery, Kenny Durrett and Joe "Jellybean" Bryant of La Salle; Paul Arizin, Hubie White, Wali Jones, Billy Melchionni and Howard Porter of Villanova; Hal Lear, Guy Rodgers, Bill "Pickles" Kennedy, Bruce Drysdale and John Baum of Temple; Ernie Beck, Corky Calhoun and Ron Haigler of Penn, Matt Goukas, Sr. and Jr., Jimmy Lynam, Cliff Anderson and Mike Bantam of St. Joseph's; on and on.

Even the incomparable Big O, Oscar Robertson, had come to the Palestra to beat Harry Litwack and Temple and set a scoring record for a visitor that stood for decades. In high school Wilt Chamberlain had played here, as had Earl Monroe and Joe Bryant's son, Kobe, whose only schoolboy loss was to my high school, Roman Catholic. Kansas had even scheduled a game here as a gift to Wilt when he played for them. For me this was the most evocative building in the world. Like Wisconsin's great coach Bo Ryan, my same age, I could not extol my boyhood experience of the Palestra enough, nor could I get enough of watching Ryan's teams play: their aggressive defense and lightning-fast passing on offense were pure Philly basketball, the teamwork total and beautiful to watch.

Despite this reverie, I heard James but knew already what he would say: "Don't give Rosen space off screens," "Remember they use a lot of handoffs instead of screens," "Watch for the switching four's and five's in the lane," meaning their post men moving across and around the paint to position themselves to get the ball for easy lay-ups. On offense James added: "Make sure you get the ball out and reverse it," "Dribble the ball to the wing, Austin, don't reverse it in the seam," where Penn would collapse on him in traps if he partially penetrated their defensive shell, and finally: "Be ready to go when the ball goes up. They always come out to fight us. We have to play right from the start. We can't come back like last night playing from behind. Now let's go."

* * * * *

It was Senior Night and Penn was pumped. Senior Night can be brutal on the visitors. The home team's seniors are desperate to go out winners and their teammates desperately want to send them out as winners. Plus, Rosen had been a four-year starter, and Tyler Bernardini and Rob Belcore, throughout their careers, whether starting or coming off the bench, had been major contributors to heaps of Penn victories. The home crowd cheered wildly for these three senior stars as they were introduced along with a fourth senior, reserve center Mike Howlett. After the celebratory photos at center court with the seniors surrounded by their parents, Jerome Allen, in a classy move, started all four along with sophomore Miles Cartwright, the sharpshooting two-guard who complemented Rosen so well at the point.

Penn had won seven straight games and eight of the last nine since losing to Harvard at the Palestra the fateful night Cornell upended us in Ithaca. Their challenging nonconference schedule had toughened them. They had won twelve of their last fourteen games, having lost only to us in JLA the week before they lost to Harvard here. Their defense had become ferocious, holding opponents to low shooting percentages and offensive totals way below their averages, usually under sixty points, sometimes even under fifty. Allen had them swarming, trapping, pressing, switching, and taking risks that led to steal after steal. They were defending like banshees on steroids.

Despite their defense we started well and were dead even at 10 apiece at the 13:50 mark when Reggie hit two foul shots. Even though Reggie swished these free throws, I had been uncomfortable watching trainer Dave DiNapoli minister to him two minutes earlier at the first media time-out. The collision the previous night in Jadwin had resulted in a painful hip pointer.

He was not moving with his usual lateral quickness and his overall athleticism. With one starter out and another impaired, we were at a disadvantage.

As if to prove this, Penn exploded for a 16-8 run to make the score 26-18 at the last media time-out with four minutes to go. By halftime they still led by eight at 30-22. They had balanced scoring: Rosen had ten points and three others had four apiece to go with Belcore's five and reserve guard Steve Rennard's three-pointer off the bench. Worse, Rosen was firmly in control. Yet we were only down eight and still in the game—provided Reggie could continue at an effective level of play.

* * * * *

At the start of the second half Jesse missed a three from the left corner and, less than a minute later, Reggie uncharacteristically threw a post feed into Jeremiah Kreisberg that went out of bounds. Belcore then hit on a driving lay-up. Miles Cartwright stole the ball from Austin and fed a pass on the right wing to Tyler Bernardini, who hit a three for his first points of the game. Then Penn went off with balanced and torrid scoring, piling up fifteen unanswered points except for a short jumper by Jeremiah Kreisberg. Suddenly the score was 50-24 at the second media time-out with a little over eight minutes gone in the half.

Penn had pulled off a 19-2 run and the game was effectively over. In the sideline huddle James was livid and scorched the guys, singling out Mangano for not getting the ball reversed out of the defended low post. Just as Princeton had done twenty-four hours earlier, Penn was collapsing on Greg on the low blocks and along the baseline. Like a batter in baseball stepping in the bucket on his swing, rendering it ineffective, Greg was again retaining the ball while struggling to get off forced shots. Seemingly unable to restrain himself from this form of panic, he hurt the team, even if his intentions were good, maybe even heroic. His determination was misplaced and counterproductive and it short-circuited our offense better than any opponent's defense, and had all season. It was a lose-lose proposition and—my worst nightmare—Penn was embarrassing us in the Palestra.

Making matters worse, Reggie had to be pulled from the game with 14:16 left to be worked on by trainer Dave. Obviously in pain, Reggie was favoring his right leg and wincing every time he made a quick move. This boded ill for us. Four minutes later he went back in the game but, gallant though his struggle was, Reggie simply couldn't make it on one good leg and had to be taken out again three minutes later with us down 52-28, a huge and insuperable deficit with only seven minutes left. Penn had simply gone off, their second-half run now standing at 22-6. It only got worse and James cleared the bench and let the younger guys get a taste of basketball in the Palestra. They acquitted themselves well: Greg Kelley scored a quick seven points in five minutes of play and Armani Cotton and Javier Duren scored three points each while Will Childs-Klein notched two and Will Bartlett added a singleton. When the horn sounded I was relieved. Injuries to two starters had undone us and Greg Mangano's attempts to take up the slack had been disastrous.

Stunned, I didn't hurry to the locker room in time to enter. Flooded with memories, I sat and listened to the Penn fans sing the school anthem, "The Red and Blue," while thrusting out their right arms. It was just as well that our locker room door was bolted by the time I got there. There was nothing to say, nothing I needed to hear: the guys deserved their privacy after our bitter ending to the regular season.

Instead, I hurried over to the press conference and caught Jerome Allen and Zack Rosen discussing the game while being pelted by the Philly press with queries about Tuesday's upcoming showdown in Jadwin with archrival Princeton, beaten easily by Penn in their first match. That night Princeton had been rusty coming off the sixteen-day mid-term break. Sitting in the postgame interview room, I wanted to tell Penn that the Princeton team I'd seen in Jadwin the night before was not the same young and inexperienced team they had handled easily back at the end of January. Sitting there I also resolved to get down to Princeton and see Tuesday's game. When the press conference ended I went back to our locker room and found James sprawled on the portable stands near it, working his cell phone, crestfallen. I stood there a few minutes, then nodded to him and meandered upstairs to roam the corridors.

I was dawdling, of course, but I always dawdle when faced with the prospect of leaving the Palestra. I lingered at the panels of vintage photos on the tiled walls, circling the corridors before exiting through the big French doors. Outside I walked along the construction site where the tennis courts used to stand and spotted Mike Grace hobbling along ahead of me on his crutches. I caught up to him and asked if he needed help. Tough and independent as ever, Mike said no. But I walked along beside him, happy for the chance to talk, and as we reached Thirty-third Street, where the team's bus was parked, I asked him to thank all the guys for playing so hard all year and to remind them that they had won nineteen games against top-flight competition. Mike grinned and said he would, but he was so quiet, unassuming, and shy that I wasn't sure he would. Maybe I was too corny anyway. I wanted to climb on the bus and tell the guys myself but I feared, as always, that it might be overstepping the bounds James had asked me always to be aware of.

So I strolled diagonally across the Drexel campus, thinking as I always did when revisiting it how lucky I had been in the teachers I had there, tolling off their names in my head: Ray Lorantas, Flora Binder Jones, Ralph C. Most, Thomas Brown, Paul Crews, Christian Lievestro, Joanne Troutman, William Hollis, and the incomparable twosome of Joel Balsham and Marty Kellman. Teachers really do make a big difference in life, and I had been privileged to witness four excellent teachers in action for five months now: James Jones, Matt Kingsley, Jamie Snyder-Fair, and Justin Simon. I hoped the players had learned from them half as much as I had.

* * * * *

In the station I was early for the train and bought coffee and, foolishly in light of my Type 2 diabetes, a chocolate croissant. Completely let down, in fact stunned and shocked, I needed comfort food. I had great memories of my father and my Uncle Bill driving my wife Lynn and me to this station many times after family visits, especially at the holidays, to return to New York. Returning alone and downcast now, I couldn't believe that our season was over. It was all quiet in my head, even my interior monologue stunned into silence.

On practice agenda #92, which I had with me in my briefcase, I read the "Word of the Day" James had included: "Disappointed—Unhappy because something was not as good as expected." A great teacher right to the end, he had warned the guys to avoid this condition, this down feeling, and we hadn't. So we had to learn to endure it. At the bottom of the page in bold type the agenda read: PRINCETON #20.

Princeton had turned out not to be win number twenty and neither had Penn. Yet, for only the eighth time in school history, Yale had won nineteen games. To that boring old saw whether your glass was half empty or half full James always ebulliently answered that his was always overflowing. I liked and admired him for that. Fighting off my tendency to depression, I often flippantly answered the same question with the sour quip that my glass was broken and wouldn't hold anything. If nothing else, James had taught me how empty my answer was.

"But we are a society today that is, like sport, entirely too hung up on numbers, figures, rankings, and statistics, so in this corporately technological world we do not so easily appreciate the odd, singular achievement anymore. Subtlety cannot be quantified, so what may be glorious can get lost nowadays if it can't be measured."

Frank Deford
"Over Time: My Life as a Sportswriter"

"By archery in the traditional sense, which he esteems as an art and honors as a national heritage, the Japanese does not understand a sport but, strange as this may sound at first, a religious ritual. And, consequently, by the art of archery he does not mean the ability of the sportsman, which can be controlled, more or less, by bodily exercises, but an ability whose origin is to be sought in spiritual exercises and whose aim consists in hitting a spiritual goal, so that fundamentally the marksman aims at himself, and may even succeed in hitting himself."

Eugen Herrigel
Zen in the Art of Archery

Epilogue: The Postseason

WE GOT ANOTHER chance to win twenty games. Twenty wins is a benchmark in college basketball, a great achievement, the equivalent of a major league pitcher winning twenty games in a single season or of a batter hitting .300 for an entire season. We received an invitation to compete in the post-season CollegeInsider.com Tournament and our first-round opponent would be near neighbor Fairfield. Having also played in the Connecticut Six Tournament at Mohegan Sun back in November, Fairfield was familiar to us. Fairfield's new head coach Sydney Johnson was familiar to us as well, having led co-champion Princeton into the NCAA Tournament the year before.

Back at Mohegan Sun I remembered watching Fairfield's win over Quinnipiac before we took the floor and beat Central Connecticut. Fairfield was a talented team that had come on strong over the latter part of the season and had just missed getting into the NCAA Tournament when they were edged out in the championship game of the MAAC Tournament. I feared them, and their star forward Rakim Sanders. The game was scheduled for Webster Bank Arena in Bridgeport on Wednesday, March 14, a week and a half after our disastrous weekend against Penn and Princeton. When I first got word that we were in the postseason I was elated but offered a quick prayer that we were not still too banged up and that Reggie especially was recovered from his hip pointer. I knew that hip pointers, like all deep bone bruises, could take forever to heal. Still, we were alive and kicking and in post-season play, always a good thing and a solid achievement, the best possible way to wind up a season.

Yet the day before the game I found myself reaching for the phone to call Bill Cloutier and get his take. He told me he thought Yale would win. Then he asked what I thought. I heard myself say, disappointing myself even as I said it, that I thought we'd lose because Fairfield had too many "superior athletes." I quickly added that we had a chance but only if we played together the way we had against Penn and Princeton the first time around. For me that had been the high point of our season, when we had played to our potential. We'd have to be at our peak again to beat Fairfield.

* * * * *

At halftime we led 39-26. I was delighted and berating myself for my lack of faith. My negativity was a lifelong problem fought off daily. Yet before I knew it my optimism surged and I was fantasizing a deep tournament run that would salvage our disappointing season. In the first half we shot a scorching 60 percent, canning fifteen of twenty-five shot attempts. We moved the ball on offense and on defense we sealed the shell, moving laterally with energy and desire. We looked to be peaking again, playing the intelligent ball we had been capable of only sporadically during the season.

Then the second half opened and Fairfield pressed us hard. Toward the end of the first half Sydney Johnson had tested his press briefly and turned us over three times. I had noted—but refused to be daunted—by this. That proved to be a mistake. Fairfield would turn us over eight times in the second half and reap fourteen points from it. The half started this way: Fairfield went on a 6-1 run, which expanded into a 13-1 run. Reggie hit a short baseline jumper to reduce the 13-1 run to a 13-3 run, but then the run mushroomed to 23-3. We had surrendered the lead midway in the half when Rakim Sanders hit a jumper from the top of the key to give Fairfield its first lead since the early minutes of the first half, 43-42. At the media time-out with six minutes left, Desmond Wade sank a foul shot and Jeremiah Kreisberg answered with a low-post, left-handed hook to make the score Fairfield 50, Yale 44. Fairfield had turned up the intensity of its defense in the second half to the point that Yale had tallied only five points in 13:37 minutes of play.

When play resumed, Rakim Sanders fouled Brandon Sherrod, who made both shots. More important, Sanders had four fouls on him. If he fouled out we might have a chance to stage a comeback. After Colin Nickerson made a lay-up, Greg Mangano pulled us within four at 52-48, but Fairfield rallied again to go up 61-50 with under two minutes to go. In the second half Fairfield had now outscored us 35-11. Austin Morgan hit two foul shots, then drove the length of the floor for a lay-up. Two Yale possessions later, Reggie followed with a driving lay-up to pull us within five at 61-56, but only because Fairfield had clanked seven straight free throws.

From there Fairfield knocked down five straight foul shots and Colin Nickerson, who had taken over the second half, stole the ball and drove in for a breakaway lay-up that made the final 68-56. The score for the second half read Fairfield 42, Yale 17. We had gone from shooting 60 percent in the first half to shooting under 17 percent in the second, hitting only five of thirty shots. Meanwhile Fairfield had gone in the opposite direction. Ironically, the win gave Fairfield number twenty for the season while we were frozen forever at nineteen.

* * * * *

After the game, I wanted to hear the interview with Sydney Johnson. He started by noting that all teams had a hard time at the end of the season because of "injuries and soreness." To a reporter's question about Yale he acknowledged that he had "some familiarity there," meaning he knew the players and the coaches from his Ivy League days, and their proclivities, tendencies, and preferences. Then he deflected most of the credit for his team's remarkable second-half turnaround to his coaches, singling out assistant head coach Tony Newsom. He mentioned the energy level his team had played with throughout the second half, remarking correctly that Fairfield had "outworked" Yale, and praising guard Colin Nickerson especially. Nickerson had butchered us on defense with five steals and on offense had scored a career-high twenty-two points, one more than Rakim Sanders, who will end up playing in the NBA or in one of the top European leagues.

Although Reggie had scored a gallant ten points to go with five rebounds, three assists, and two steals, he had been attended to heavily before the game by trainer Dave DiNapoli. Dave had rubbed his sore right hip with Thera-Gesic, a high-powered heat treatment ointment, a kind of super Ben-Gay, and had also injected the hip with Toradol, a non-steroidal, anti-inflammatory drug, a potent painkiller. Neither measure restored Reggie's full athleticism and his lateral movement was curtailed. He was unable to defend with his usual proficiency. The result was that Nickerson, four inches taller and rangier than Austin, had been able to have a spectacular game. Had a healthy Reggie been on him things might have been different. On offense Austin was again playing out of position at point guard, and that explained why we could not get the ball up court with any effectiveness in the second half against their swarming press. Though off crutches, our starting point guard Mike Grace was wearing a big blue orthopedic "boot" on his injured left ankle and foot.

As Greg Mangano remarked postgame: "It's a tough way to end. You always want to win your last game, but we won nineteen games and had the opportunity to play in the postseason. There is certainly nothing to be ashamed of." That was correct as well as eloquent. Yale had played in the postseason for only the fifth time in school history. Yet we did fall shy of winning twenty games, something Harvard, Penn, and Princeton, who all finished ahead of us in the Ivy League standings, managed to do. Penn and Princeton notched their twentieth wins in the postseason. Penn beat Quinnipiac at the Palestra in the opening round of the College Basketball Invitational Tournament while Princeton topped Evansville on the road. Each then lost in the CBI quarterfinal round, Penn to Butler, again at home, and Princeton to Pittsburgh, again on the road.

Earlier, on March 6, in the last Ivy League game of the season, I had watched Princeton pay back Penn for the drubbing they had endured at the end of January in the Palestra. Penn's loss meant Harvard won the Ivy championship outright and the automatic NCAA bid. In the first round they drew Vanderbilt, a team that four days earlier in the SEC Tournament had upended eventual national champion Kentucky. In a competitive game, Vanderbilt eliminated Harvard, which I hated to see. Despite losing, Harvard acquitted itself admirably. Their 26-5 record spoke volumes for Coach Amaker's program. It was unfortunate they drew such a strong opening round opponent. With a kinder draw they were capable, like Cornell two years before, of reaching the Sweet Sixteen. Drexel, my beloved alma mater, I'm happy to report, made the postseason too, only to fall two points short of appearing in a Madison Square Garden NIT semifinal when UMass topped us on our own floor.

After the season, I spoke to Cornell's convivial and talented Sports Information Director, Jeremy Hartigan, checking some facts. When Cornell upset us there on that snowy and inhospitable February night, he couldn't have been a better host. On the phone half a year later, in rehashing the season, he articulated a feeling I share: "After an Ivy League loss I never walk out of the gym feeling bad because you get the opportunity to meet the kids and know the future is in good hands." That's why I was happy for Harvard ending its sixty-six year drought in NCAA appearances and winning its first outright Ivy League championship since the league started formal play in 1956.

* * * * *

In Webster Bank Arena I hung around, unable to leave, wanting to say a thousand things to the Yale players about what a magical gift they had laid on me all season long. The assistant coaches too, the Three Wise Men. But most of all I wanted to see James, who already knew how grateful I was. I just wanted to lend him support. Earlier, when he had come out of the locker room into the corridor to answer media questions, his eyes had been slightly red and puffy. I had seen at Alumni Weekend how much he loved his players and how much they loved him. I knew it had been excruciating just now to say goodbye to his seniors after their final game.

As the Yale players filtered out, I managed to thank them and get their emails and phone numbers for any follow-up questions. Then James came out holding Quincy's hand. He and I nodded and shook our heads and then I said goodbye to Q. When Q kept walking out of the building without acknowledging me, James stopped dead still and said, "Did you not hear Ed talk to you? Look at someone when they talk to you and respond." Quincy turned back and did. That's James, I thought, teaching right to the end, straight through an aching heart.

Eventually I drifted back through the building, my head spinning and a bit spacey. When I got home, still stunned and disoriented that the whole shebang was over, I emailed Bill Cloutier, who had a conflict that night and couldn't be at Webster Bank Arena: "After the game I waited and said goodbye and thanks to all the Yale players and coaches and then told Fairfield Coach Johnson and his kids that I hope they go all the way. I walked along that enclosed tunnel with the white trusses toward the train station and stood still and watched as the Yale bus disappeared along the waterfront drive on its way back to Payne Whitney. It's too trite to say it but I'll say it anyway: not with a bang but a whimper."

* * * * *

Getting this whole enlightening experience behind me has proved harder than I thought. In fact I'm still working on it. Indeed, I may never get over it. For me that could be a very good thing. Yesterday I went up to New Haven and spent four hours in Lanman Recreation Center watching Yale Junior Basketball Camp, snapping pictures of James with Q and surrounded by other aspiring roundballers aged mostly six to ten, with a few stray eleven-, twelve-, thirteen- and fourteen-year-olds thrown in. Justin Simon, delegated by James as the man in charge, was getting a workout impersonating college basketball's answer to Captain Kangaroo. Matt Kingsley was there helping out while also keeping an eye on daughter Amelia and son Eli, with Amelia just emerging from the toddler stage and Eli steeped in it. The young attendees with injuries, real and imagined, many exaggerated, kept trainer Dave DiNapoli going to his ice chest to fill plastic bags and put ice wraps on twisted ankles and swollen fingers. I nearly injured myself laughing all day.

Two months earlier I had driven to New Haven on a rainy Saturday to witness seven hours of Yale Basketball Elite Bulldog Camp wrapped around lunch with James to discuss the upcoming year. The elite camp is for older high-school kids and their parents to look over the facilities at Yale while James and the Three Wise Men look over the players and evaluate them as potential Yale prospects. That camp had many other coaches helping out, like the wizard Larry Anderson, the man who led MIT (no less!) into the Division III playoffs last year and intends to do it again this season, aiming to walk off with the championship of that no-scholarships-allowed division.

Watching the prospects play was entertaining, and getting to meet their parents was a privilege. I met a set of parents who could not have been more exciting and fortuitous: published poet and college professor Todd Davis and his wife Shelly. Their son, an athletic forward named Noah, hopes to get an offer to attend Yale in the fall of 2013. A week later Todd and I exchanged books and his poetry was superb. Using charged language to deliver pithy and spiritual insights on life, love, death, grief, perseverance, endurance, art, and courage, the poems were as celebratory as Whitman, as plain as Williams, as sturdy as early Pound and as eloquently demotic and inspirational as late Yeats. I loved reading them. Todd and Shelly had both played college basketball and their two sons, Noah and Nate, had inherited their passion for the game as well as their skills. Todd also sent me a book he co-edited of essays on basketball written by poets.

It was fun to be back in the gym that day and to have lunch with James and discuss the upcoming season. I told him he would be surprised at how well his 2012–2013 team would do. As much as his two stars this past season had provided great senior leadership, they had also too often imbalanced the offense by going freelance and aborting ball movement. The Flex offense can't function that way. The ball must circulate until the opening appears. Too often this past season when the ball should have been whipped around to the weak side, where Jeremiah Kreisberg was usually open on the low blocks or at the elbow, or where Mike Grace or Jesse Pritchard was open on the perimeter, it was instead trapped on the strong-side low blocks or the baseline. There, too often senior stars Greg Mangano or Reggie Willhite went freelance, forcing a shot, or turning the ball over off a steal or an errant pass, or simply by being tied up by multiple defenders converging on them. The ball needed to be moved and recycled for the open shot. Reggie, the far less frequent offender, had 114 assists, a really handsome number, but Greg, usually the entry pass first option in the Flex, had a hundred fewer, or less than half an assist per game. The 2011–2012 Yale team, blessed with more potential, never achieved the cohesion and teamwork the previous year's team exhibited with Porter Braswell, a true point guard, at the helm.

This coming 2012–2013 season I believe Jeremiah Kreisberg will blossom into one of the best big man in the Ivy League. Javier Duren, if fully recovered from his concussion, will show himself to be a multitalented point guard capable of conducting a symphonic team effort. The peerless Austin Morgan will shine again as a standout shooting guard, and mighty Michael Grace will alternate with Javier at the point. Scrappy team captain Sam Martin will back up Austin at the two. Sophomore Brandon Sherrod will be an All-Ivy forward, second team. Jesse Pritchard will be a gifted swingman, at small forward or at shooting guard or even as the third guard in a three-guard offense. Matt Townsend and Greg Kelley will flourish at the four and three spots respectively, Matt spelling Brandon and Greg injecting instant offense at the three. Greg has a solid offensive game and is fully recovered from a devastating injury suffered two year ago as a freshman. He's ready to go. Armani Cotton, the "Baby Raptor," with his flighty quickness and enormous wingspan, will assert himself as a defender in the Reggie Willhite mold and as a swingman whose offensive talents will complement Jesse Pritchard's perfectly. Feisty Will Bartlett will contribute at small forward where his scoring ability and his fearless rebounding will make a difference. While waiting to fill out more, Will Childs-Klein will play instructive minutes as the backup center. Throughout the season I will mourn the loss of super-gifted guard Isaiah Salafia.

James and the Three Wise Men have snared three talented recruits, who may be able to help as freshmen. One, Jack Montague from Brentwood, Tennessee, is a nifty point guard, a good ballhandler and passer who can score as well. Justin Sears is a six-eight athletic forward from Plainfield, New Jersey, who scored more than a thousand points and grabbed more than a thousand rebounds in high school. At six-five Nick Victor, from Dallas, Texas, is a tall guard who can score, rebound, and dish for assists. Last year playing in the New England Prep School Athletic Conference he earned honorable mention. A fourth freshman, added late, is six-five walk-on Khaliq Bedart Ghani from Inglewood, California, another tall and quick guard with solid skills and considerable promise.

Yale will be in good shape and in good hands this coming season, and for many to come, I hope. The oh-so-articulate Jeremy Hartigan in our recent telephone conversation summed up my feelings on this score when he said of Yale basketball: "They'll have a breakthrough and win again. James is too good a coach."

* * * * *

Not being intimately involved with the upcoming Yale season I'll be lost. I wish I could move even closer and be part of the coaching staff. I wish I could have that much fun again and feel that alive and that far above the winter blues. This winter may be rough as I scramble around scrabbling for bucks, having exhausted my coffers by footing the nearly year-long bill to pursue my Walter Mitty coaching fantasy. But what I learned was worth it. Instead of wondering in agony if I've mis-lived my life by renouncing graduate school foolishly over four decades ago, I have resolved to set up somehow, some way, as a teacher of writing, provided I can get over my doubts about myself in that area, both as practitioner and as teacher. After all, I had not only the one crisis of nerves about my ability to write this book back on December 2 when I fled into the comfort of Trinity Church on the New Haven Green, but also in Gainesville before the Florida game when I found myself reading the Book of Job in the hotel Bible and taking massive comfort in knowing my problems were minor, and manageable, just like my doubts. Despite these doubts I am going to throw myself into the teaching of writing.

I have met a wonderful set of professors and administrators at CCNY who may well give me the chance to teach a writing course or two beginning in the fall of 2013. While I was up at Yale Junior Basketball Camp yesterday, in talking to Justin Simon he mentioned that Austin Morgan and Armani Cotton would be playing in the championship game of the Nike Pro City AAU Tournament that night at Baruch College's gym. I went straight down there on the subway from Grand Central Terminal and enjoyed a fabulous game. Gary Ervin, a former collegiate star currently playing in the Russian professional league, won it in overtime on a three-point shot.

As Gary's buzzer-beater dropped through the hoop, the backboard lit up. The shot propelled his Franchise team to victory over Austin's and Armani's Dyckman team. Significantly, when Dyckman found itself trailing in the closing minutes, their coach went to a full-court press. Armani made two pickpocket steals exactly in the Reggie Willhite mold. Only that afternoon in Lanman I had told Matt Kingsley that Armani is fully capable of doing this. Two months before, when I had lunch in the Educated Burgher with James, I had told him the same thing.

Baruch plays in the league for City University of New York teams. CCNY is in that same league, as are Hunter, York, Brooklyn and a handful of other colleges. Each has a banner hanging in the rafters in Baruch's gym. After a postgame chat with Austin, on my way home on the subway I made a decision. I would pursue my chance to teach at CCNY and I would make it a point to go to a CCNY game at their gym and introduce myself to the coach. I wanted to give something back. I didn't want to live the life anymore of a solitary writer, at least not exclusively.

In West Philly before the Penn game on March 3, I had browsed the Drexel bookstore, something I do every time I visit University City. I found a pocket calendar emblazoned with the Drexel Dragon on the cover. For recording my noisome glucose readings it was perfect. I bought it and discovered pithy, witty, and insightful quotes inside, one for each week. One quote struck me, by Albert Einstein: "Only a life lived for others is worth living."

How come James Jones knew that very thing all his life and I took sixty-four years to catch on? I don't know and it doesn't matter. Starting now I was going to strive to help others by teaching writing and if I got lucky maybe I'd get to do some real if marginal coaching of basketball as well. If nothing else I was going to look into one of these junior league things. Those kids at Lanman shooting at a lowered eight-foot basket had reminded me of myself at that age, heaving up my first awkward shots like boulders, patty-caking my first wayward dribbles. I wanted to be a part of something like that. Not just peripheral, but a participant. Maybe even a mentor. Basketball is eminently worthy of being taught. In what other game can you learn to meld the thrill of individual mastery with the ecstasy of collective excellence? In what other game does this divine secret to attaining human happiness reveal itself so well?

Anyway, fearing the wrath of six-nine, two-hundred-and-fifty-pound Jamie Snyder-Fair as I do, I'm happy to report that I never stepped on the Y.

ACKNOWLEDGMENTS

WITHOUT JOEL E. Smilow, Class of 1954 Yale Men's Head Basketball Coach James Jones this book would never have been written. So the debt of gratitude I need to acknowledge to him is impossible to express. It's why I think of him as my co-author and of assistant coaches Matt Kingsley, Jamie Snyder-Fair, and Justin Simon as my collaborators. The Yale players themselves were the greatest supporting cast imaginable. Thanks also to Yale Athletic Director Thomas Beckett for granting permission to write this book and to Associate Athletic Director Forrest Temple for aid and assistance with it. Associate Athletic Director Natalie Gonzales helped in varied and many ways, as did team trainer Dave DiNapoli, always cheerful and patient in answering my questions and raising my spirits. Will Manville, the team's student manager, was Johnny-on-the-Spot every time, with anything I needed. That holds true as well for student team statistician Zan Tanner, with his boxcar-serial-number IQ and his quick and unfailing impulse to save me from mistakes.

Yale Sports Information Director Tim Bennett contributed to the book so unstintingly, energetically, and magnificently that he too fits in the inexpressible category when it comes to my debt of gratitude. I cribbed from him shamelessly. Indeed, the Sports Information Directors of all the schools Yale played during the 2011–2012 season were universally helpful and kind, and I send them a big salute. The seven other Ivy League SIDs were so outstanding they need to be named: Chris Humm, Brown; Pete McHugh, Columbia; Jeremy Hartigan, Cornell; Rick Bender, Dartmouth; Tim Williamson, Harvard; Mike Mahoney, Penn; and Andrew Borders, Princeton. In addition, the assistance given by the effervescent and knowledgeable Scottie Rodgers, Associate Executive Director, Communications and External Relations, The Ivy League, was inestimable. At West Point, Army SID Brian Gunning was especially welcoming and supportive in every way possible. And at Cornell, Brandon Thomas, Assistant Director of Athletic Communications, came through for me in a big way. At every game, the student media teams were exceptional, none more than the Fairfield Student Media Team, who hosted our final, hectic, postseason game: Ivey Speight, Eric Bernsen, and John Tessitor. All the coaches, throughout the season, were a big help, none more than those in the Ivy League. And Joe Jones, now the head coach at Boston University but then the head coach of Columbia University, in spring of 2010 got the whole ball rolling through kindness and graciousness, characteristics he shares with his brother James.

The sportswriters whose company I enjoyed and whose help I exploited include Bill Cloutier, Assistant Sports Editor, the *New Haven Register*; Mike Anthony, the *Hartford Courant*; Bob Ryan, the *Boston Globe* and ESPN; Mark Blaudschun, then of the *Boston Globe*, now of his own site, *ajerseyguy. com*; Bill Reynolds, the *Providence Journal*; Kevin McNamara, also of the *Providence Journal*; Charles Condro, the *Yale Daily News*; Bill Kiser of AP, a huge help at the Wake Forest game; Naveen Reddy, of *rush the court.net*; and last but not least, so special was he, Brian Delaney, of ESPN Radio and the *Ithaca Journal*. Yale radiocasters Joey Rosenberg and Evan Frondorf offered brilliant commentary and peerless companionship.

The three photographers whose work enhance this book are: Sam Rubin, Yale's Assistant Director of Sports Publicity; Ron Waite, Chair of the Department of Communications, Albertus Magnus College, and an independent photographer based in New Haven, Connecticut; and Dave Silverman of David Silverman Photography, headquartered in Cranston, Rhode Island. Among Dave's many achievements, he is the official photographer for the New England Patriots. His outstanding panoramic photo of JLA graces the cover of this book. My gratitude to these three maestros is off the charts.

With research, as ever, the Heermance Memorial Library in Coxsackie, New York proved invaluable, as did their affiliation with the Mid-Hudson

Library System. Heermance Director Linda Deubert and her staff extended themselves all-out on my behalf on countless issues and on numerous occasions. I thank them one and all: Linda herself, Lynn Erceg, Juliana Ferenczy, Lorri Field, Christine Reda, Sandy Stephen, and Jacqueline Whitbeck. Also of enormous help with research was Denise LePera, Executive Director of Institutional Advancement at Roman Catholic High School in Philadelphia, Pennsylvania.

For help with the quotations that appear as epigraphs throughout this book, I thank the authors and personalities quoted: the late Leonard Michaels, George Plimpton, and Eugen Herrigel, and the very much still alive Senator William Warren Bradley, Coach Pete Carril, Coach Bob Knight, and the incredibly gifted writer, Frank Deford. Those assisting in securing permission to use these quotes include Babe Liberman of Farrar, Straus & Giroux; Derek Parsons and Will Lippincott of Russell & Volkening, Inc., literary agents; Anna Sacca of FSBAssociates and Claire Falkner of Senator Bradley's staff; Leif Milliken of the University of Nebraska Press; Deana Dupree of St. Martin's Press; Dara Hyde and Morgan Entrekin of Grove, Atlantic, Inc; and Melanie Flaherty of Random House, Inc. I tip all of them the wink for coming through so generously with their time and expertise.

With an assist from his super agent, IMG's Susan Lipton, and another from his lovely wife Lorraine, Coach Dick Vitale came through with an endorsement like the PTPer he is: Prime Time Person. Nothing is put on about Dick Vitale except the outfit he's wearing: he's genuine through and through, and the most astute, passionate, and entertaining commentator on basketball ever. Coming through as well with an endorsement was former La Salle standout guard Fran Dunphy, now head coach of men's basketball at Temple University and formerly ten-time Ivy League champion coach at the University of Pennsylvania. Rick Telander's foreword left me paralyzed with gratitude. He's as great a writer as he is generous as a man. And who can gainsay Barack Obama's pronouncement that *Heaven Is a Playground* is the best book he ever read on basketball?

I thank heartily Richard "Doc" Sauers, the legendary retired head coach of men's basketball at the State University of New York at Albany for taking time to chat with me—enthusiasm and pride evident in every word—about protégé James Jones, who had played his college ball for Coach Sauers. Take note: Doc is a member of the exclusive 700 wins club among collegiate basketball coaches. My thanks go out as well to Malcolm Wesselink, also now retired but for years the respected and celebrated coach at Phillips Exeter

Academy, who patiently answered my questions about Yale's Reggie Willhite and Dartmouth's Jabari Trotter, both former prep school stars for him.

For support and encouragement throughout this project, friends Frank Curtis, Yvette Durant, Jeanette Fintz, Michael Goedhuis, Christine Hughes, John Lees, Ruth Leonard, Gene Mydlowski, Margaret S. Neilly, Jerry Orter, Ahouva Rubinstein, and D. Jack Solomon never wavered. Early readers Joan Alden, Eddie Bell, Ed Carpenter, Larissa Noon Dougherty, Shelly Hebert, Ed Hoff, and Ed Scott all contributed incisive comments that improved the book. For hands-on editing I thank two incredibly loyal friends, Mike Cunningham, whose insight matched the size of his heart, which is immeasurably large; and I salute as well my prose connoisseur of an agent, Alex Hoyt. Seven friends at St. Martin's Press came through, as always, with crucial early enthusiasm and support: Sally Richardson, Tom Dunne, Elizabeth Beier, Chris Holder, Marcia Markland, Michelle Richter, and Kat Brzozowski. Editorial wizards Jon Segal at Knopf and George Gibson at Walker each gave me a subtle boost I much appreciate.

Four parents of the Yale players were exceptionally good company at nearly every game: Carol Martin, Reverend Kelley, and Sherry and Jay Morgan. Jay's knowledge of the game and acute powers of observation were a big plus when discussing halftime strategy and drawing postmortem conclusions. Assistant Coach Justin Simon's dad, Richard, was also invaluable in these respects.

My own parents played a key role here. My mother, Margaret Marie Kelly Breslin, my father, James Bernard Breslin, and my preternaturally kind uncle, William F. Kelly, proved to be posthumous angels with generous financial underwriting that made this book possible. With superlative advice—beyond wise and sagacious—the great Jack Lichtenstein, an extraordinary friend and another financial backer, contributed in a comparable way, as did Warren S. Gold on these same two fronts, financial and advisory.

I never entered the Payne Whitney gym without the unfailingly genial Vernon, manning the reception desk, beaming me up with one of his sunburst smiles, and that goes too for all the security guys and gals, especially when they manned the security office just off the lobby and kept a watchful eye on Yale athletics, as did their constant companion, the stuffed and mounted original Handsome Dan in his glass-enclosed case. Whenever I rode the team bus, eminently professional Raoul was masterful at the controls and fun to kid and laugh with.

The professors at the Divinity School and the School of Architecture were generous and kind in allowing me to audit, and thereby sample, what acquiring a sterling education in theology and architecture—two subjects that interest me inexhaustibly—was truly like. Every time I walked through the quad of Old Campus and saw the modest memorial stone honoring the memory of Dr. Kingman Brewster, under my breath I murmured my thanks to him all over again for courageously and relentlessly trying to stop the Southeast Asian tragedy in the late sixties and early seventies.

Then came this supreme celestial experience: on a cold and overcast winter afternoon, when I finally remembered to leave extra early for that night's game and also to bring along my passport, as a second photo ID security requirement, four staffers at the Beinecke Rare Book & Manuscript Library gave me an enduring thrill when they let me hold Gertrude Stein's original Paris notebooks and read her handwritten draft of *Three Lives*, a book I love. Great Gertie's wit and panache and her plain and nonpareil prose—with the tensile strength of suspension bridge cable—got me going to the point I grinned like Joe E. Brown on crystal meth and actually forgot myself and laughed aloud (more than once, I regret to add) amid all those admirable and devout scholars, for which faux pas I sincerely apologize. It's a case of that old chestnut: you can take the boy out of North Philly but you can't take North Philly out of the boy. Those four magnanimous and magnificent librarians were: John M. Monahan, Maria Rossi, Laurie Klein, and Mary Ellen Budney. I'll never be able to repay them for what they did for me that day. Love basketball as I do, the game that night was anticlimactic.

Big ups to my brilliant all-around editor at Skyhorse Publishing, the redoubtable Niels Aaboe, and to the able and gracious Skyhorse publisher Tony Lyons, as well as to the entire staff, for doing such a first-class job of designing, printing, and packaging this book.

It's impossible to encompass the totality of help and work done on this book by the man I refer to as my writing coach: over the course of three months Geoff Hannell helped to shape, prune, and polish my writing to the point where I would gladly plead nolo contendere were he to seek co-author credit. Geoff is a gift from the gods when it comes to rendering prose sharp, clean, clear, tight, lively, and forceful. As a friend he's exactly the same way: a deus ex machina to smooth all the dramatic problems away.

My wife Lynn, as ever, was patient, supportive, encouraging, kind, and helpful throughout the two-year process of researching and writing this book. When it came to fine-tuning the writing, she was unfalteringly on the mark, as always.

For their patience and understanding I thank James Jones's family: beautiful wife Rebecka, a talented actress in her own right; equally beautiful daughter Rachel, already a published and award-winning poet though not yet out of high school; and the irrepressibly energetic, uplifting, and entertaining James Quincy Jones, the one-of-a-kind Q, who added to the fun of covering Yale games in too many ways to enumerate. He was as adept at equipping me fully to do my job as his namesake was for James Bond.

Speaking of family and Yale, the young men on the hockey team who cordially chatted with me one lunchtime in the Au Bon Pain on the corner of York and Broadway steered me wisely to check out Ingalls Rink, an architectural marvel by Yale alumnus Eero Saarinen, and, fifteen months later, the home of the NCAA National Champions in hockey. Those kids were champions long before the NCAA ever formalized that status. When I walked up to the rink and entered, the building manager in work blues gave me the full tour, then refused to give me his name out of self-effacing modesty. No matter, I'm grateful to him. Just as I'm grateful to Bruce Rossini and Bucky No-name, who added to my pleasure at being in JLA every time I saw them, which was frequently. Like the terrific building manager at Ingalls, Bucky was too modest to surrender his name and seek recognition, but he's getting it here anyway.

Just as the whole Yale community is. As James Jones said to me one day when I remarked on the unwavering pleasantness of Yale people, none more than James himself, a sentiment I didn't voice at the time: "Ed, I tell you, you meet the best people around here." So true did I find this, I have only two words to add to "Thank you":

"Boola, boola!"

2011-12 Yale Men's Basketball Roster

No.	Name	Pos.	Cl.	Ht.	Wt.	Hometown/High School
15	Rhett Anderson	F	Sr.	6-8	230	La Canada, CA / La Canada
3	Will Bartlett	F	So.	6-6	200	New York, NY / Collegiate School
34	Will Childs-Klein	C	Fr.	6-11	225	St. Louis, MO / Ladue
12	Armani Cotton	G	Fr.	6-7	215	New York, NY / Northfield Mount Hermon
20	Javier Duren	G	Fr.	6-4	175	St. Louis, MO / Oakville
5	Michael Grace	G	Jr.	6-0	180	Winston-Salem, NC / Mt. Tabor
10	Brian Katz	G	Sr.	6-4	200	Woodbury, NY / St. Dominic
32	Greg Kelley	F	So.	6-8	215	Newton, MA / Newton North
50	Jeremiah Kreisberg	C/F	So.	6-10	230	Berkeley, CA / Head-Royce School
44	Greg Mangano	C	Sr.	6-10	240	Orange, CT / Notre Dame-West Haven
25	Sam Martin	G	Jr.	6-3	195	West Warwick, RI / Worcester Academy
1	Austin Morgan	G	Jr.	5-11	185	Reno, NV / Reno
11	Jesse Pritchard	G	So.	6-5	215	Ames, IA / Blair Academy
23	Isaiah Salafia	G	So.	6-3	185	Cromwell, Conn. / Cromwell
35	Brandon Sherrod	F	Fr.	6-6	230	Bridgeport, CT / Choate Rosemary Hall
42	Matt Townsend	F	Fr.	6-7	235	Chappaqua, NY / Horace Greeley
22	Reggie Willhite	G/F	Sr.	6-4	194	Elk Grove, CA / Phillips Exeter

Joel E. Smilow, Class of 1954 Head Coach: James Jones
Assistant Coaches: Matt Kingsley, Jamie Snyder-Fair, Justin Simon
Athletic Trainer: David DiNapoli
Captain: Reggie Willhite